THE CREATIVE PROCESS:
A Computer Model of
Storytelling and Creativity

THE CREATIVE PROCESS:
A Computer Model of
Storytelling and Creativity

SCOTT R. TURNER
University of California, Los Angeles

 LAWRENCE ERLBAUM ASSOCIATES, PUBLISHERS
1994   Hillsdale, New Jersey   Hove, UK

PN
171
.D37
T87
1994

Lawrence Erlbaum Associates, Inc., Publishers
365 Broadway
Hillsdale, New Jersey 07642

Library of Congress Cataloging-in-Publication Data

Turner, Scott R.
    The creative process: a computer model of storytelling and
creativity / Scott R. Turner.
        p.   cm.
    Includes bibliographical references and indexes.
    ISBN 0-8058-1576-7
    1. Authorship--Data processing. 2. Storytelling--Data processing.
I. Title.
PN171.D37T87 1994
808'.02'0285--dc20   94-22481
                                                               CIP

Books published by Lawrence Erlbaum Associates are printed on acid-free paper,
and their bindings are chosen for strength and durability.

Printed in the United States of America
10 9 8 7 6 5 4 3 2 1

Contents

Preface

Someday computers will be artists. They'll be able to write amusing and original stories, invent and play games of unsurpassed complexity and inventiveness, tell jokes, and suffer writer's block. But these things will require computers that can both achieve artistic goals and be creative. These capabilities are far from accomplished.

This volume presents a theory of creativity that addresses some of the many hard problems that must be solved to build a creative computer. It also presents an exploration of the kinds of goals and plans needed to write simple short stories. These theories have been implemented in a computer program called MINSTREL which tells stories about King Arthur and his knights. While far from being the silicon author of the future, MINSTREL does illuminate many of the interesting and difficult issues involved in constructing a creative computer.

The results presented here should be of interest to at least three different groups of people. AI researchers should find this work an interesting application of symbolic AI to the problems of storytelling and creativity. Psychologists interested in creativity and imagination should benefit from the attempt to build a detailed, explicit model of the creative process. Finally, authors and others interested in how people write should find MINSTREL's model of the author-level writing process thought provoking.

The research presented in this volume was done while I was a graduate student at the University of California, Los Angeles. I owe much to the environment there, and particularly to my thesis advisor, Michael Dyer, who set the tone and direction of my studies. I am also grateful to John Reeves, who not only taught me a great deal about critical thinking, but also helped implement the tools package upon which MINSTREL is written. Others who provided invaluable support include Gerald Estrin, Charles Taylor, David Jefferson, Maria Pozzo, Michael Pazzani, Matthew Merzbacher, and Mark Banilower. I also owe a debt to The Aerospace Corporation, which provided me with financial support and a stimulating work environment. Deserving of special thanks is my manager, Patricia Mangan, who was notably understanding and supportive. This research was also supported in part by the Hewlett-Packard Corporation.

Lastly, words cannot express the debt of gratitude I owe my wife Jennifer, whose love and encouragement contributed more to this research than any small skills I possessed.

Scott R. Turner

1

Storytelling and Creativity

1.1 Introduction

During my senior year in college, I was browsing the stacks in the research library and quite by accident came across a small but intriguing book called *The Morphology of the Folktale* (Propp, 1968). The author, Vladmir Propp, had studied common Russian folktales and distilled the form[1] of those tales into cryptic equations:

$$S \rightarrow ABC \uparrow DEFG \frac{HJIK \downarrow Pr - Rs^0 L}{LMJNK \downarrow Pr - Rs} QExTUW *$$

Using letters to represent story elements such as "One of the members of a family absents himself from home," each equation captured a common pattern Propp had found in the folktales he studied. Altogether the equations in Propp's book formed a definitive description of the form of Russian folktales.

As a computer scientist, I found this fascinating. Propp had reduced the folktale to a grammar—a set of well-defined rules. Grammars are used throughout computer science to formalize structure and to understand well-structured input. Compilers, for example, use grammars to translate computer programs in languages like FORTRAN—which are easily understood by humans—into the binary "ones and zeros" understood by computers. In theory, Propp's grammar

---

[1]Morphology is the study of form and structure.

could be programmed into a computer and used to recognize folktales—provided someone first translated each folktale into Propp's notation.

But what was more intriguing to me was the notion of running Propp's grammar "backwards." Propp's grammar was intended as a tool for recognizing and understanding the underlying forms of folktales. But, I reasoned, the same grammar could be used in reverse to *create* folktales. By starting with an initial rule and then randomly choosing the next rule to apply, Propp's grammar could be used to "grow" a story from seed to completion. The random choices would ensure that the story created would likely be different from any actual folk tale, while the rules would ensure that the resulting story had the form of a folk tale. And programming a computer to do this would be trivial. A few hours in the Computer Lab and I would have a computer program that could tell stories!

Or so I thought.

I did eventually write a computer program that tells stories. But it took years, not hours, and in the end, Vladmir Propp's intriguing little grammar was nowhere to be seen.

This volume is the story of the program I wrote and what I learned in the process. It looks at the myriad problems an author faces when he sits down to write a story, and presents the processes, techniques, and knowledge needed to address these problems. Like all authors, I hope you find my story both interesting and enlightening.

1.2 The Storytelling Problem

It is surprisingly difficult to tell a story. Even young children can *understand* stories. By four or five, children understand most aspects of folktales like the ones Propp studied. Indeed, the primary use of folktales is to teach the young principles they'll need as adults.

But *telling* a story is a different matter. It seems an easy enough task. Surely an adult should be able to easily create what a child can easily understand. But more than a few educated, intelligent adults have learned differently when put on the spot by their children. Most can manage little more than an embarrassing hodge-podge of stereotypical cliches, inevitably starting "Once upon a time...." They sputter out a trite beginning and are soon lost. And if grown adults find it difficult to tell a story, imagine how much more difficult it must be to build a computer program to tell stories.

Why is storytelling so difficult? Storytelling appears simple because at a surface level, stories *are* simple. As Propp showed, the form of a story can be captured by a simple, easily understood formalism. But there is more to a story than form. Underlying the form is the story content—the meaning of the story. And it is here that the difficulties arise.

Because in this case, form does not reflect function. Underlying the form of a story is a complex web of author goals, reader expectations, and cultural knowledge. Just as an elegant mathematical proof does not reveal the knowledge and effort that went into its making, neither does the form of a story reflect the difficult process of its creation.

Authors craft stories to achieve a wide variety of complex and often competing goals. To understand why storytelling is so difficult, we must understand what an author is trying to achieve. To build a computer program to tell stories, we must understand and model the processes an author uses to achieve his goals. Both of these are difficult tasks.

The next few sections of this chapter illuminate some of the problems an author faces in telling a story. In the second part of this chapter we'll take a quick look at how these problems can be solved by a computer program.

1.2.1   Why Form Alone is Insufficient

Around 1958, Roger Price and Leonard Stern came out with a party game called *Mad Libs®* (Price & Stern, 1958) that became an instant classic. Each Mad Lib was a story with key words missing:

A Fable

Once upon a time there was a very curious girl who was always sticking her nose into everybody's _____ (plural noun). She kept company with a/an _____ (adjective) man named Dave, who was always buying her _____ (adjective) presents...

The game is played by having people fill in the blanks knowing the proper type of word, but not the surrounding context. The result is often funny and occasionally hilarious.

Like Propp's work, each Mad Lib is a kind of grammar. It specifies the form of a story without specifying the exact content of the story. Mad Libs works as a party game because the final story has a legitimate form combined with an absurd meaning. That's a combination that is, at least in small doses, quite amusing.

But as a way to create stories, Mad Libs leave much to be desired. Mad Libs are amusing, but they aren't good stories. Propp's grammar, although more complex, has the same failing. It captures the form of a story but not the content of a story. And like Mad Libs, Propp's grammar can produce stories that have good form but absurd meanings. The fundamental failing of story grammars is that they capture form without meaning.

Of course, the form of a story is important. We can appreciate a well-crafted story, or admire a good turn of phrase. We also expect a story to have a certain form, and may classify it as a "bad" story if it does not. But most of our appreciation of stories comes from the content level. Storytelling is an act of communication between the author and his or her readers. It is what the story tells—the message—that matters most to both the author and the readers. What Mad Libs and Propp's grammar fail to capture is the message level of storytelling. Any storytelling system based solely on the surface features of stories—whether a complex system like Propp's or a simple system like Mad Libs—will inevitably fail to be successful. A story that doesn't mean anything is not a story, even if it has the proper form.

A storyteller must have an in-depth understanding of the stories he or she tells.

An author must understand the meaning of the stories he or she tells. One reason storytelling is difficult is because it requires the storyteller to understand the story at every level: the surface format, the message or point of the story, the actions of the characters, the events in the story world, the literary values in the story.

For human authors, this task isn't difficult. Humans spend the first 20 years of their lives learning about the world, about how people act, and about ways to understand the world. They are skilled and experienced at using this knowledge, whether to manage their day-to-day life or to understand a story.

But for a computer program this represents a tremendous barrier. To a certain extent a story is a model of a tiny world, peopled with story characters, natural forces, locations, and inanimate objects. To understand these things and their interrelationships requires a tremendous amount of knowledge that humans take for granted. Consider, for example, the simple sentence:

> When Galahad saw the dragon charge, he drew his sword and jumped to the side.

To understand this sentence in depth requires an enormous amount of knowledge:

- What is a dragon? What is a knight?
- What does "charging" mean in this context? "Drawing?"
- What is the dragon trying to accomplish? Galahad?
- What will Galahad do next? The dragon?
- What is Galahad feeling? The dragon?

Capturing and applying all this knowledge to the task of storytelling is one of the challenges of building a computer program that can tell stories. But this is necessary because a story is more than just a form; it has in-depth meaning to both the author and the reader.

1.2.2 Purpose and Message

Meaning is important to storytelling because storytelling is a form of communication. The author of a story isn't simply stringing together words randomly, or even according to a grammar. Storytelling is a purposeful activity. The storyteller constructs his story to bear a message to his or her readers.

Consider the following story:

Rainy Day

One day, Tom got up in the morning and saw that it was raining. He went downstairs and had breakfast. Then he sat by the window and read a book for a while. It was still raining. Later, Tom fixed himself a sandwich for lunch.

Rainy Day isn't much of a story. The problem isn't that it lacks form (the sentences are all grammatical) or that it has an absurd meaning (it's quite understandable). It's just boring. It has a message, but the message isn't interesting. As a story *Rainy Day* is a failure because the message conveyed isn't worth the work required to extract it.

So what makes a message worth the effort? What makes a message interesting?

Certain topics are inherently interesting. Sex and danger—both of which appeal to primitive drives—arouse interest in almost any context. Novelty and new ideas are also interesting—mankind has retained curiosity as one legacy of his primate heritage. Useful information is also interesting. An article on how to reduce your tax bill is likely to interest you for this reason. Still other topics appeal only to some readers. Presumably the reader of this book is interested in artificial intelligence. Or perhaps you are a member of my family, and your interests are aroused for other reasons. There are many ways a story can be interesting.

Sometimes life provides an interesting message. The author of *Adrift* (Callahan, 1986) was lost at sea for 76 days without food or water. The story of his experience is interesting because he faced danger, invented novel solutions to his problems, and learned useful information about survival under the most difficult of circumstances. But when life doesn't provide an interesting story, the author must create his own message:

A storyteller must fashion his story to convey
an interesting message.

Finding, formulating, and conveying an interesting message is one of the reasons that storytelling is such a difficult task. To build a computer program that can tell stories, we must build a model of communication. The computer program must (1) know what an interesting message is, (2) be able to select a message to convey, and (3) be able to create a story that illustrates the message. Building a model of "messages" and designing the processes that can illustrate a message is one of the challenges of creating a program that can tell stories.

1.2.3 Creativity

In literature, as in all the arts, there is a premium placed on creativity. To be art, a work must be new and different in significant ways. No publisher would accept a copy of *Romeo and Juliet* with only the names changed. Even an author who tells consistently interesting stories inevitably loses popularity if his stories are all very similar. One of the reasons that storytelling is so difficult is that the author is challenged to be creative. It isn't enough to tell an interesting story; the author must also strive to make the story new and different.

A storyteller must be creative.

But being creative is hard. Even judging whether or not something is creative is difficult. Surely copying *Romeo and Juliet* with only the names changed is not creative. But what if an author copied *Romeo and Juliet* and changed the setting to, say, the west side of New York City? The musical *West Side Story* was a tremendous Broadway hit and award-winning movie. Was Leonard Bernstein being creative when he wrote *West Side Story*? Or does Shakespeare deserve the credit for that success?

Whether or not something is creative depends on the number and quality of its differences from similar works. But how can we distinguish inspiration from plagiarization? How can we judge when something has enough differences from previous work to be creative? And how can we determine if the differences are significant? These are just some of the problems in determining whether something is creative.

And if judging creativity seems difficult, *being* creative seems almost impossible. The creative person performs an almost miraculous feat: the bringing forth of something new and novel, something never before seen. The average person cannot write a creative story, paint a masterpiece, or invent a new device. The few people who are consistently and greatly inventive—William Shakespeare, Albert Einstein, Leonardo da Vinci, Thomas Edison—are revered as geniuses. And yet storytelling is an activity that demands creativity. No wonder then that it is so difficult to tell stories.

What is the source of creativity? The ancients believed that creativity was the work of a supernatural Muse who spoke into the artist's ear. Although few artists today would profess to believe in a literal Muse, many do believe that creativity originates in processes that are beyond human comprehension. Is creativity a mystery that can never be explained by man, nor expressed in language? Or does creativity have a natural explanation in the cognitive processes of the human mind?

Many psychologists and cognitive scientists today believe that creativity is the result of cognitive processes that bring together pieces of old knowledge in new ways. But that is hardly a full explanation of creativity. To embody this model of creativity in a computer program requires addressing a myriad of difficult issues:

• How is knowledge organized and searched?
• How is knowledge combined to form new knowledge?
• How does creativity interact with other cognitive processes?
• Are there different types of creativity?
• Is imagination different from creativity?
• How does the creator recognize something new?
• How does the creator guide his creativity?
• How does the creator evaluate his creation?

The requirement to be creative is one reason that storytelling is such a difficult task for humans; the requirement to understand and model creativity is one of the reasons that building a computer program to tell stories is so difficult.

1.2.4 Art and Language

The sciences distinguish between content and presentation. We can and do speak of research as "important but poorly presented" or "polished but lacking substance." In the arts, however, it is much more difficult to separate presentation from content. In the sciences, presentation is a secondary concern, needed only to communicate content. But in the arts, presentation is part of the content. Art demands good presentation in a way that science does not.

This is true in literature as in the other arts. An author is expected not only to present a meaningful, interesting, and creative story, but also a well-crafted story. At one level, this requires that the author use language well by following the rules of grammar and punctuation while accurately conveying his meaning. At another level, this requires that the author present his story beautifully, by using language in poetic ways and by using dramatic writing techniques such as characterization and foreshadowing. In addition to all the other goals he is trying to achieve, a storyteller must try to create an artistic story.

A storyteller must create stories
that are aesthetically pleasing.

Of course, this further complicates the problem of creating a storytelling program. To tell a story that meets literary standards as well as standards of comprehension, interest, and creativity, a storytelling program needs knowledge of both language and drama. To use language well, a computer storytelling program requires knowledge about words and what they mean, an understanding of grammar, and a model of how language is produced—how concepts are expressed in language. To produce a story that is artistically pleasing, a computer storytelling program requires knowledge about the structure and parts of a story, knowledge about dramatic writing techniques (including how they are applied and what they achieve) and a model of dramatic writing that captures how an author uses dramatic writing techniques to improve the artistic value of his stories.

1.3   MINSTREL: A Computer Model of Storytelling

Clearly, telling a story is very difficult. A good story must be understandable, interesting, creative, and artistic. Alone each of these goals is difficult to achieve; together they are truly formidable. It is no wonder that most adults are not good storytellers.

And as we have seen, the task of building a computer program to tell stories is even more daunting. Building a computer storyteller requires capturing all the knowledge a human author uses to tell a story, building models of storytelling, creativity, interestingness, and art, and executing the plans and processes an author uses to tell a story. If not outright impossible, this is at least an enormous job.

In this section, we give a brief overview of MINSTREL, a computer program that tells stories about King Arthur and his Knights of the Round Table. As one might expect from the difficulty of the storytelling task, MINSTREL is a large and complex program representing many years of research. It isn't possible to give a detailed description of MINSTREL in just a few pages. Instead, we hope to give the reader a general overview of MINSTREL's design and structure, and a preliminary glimpse into the kinds of knowledge and processes MINSTREL uses to tell stories. Hopefully this prelude will entice the reader deeper into this book to discover the inner workings of MINSTREL.

1.3.1   What is MINSTREL?

MINSTREL is a computer program written in Common Lisp that tells stories about King Arthur and the Knights of the Round Table. MINSTREL is about 17,000 lines of code, and is built upon a tools package called Rhapsody (Turner & Reeves, 1987) that is itself about 10,000 lines of code.

The stories MINSTREL tells are one-half to one page in length. MINSTREL begins with a small amount of knowledge about the King Arthur domain, as if it had read one or two short stories about King Arthur. Using this knowledge, MINSTREL is able to tell more than ten complete stories, and many more incomplete stories and story fragments. In addition to storytelling, MINSTREL has been used to invent mechanical devices and to solve planning problems.

1.3.2 A Story

When they first hear about MINSTREL, most people are curious to read a story that MINSTREL has written, so that they can judge for themselves whether or not MINSTREL is a competent author. Accordingly, we present here a representative story so that you can judge for yourself MINSTREL's capabilities. This story and other stories throughout the volume are presented exactly as produced by MINSTREL, with the exception of the titles, which were added later by the author. Here then, is one of MINSTREL's stories:

The Vengeful Princess

Once upon a time there was a Lady of the Court named Jennifer. Jennifer loved a knight named Grunfeld. Grunfeld loved Jennifer.

Jennifer wanted revenge on a lady of the court named Darlene because she had the berries which she picked in the woods and Jennifer wanted to have the berries. Jennifer wanted to scare Darlene. Jennifer wanted a dragon to move towards Darlene so that Darlene believed it would eat her. Jennifer wanted to appear to be a dragon so that a dragon would move towards Darlene. Jennifer drank a magic potion. Jennifer transformed into a dragon. A dragon moved towards Darlene. A dragon was near Darlene.

Grunfeld wanted to impress the king. Grunfeld wanted to move towards the woods so that he could fight a dragon. Grunfeld moved towards the woods. Grunfeld was near the woods. Grunfeld fought a dragon. The dragon died. The dragon was Jennifer. Jennifer wanted to live. Jennifer tried to drink a magic potion but failed. Grunfeld was filled with grief.

Jennifer was buried in the woods. Grunfeld became a hermit.

MORAL: Deception is a weapon difficult to aim.

The reader will probably have a number of immediate first impressions about this story:

- The story has a "point."
- The story is understandable and consistent.
- The story is reasonably clever, particularly the deception and how it leads to grief.
- The use of English is not as polished as that of a human author.

Most people judge MINSTREL's stories to be competent but not brilliant, equivalent to the kinds of stories people expect from children 10–15 years-of-age.[2] However, the reader will soon realize that it is difficult to evaluate MINSTREL's performance solely by looking at the stories it creates. As important as *what* MINSTREL creates is *how* it creates. Certainly *The Vengeful Princess* is less impressive if it was produced from canned text hidden in MINSTREL's code. To understand MINSTREL we have to look deeper. We have to look at the processes and knowledge MINSTREL uses to create stories.

1.3.3 The Architecture of MINSTREL

MINSTREL is based on a model of the author as a *problem solver*. We are not accustomed to think of art as problem solving. The phrase *problem solving* brings to mind scientific disciplines, logic, and schoolwork. And yet there are few fundamental differences between creative domains such as storytelling, art and music and more mundane problem domains, such as science and day-to-day problem solving. In art as in day-to-day life, people have goals, find or create plans to achieve those goals, apply the plans, evaluate the results, and so on. To be sure, the arts are generally more creative than other problem domains. But anyone who has performed scientific research or jury-rigged a temporary fix to a household problem knows that creativity is both possible and necessary in science and day-to-day life.

In MINSTREL, storytelling is treated as problem solving. The same architecture and processes are used to write stories, to solve problems in the story world (such as how a knight can kill a dragon), and to invent mechanical devices. It is a basic tenet of this research that the problem solving process is invariant across problem domains, whether they be mundane or artistic, creative or noncreative:

The problem solving process is invariant
across problem domains.

---

[2]See Chapter 8 for a discussion of a survey in which subjects were asked to evaluate MINSTREL's output.

How then does MINSTREL solve problems?

MINSTREL is a type of *case-based reasoner* (Reisbeck & Schank, 1989; Slade, 1991). The fundamental principle of case-based reasoning is that reasoners remember past problem solving situations ("cases") and use that knowledge to solve current problems. One of the major values of the case-based reasoning paradigm is that it explains how reasoners can learn from experience: They remember what happens and reuse that knowledge when appropriate.

MINSTREL's case-based problem solving process is illustrated in Figure 1.1. Problem solving proceeds in three steps: (1) The current problem is used to recall similar past problems, (2) The past solution is adapted to the current problem, and (3) The recalled solution is then applied to the current problem. Because there is nothing specific in this model to the storytelling problem domain, this same process can be used to solve both author-level storytelling problems and character-level planning problems, as well as problems in mechanical device invention.

MINSTREL's model of problem solving is discussed in more detail in Chapter 3. However, one major shortcoming of this model should already be obvious. Case-based reasoners solve problems by reusing past solutions. A case-based storyteller would tell the same story over and over again—repeatedly solving the storytelling problem by reusing an old solution. Such a storyteller would be the opposite of creative. What do we need to add to a model of case-based reasoning to support creativity?

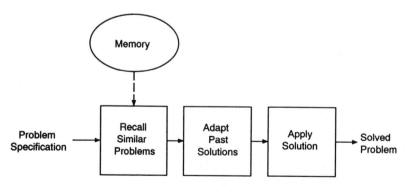

Figure 1.1 Case-Based Problem Solving

1.3.4   The Challenge of Creativity

The challenge of creativity is to find and use old knowledge in new ways to form a novel and useful solution to a problem. What processes and knowledge do we need to be able to create *new* problem solutions from *old* knowledge? How can we extend the case-based model of problem solving to include creativity? To begin answering these questions, let's look at an example of creativity. The following story concerns a UCLA engineering professor:

> One night, the professor and his wife were out late at a party. Returning home along a lonely road, the car they were driving slowly lost its electrical power. Looking under the hood, the professor discovered that the fan belt had broken.

> After a perfunctory search in the trunk for a spare fan belt, the professor returned to the car and asked his wife to remove her pantyhose. The professor tied a series of knots in the pantyhose, and then tied the pantyhose into a loop somewhat smaller than the fan belt. He forced the loop over the crankcase pulley and the alternator pulley. The elasticity of the pantyhose kept it on the pulleys; the knots provide traction so that the improvised belt wouldn't spin uselessly.

> After giving the battery a few minutes recovery, the professor started the car and successfully made it home.

In this example, the professor brings together things he already knows—requirements for a fan belt, available materials, the properties of pantyhose, and knowledge of knots—to create a new and useful solution to the "fan-belt" problem. From everything the professor knew, he somehow picked out the knowledge that when combined in a new and unique way would result in a solution to his problem.

This process of finding and combining knowledge seems paradoxical. On the one hand, if the professor randomly grabs at old knowledge to try to create a new solution, he has an impossibly hard task in applying the knowledge he finds. Suppose the professor had recalled what he knew about grading papers, eradicating garden pests, and the rules of ping-pong and tried to apply that knowledge to the fan-belt problem. Surely he would fail. On the other hand, if the professor uses only knowledge that he knows how to apply to the current problem, he is unlikely to create a new solution. The professor's knowledge of normal car repair procedures and the tools and parts used can be easily applied to the fan-belt problem. But it is unlikely to result in a new solution.

This is a classic "Catch-22" situation. The creator must somehow search everything he knows to find knowledge that can be adapted to create a new solution. But without knowing what knowledge can be adapted, how can the creator recognize what knowledge is useful? Conversely, once the knowledge has been found, the creator must somehow adapt it to the current problem. But without knowing how the knowledge is related to the current problem, how can the creator adapt it? The challenge of creativity is to define a creative process that (1) will find and recognize useful knowledge, and (2) know how to adapt that knowledge to create a new solution.

The MINSTREL solution is to *integrate* the search and adapt processes of creativity. By integrating the search and adapt processes, search can be guided by adaptation knowledge and adaptation guided by search knowledge. The search process finds only knowledge that it knows how to adapt; the adaptation process knows what adaptations to apply because it knows how the knowledge was found.

Creativity is an integrated process
of search and adaptation.

In MINSTREL, the search and adaptation processes of creativity are integrated in heuristics called Transform-Recall-Adapt Methods, or TRAMs. Each TRAM bundles a search method with a corresponding adaptation. "Transform" takes a problem and changes it into a slightly different problem. "Recall" takes the new problem description and tries to recall similar past problems from memory. "Adapt" takes the recalled problem solutions and adapts them to the original problem.

One of MINSTREL's TRAMs is TRAM:Cross-Domain-Solution. This TRAM is based on the idea that there are often enough similarities between two problem domains that solutions from one domain can be applied in the other. For example, military tactics can be applied to business problems—as evidenced by the popularity of *A Book of Five Rings* (Miyamoto, 1982) with both Japanese and American businessmen. TRAM:Cross-Domain-Solution suggests that a creative person can take advantage of this by translating a problem into a new domain ("Transform"), solving the problem in that domain ("Recall"), and then translating the solution back into the original domain ("Adapt").

MINSTREL uses TRAM:Cross-Domain-Solution when telling a story called *The Mistaken Knight*. In the course of telling this story, MINSTREL has to create a scene in which a knight accidently meets a princess. As it happens, MINSTREL doesn't know any way in which a knight can accidently meet a princess, so it must use creativity to solve this problem. To do this, MINSTREL uses TRAM:Cross-Domain-Solution.

The first step of the creative process is to search for new knowledge to apply to the current problem. TRAMs do this by transforming the current problem into a new problem, and finding the problem solutions that have been previously used for the transformed problem. These problem solutions are "new" in the sense that they've never before been applied to the current problem. By transforming the current problem into a different problem, TRAMs search new areas of knowledge.

The "Transform" part of TRAM:Cross-Domain-Solution translates the original problem into a new problem domain. In this case, TRAM:Cross-Domain-Solution transforms the current problem ("A knight accidently meets a princess") from the domain of medieval stories into the modern day-to-day domain ("A businessman accidently meets a person"). TRAM:Cross-Domain-Solution does this by translating the original problem element by element, trying to find correspondences between the two domains. In this case, TRAM:Cross-Domain-Solution translates a knight into a businessman, leaves "accidental meeting" unchanged, and translates a princess into a person.

The second step of the creative process is to use the transformed problem as an index for recall, to see if the creator has ever encountered a similar problem before. In this case, the transformed problem recalls this story:

Walking The Dog

John was sitting at home one evening when his dog began scratching at the door and whining for a walk. John decided to take the dog for a walk. While they were out, John ran across his old friend Pete, whom he hadn't seen in many years. John realized that he would never have run into Pete if his dog hadn't wanted a walk.

The final step of the creative process is to adapt the recalled solution to the original problem. Because TRAM:Cross-Domain-Solution knows that the recalled solution was found by translating the original problem into a new problem domain, adaptation is easy. TRAM:Cross-Domain-Solution needs only translate the recalled story back into the original domain, creating this scene:

```
One day while out riding, Lancelot's horse went
into the woods. Lancelot could not control the
horse. The horse took him deeper into the woods.
The horse stopped. Lancelot saw Andrea, a Lady of
the Court, who was picking berries.
```

The resulting scene is new and original, illustrating how TRAM:Cross-Domain-Solution can create a new solution by adapting knowledge from another problem domain.

MINSTREL's TRAMs integrate the search and adapt processes of creativity. This ensures that (1) Any knowledge found will be useful, and (2) The creator will know how to apply the knowledge found. Thus MINSTREL's TRAMs provide a model of creativity which resolves creativity's seeming paradoxes.

MINSTREL's model of creativity is discussed further in Chapters 2 and 8. Those chapters address a variety of other issues in creativity, including:

- How TRAMs incorporated into the case-based model of problem solving.
- How multiple TRAMs can be used simultaneously to increase the power of creativity.
- How a problem solver can recognize a creative solution.
- How creativity can be integrated into a model of episodic memory to create an *imaginative memory*.
- Descriptions and discussions of the TRAMs MINSTREL uses.
- Descriptions of experiments with the MINSTREL model of creativity.

1.3.5   Author Goals in Storytelling

The previous section illustrated how MINSTREL solves problems by using a case-based problem solver augmented with creativity heuristics. Let's return now to the particular problem of storytelling and look at the kinds of problems an author has to solve when he tells a story.

Earlier we identified four concerns of an author. An author wants to make his story (1) interesting, (2) understandable, (3) artistic, and (4) creative. We have already seen how MINSTREL achieves the last goal. How are the other three goals achieved?

MINSTREL has four classes of author-level goals corresponding to the major concerns of an author. They are:

- Thematic Goals
- Consistency Goals
- Drama Goals
- Presentation Goals

Thematic goals are concerned with the selection and development of a story theme. The story theme is the point or moral of the story. These goals assure that the story MINSTREL tells will have an interesting message. Consistency goals focus on creating a story that is plausible and believable. Drama goals are concerned with the use of dramatic writing techniques to improve the artistic quality of a story. These goals represent MINSTREL's desire to tell a story that is aesthetically pleasing. Finally, presentation goals are concerned with how a story is presented to the reader, and represent MINSTREL's desire to tell the story in a pleasing and effective way.

These four classes of goals combine to create a complete story. In the following four sections we'll look briefly at each class of goals, what it contributes to a completed story, and how MINSTREL achieves each type of goal.

1.3.5.1 Theme in Storytelling

The theme of a story is the point, moral, or general truth that the story illustrates. Some stories, like fables, have an easily identifiable theme. Other stories, such as novels, may have several themes. In general, we assume that an author tells a story in order to present some point to the reader, or to illustrate some truth. We call this the theme of the story.

Themes help make stories interesting. Partly this is curiosity: If the reader realizes that a story has a purpose or point, he is curious to discover what it is. Partly it is self-interest. If the theme represents useful knowledge, such as a general truth about how the world works, the reader is interested in learning the theme so that he can use it to improve his life. Themes are thus one way an author can give his stories purpose and make them interesting.

MINSTREL's stories have very specific themes called Planning Advice Themes, or PATs. Each PAT represents a stereotypical planning situation and advice about how to handle the situation. Each PAT is a morsel of planning advice, and can often be summarized by an adage.

For example, the theme of *The Vengeful Princess* is summarized by the adage "Deception is a weapon difficult to aim." This theme is called PAT:Juliet, and is based on one of the themes in *Romeo and Juliet*. In the last act of *Romeo and Juliet*, Juliet takes a potion that makes her appear to be dead. Her intention is to deceive her family, but she deceives Romeo instead. Romeo, stricken with grief at the apparent loss of Juliet, kills himself. PAT:Juliet captures the mistake that Juliet made, and advice for planners considering a similar plan: "Be careful with deception plans because you may fool someone unintended."

MINSTREL's primary goal when storytelling is to tell a story that illustrates a particular Planning Advice Theme. By making this its primary storytelling goal, MINSTREL ensures that the stories it tells will (1) have a point or purpose, and (2) be interesting.

MINSTREL's plan for illustrating a theme involves creating story events that form a specific example of the planning advice the theme represents. This can be seen in *The Vengeful Princess*, where MINSTREL has created story events to illustrate the theme "Be careful with deception plans because you may fool someone unintended":

```
Jennifer wanted to appear to be a dragon [to
fool Darlene]. Jennifer drank a magic potion.
Jennifer transformed into a dragon...

Grunfeld was near the woods. Grunfeld fought a
```

```
dragon.   The  dragon  died.   The  dragon  was  Jen-
nifer.   Jennifer  wanted  to  live...
```

These events illustrate the story theme by showing how Jennifer's deception plan leads to grief when Galahad is fooled instead of Darlene. And by including an example of the theme in the story, MINSTREL makes the story purposeful and interesting.

MINSTREL's use of themes is discussed in more detail in Chapter 4. Among the issues addressed are:

- The structure and representation of Planning Advice Themes.
- How a theme is selected for storytelling.
- How the events that illustrate a theme are created.
- How new story themes can be invented.
- How story themes function as advice.
- Descriptions of the story themes that MINSTREL knows.

1.3.5.2   Consistency in Storytelling

As the reader may have noticed, the story events that illustrate the theme are only a small part of the final story. *The Vengeful Princess* is about 30 sentences long, but only 10 of those sentences concern the story theme. Even though illustrating a theme is MINSTREL's primary purpose in storytelling, a good story requires that MINSTREL be concerned with many other goals. One of these is story consistency.

A good story must be consistent at many levels. The author must have an in-depth understanding of both story form and of the world in which the story takes place. The characters and the world should act consistently and predictably. MINSTREL tries to create stories in which the characters act as rational and intelligent planners, in which the characters show the proper emotional reactions to events in their lives, and in which the story world is consistent and plausible. These concerns are apparent in several places in *The Vengeful Princess*.

To illustrate the story theme, MINSTREL creates a scene in which Galahad kills a dragon (which turns out to be Jennifer). This story scene satisfies the thematic requirement that Jennifer's deception leads to grief. But in other ways the scene is inconsistent. There is no explanation of why Galahad killed the dragon, or how he reacts to the discovery that the dragon is really Jennifer.

To correct these problems, MINSTREL adds new story scenes. First MINSTREL adds scenes to explain why Galahad kills the dragon:

```
Grunfeld  wanted  to  impress  the  king.
Grunfeld  wanted  to  move  towards  the  woods  so
```

> that he could fight a dragon. Grunfeld moved
> towards the woods. Grunfeld was near the
> woods. Grunfeld fought a dragon...

MINSTREL uses knowledge about knights, what their typical goals are, and how they achieve those goals to create story scenes which explain why Galahad fights a dragon.

By detecting and correcting story inconsistencies such as this one, MINSTREL tells stories that are plausible and understandable. Story consistency is discussed in more detail in Chapter 6. Among the issues addressed are:

- How story consistencies arise.
- The types of planning inconsistencies MINSTREL can detect and correct.
- The types of story world inconsistencies MINSTREL can detect and correct.
- How emotions are modeled in MINSTREL.
- How emotional inconsistencies are detected and corrected.

1.3.5.3 Art and Drama in Storytelling

Another major concern of a storyteller is to create a story that has aesthetic appeal. By writing a story with literary values, an author helps make his story interesting and increases the emotional and intellectual impact of his story.

Human authors have many literary writing techniques: pacing, characterization, dialogue, suspense, foreshadowing, description, and many others. A look at the creative writing section of any bookstore will reveal that there are as many writing techniques as there are authors to expound them. Every human author develops a combination of literary writing goals and techniques that create a particular writing style.

It would be impossible to model all these techniques and their myriad combinations in MINSTREL. Instead, MINSTREL implements a few representative techniques: suspense, tragedy, characterization, and foreshadowing. This particular combination of techniques represents, if you will, MINSTREL's writing style.

One of the techniques that MINSTREL uses in creating *The Vengeful Princess* is tragedy. Tragedy is a literary form that evokes feelings of pity and regret in the reader, and often involves a character suffering a downfall because of a tragic flaw. MINSTREL has the ability to recognize when a story has the potential to be tragic, and has techniques it uses to emphasize the tragedy. The seed of a tragic situation occurs in *The Vengeful Princess* when Galahad accidently kills Jennifer. The tragedy here is that Jennifer's temper leads her to seek revenge for a trivial reason, and eventually results in her own death.

MINSTREL has several plans for accentuating a tragic situation. One of these plans increases the impact of a tragic situation by making the tragedy occur at the hands of a loved one. This plan was used in the telling of *The Vengeful Princess* by making Galahad and Jennifer lovers:

```
    Once upon a time there was a Lady of the
Court named Jennifer.  Jennifer loved a knight
named Grunfeld.  Grunfeld loved Jennifer...

    ...Grunfeld fought a dragon.  The dragon died.
The dragon was Jennifer...
```

The fact that Jennifer's tragic flaw leads to her death at the hands of someone who loves her intensifies the tragic aspect of this story.

By applying dramatic writing techniques like tragedy, MINSTREL creates stories that have literary value and are aesthetically pleasing. MINSTREL's dramatic writing goals are discussed in more detail in Chapter 5. The writing techniques described are:

- Suspense
- Tragedy
- Characterization
- Foreshadowing

1.3.5.4 Presenting the Story to the Reader

The final task of an author is to present his story to his readers. He must express the story in language, in a manner that is both pleasing and understandable. A good author will also fashion his story presentation to reflect and accentuate the purposes of his story.

To express a story in English, MINSTREL must accomplish several tasks. First, MINSTREL must select an order in which to relate the events of the story. In many cases, this ordering can be guided by the temporal ordering of story events. In other cases, such as foreshadowing, MINSTREL must make specific decisions about the order in which to present story scenes. Second, MINSTREL must generate the story events in English. This requires selecting words to express concepts, building up grammatical sentences, paragraphing, and many other tasks. Finally, MINSTREL may also create new story scenes in order to improve the presentation of the story.

In *The Vengeful Princess*, MINSTREL creates a story scene to introduce the reader to the main character of the story:

```
Once upon a time there was a Lady of the Court
named Jennifer...
```

and story scenes to resolve character fates:

```
Jennifer was buried in the woods.  Grunfeld
became a hermit.
```

These scenes are created to improve the story presentation. The introductory scene is created to ease the reader's transition into the story by providing an immediate identification of the main character and the story genre. The final scenes are created to resolve the reader's expectations about the fates of the story characters and create a sense of closure.

MINSTREL achieves a number of difficult tasks in presentation. These tasks include:

- How introduction scenes are created.
- How denouement scenes are created.
- How story events are ordered, both implicitly and explicitly.
- How paragraphing is used to reflect thematic structure.
- How natural language is generated from concepts.

Further information about how MINSTREL achieves its presentation tasks can be found in (Turner, 1993).

1.4 A Reader's Guide

The remainder of this volume is divided into three sections.

Chapter 2 describes MINSTREL's model of creativity, how creativity is used to augment case-based reasoning, and gives examples of MINSTREL's creativity in planning and storytelling. Chapter 3 also discusses a variety of related issues, including errors in creativity and learning.

Chapter 3 introduces MINSTREL's model of storytelling. Chapters 4, 5, and 6 describe MINSTREL's author-level goals and plans for theme, drama, and consistency.

Chapter 7 presents an extended example of how MINSTREL tells a story. A detailed trace of MINSTREL creating a story is analyzed to reveal the exact sequence of author goals and plans that leads to a finished story.

Finally, Chapter 8 evaluates the MINSTREL model by comparing it to previous work in psychology and artificial intelligence and by analyzing MINSTREL's performance as a storyteller and creator. Chapter 9 contains conclusions and some thoughts on future work.

2 | A Model of Creativity

2.1 Introduction

Creativity—the bringing forth of an original product of the human mind—is the pinnacle of human cognition. Artists, writers, and scientists are treated with intellectual awe, and the word itself brings to mind the roll of men whose discoveries changed their social and scientific cultures: William Shakespeare, Albert Einstein, Leonardo da Vinci, Thomas Edison.

And yet creativity has a mundane side as well. From small child to adult, we are all creative in every aspect of our lives. Faced with a problem we have never before encountered, we combine past knowledge in new ways to create a solution. We fix our cars using hangers and baling wire, invent jokes based on the latest domestic crisis, and make up bedtime stories for our sons and daughters. Far from being the sole province of extraordinary thinkers, the ability to create new solutions to problems is one of the cornerstones of human problem solving.

To understand human cognition, it is essential that we understand the processes of creativity: the goals that drive people to create and the mechanisms they use to create. And because creativity spans the intellectual spectrum from the highest peaks to everyday cognition, it is likely that studying creativity will provide special insights into human thought.

Understanding creativity also has practical value to computer scientists. Current computer programs have little adaptability. Faced with new situations, they act incorrectly or fail completely. Implementing the fundamental processes of creativity in computer programs has the potential to greatly increase the scope and power of the modern computer.

This chapter presents a process model of creativity. A case-based problem solver is augmented with evaluations that act as a creative drive, and a set of creativity heuristics called Transform-Recall-Adapt Methods (TRAMs). TRAMs create new solutions to problems by transforming problems into slightly different problems, solving the new problems, and then adapting any solutions found to the original problem. Repeated application of TRAMs enables the problem solver to make elaborate problem transformations by small steps, invent new solutions substantially different from old ones, and greatly extend the range of problems that can be solved.

The second part of this chapter discusses the implementation of this model in MINSTREL. Although MINSTREL is primarily a storytelling program, MINSTREL's model of creativity is independent of the storytelling domain. Consequently, the creative problem solving portion of MINSTREL can be applied to other domains and problem tasks. This chapter presents examples of MINSTREL's model of creativity applied to different problems, and discusses some of the important issues of modeling creativity.

2.2   Creativity and Problem Solving

The goal of this research is to develop a model of creativity and answer the question: What are the processes of creativity common to many problem solving domains? The first step to answering this question is to understand what it means to call the solution to a problem "creative."

According to psychologists, people recognize a solution as creative if it (1) has significant novelty and (2) is useful (Koestler, 1964; Wallas, 1926; Weisberg, 1986).

We all recognize that creative solutions must be original. They must be new and different from old solutions. But the differences must also be *significant*. If an artist were to paint the Mona Lisa in a red dress instead of a blue one, the resulting painting would not be considered creative, despite its differences from the original. Significant novelty distinguishes creative solutions from ones that are only adaptations of old solutions.

Usefulness is the second characteristic of a creative solution. We expect problem solvers to be capable: They must develop solutions that solve their problems. Replacing a flat tire with an air raft is novel but not creative, because it doesn't effectively solve the original problem. Creativity must be purposeful and directed. Creative solutions must have bearing and utility on the problems to which they are applied.

Creative solutions are, therefore, both useful and significantly novel. How are these features reflected in the creative process? Consider the following anecdote concerning the 7-year-old niece of the author:

One day, while visiting her grandparents, Janelle was seated alone at the dining room table, drinking milk and eating cookies. Reaching for the cookies, she accidently spilled her milk on the table. Since Janelle had been recently reprimanded for making a mess, she decided to clean up the spill herself.

Janelle went into the kitchen, but there were no towels or paper towels available. She stood for a moment in the center of the kitchen thinking, and then she went out the back door.

She returned a few minutes later carrying a kitten. The neighbor's cat had given birth to a litter about a month ago, and Janelle had been over to play with the kittens the previous day. Janelle brought the kitten into the dining room, where he happily lapped up the spilled milk.

Most people find Janelle's solution to her problem creative. The use of a kitten as an agent and the substitution of "consumption of milk" for "removal of milk" are significant differences from Janelle's known solution to the "spilled milk problem", and the success of the new solution shows its usefulness. Janelle's example illustrates three important principles of creativity:

Creativity is driven by the failure of problem solving.

When Janelle could not find a towel, her old plans for cleaning up a spill became unusable, forcing her to invent a new solution. The need for creativity arises from the failure of problem solving (Weisberg, 1986).

Creativity is an extension of problem solving.

Janelle's solution to the spilled milk problem arises as part of her problem solving process, and even the creative aspects of her solution—using a kitten as an agent and substituting consumption of the milk for removal of the milk—are broken down into subtasks in the manner of a classical problem-solving strategy (divide and conquer). Although some theorists (e.g., Koestler, 1964; Wallas, 1926) have suggested that creativity is a process fundamentally different from problem solving, there is ample evidence to indicate that creativity is an outgrowth or extension of problem solving (Weisberg, 1986).

New solutions are created by using old knowledge in new ways.

Creative solutions do not spring forth newborn from the head of Zeus; they make use of what the problem solver already knows. Janelle knew that the neighbors had kittens, that kittens like milk, and that the goal "consumption of milk" could subsume the goal of "removal of milk," and she combined this information into a new solution by using her general knowledge about agents. The significant novelty of creative solutions arises from the problem solver's application of knowledge in a new way to the problem (Koestler, 1964; Weisberg, 1986).

The model of creativity presented in this chapter incorporates these principles into a model of case-based problem solving.

2.3 Case-Based Models of Problem Solving

MINSTREL's model of creativity is built on a case-based model of problem solving (Hammond, 1988; Kolodner, 1987; Schank, 1987).

Case-based reasoning systems are driven by an episodic memory of past cases rather than a base of inference rules or knowledge-intensive heuristics. Given a problem, a case-based problem solver (1) *recalls* a past problem with the same features and its associated solution, (2) *adapts* the past solution to the current problem, and then (3) *assesses* the result. To drive home from work, a case-based problem solver recalls a previous time he or she drove home and the route he used, modifies the route in light of changing road conditions (perhaps a particular street is closed for repair) and then assesses that route according to his or her general knowledge about driving.

This model is illustrated in Figure 2.1. Problem specifications are input at the left side, where they are used to recall similar past problems. The solutions from these past problems are then adapted to the current problem. Finally, the adapted solutions are assessed to determine if they are useful and meet other domain-specific considerations (e.g., a mechanical engineer might want to create efficient solutions). (A more complete review of case-based reasoning can be found in Slade, 1991.)

Case-based problem solving has several benefits. First, case-based problem solving is similar to the reasoning done by human experts (Riesbeck & Schank, 1989). Expertise depends on experience, and case-based reasoning captures this connection.

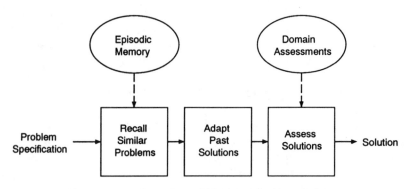

Figure 2.1 A Case-Based Model of Problem Solving

Second, case-based problem solving explains how a problem solver can use new experiences to extend his knowledge. Planning and storytelling systems that capture problem solving knowledge as static rules (i.e., Lebowitz, 1985; Meehan, 1976; Warren, 1978) require additional mechanisms to explain how that knowledge can be extended.

A final advantage of case-based problem solving is efficiency at solving routine problems. By recalling a past problem that shares all the features of the current problem, the problem solver is assured (1) that the solution from the recalled problem will apply to the current problem, (2) that adapting the recalled solution to the current problem will be simple, (3) that little or no assessment of the adapted solution will be necessary, and (4) that the recalled solution is very likely to work. Re-using past solutions under identical circumstances requires little effort and results in a high degree of success.

However, case-based problem solving has an obvious shortcoming: It fails when faced with a new problem. If a similar past problem cannot be recalled, the case-based problem solver has no way to discover, build, or create a new solution. Using old solutions over and over again is acceptable and efficient in many domains. It would be tiresome, for instance, to create a new route home from work each day. But when no old solution is known, a problem solver must be able to create a new solution. Furthermore, case-based problem solving has difficulty explaining domains such as art and literature. In these domains, problem solvers often reject solutions simply because they are old or repetitive.

To capture the creative process, case-based problem solving must be extended to include (1) a creative drive, and (2) processes that can combine old knowledge in new ways to create problem solutions.

2.4   Failure-Driven Creativity

People are conservative problem solvers. They expend the effort to create new solutions when familiar, known solutions fail (Weisberg, 1986). Janelle created a new solution to the spilled milk problem only because the lack of a towel prevented her from applying an old plan.

Old solutions may fail for a number of reasons. They may not solve the problem, or may solve the problem inefficiently. Or they may be rejected simply because they are old, as in literature and art, where a premium is placed on new ideas. Whatever the cause, it is the failure of old solutions that drives the problem solver to create a new solution. A model of creative problem solving needs a mechanism for detecting planning failures and using that to drive the creative process.

Case-based problem solving can fail at each of the three steps shown in Figure 2.1: (1) if a past problem situation similar to the current problem situation cannot be recalled, (2) if a recalled solution cannot be adapted to the current problem, or (3) if the adapted solution fails a domain assessment. In the

MINSTREL model of creativity, a failure at any of these steps causes MIN-STREL to attempt to create a new solution to the problem. Like Janelle, MIN-STREL is creative when it encounters a problem for which its past solutions fail.

Because MINSTREL is a model of storytelling as well as creativity, MIN-STREL also implements an artistic drive to create. Unlike their counterparts in traditional problem solving domains such as engineering, artists sometimes reject solutions even when problem solving is successful. Artists create for the sake of creation; they find repetition of solutions boring and unacceptable. (In fact, all human problem solvers get bored with repetitive solutions, but particular emphasis is placed on this motivation in the arts.) MINSTREL implements the artistic drive to create as a *boredom assessment*.

The boredom assessment operates during the Assess step of problem solving (see Figure 2.1). The boredom assessment examines proposed problem solutions to determine if they've been used too many times previously, that is, have become boring. To do this, MINSTREL uses episodic memory.

Episodic memory is the autobiographical record of the events and experiences that make up a person's personal history (Cohen, 1989; Tulving, 1972). MINSTREL uses a model of episodic memory based on work by Schank (1982) and Kolodner (1984), and elaborated and tested by Reiser, Black, and Abelson (Reiser, 1983, 1986; Reiser, Black, & Abelson, 1985), who term it the "context plus index" model. In this model, episodes are organized according to their distinctive differences. Two episodes with significant differences fall into different memory categories and will not be recalled together. Episodes with no significant differences fall into the same memory category and are recalled as a group.

To determine if a solution has become boring, MINSTREL indexes the solution in episodic memory and counts how many times similar solutions have been used. If the solution has been used more than a small number[3] of times, it is judged boring and rejected.

To illustrate this process, suppose that MINSTREL is building a story scene in which a knight's life is endangered. MINSTREL's episodic memory contains scenes about King Arthur and his Knights. Some of these scenes are initially seeded into MINSTREL's memory, as if MINSTREL had read several short stories about King Arthur. Others are from stories MINSTREL invented during earlier storytelling sessions. In this example, MINSTREL's episodic memory contains only one scene. In this scene, a knight fights a dragon. To build a new scene in which a knight's life is endangered, MINSTREL tries to recall a similar scene from a previous story. This recalls the scene in which a knight fights a dragon. Because the recalled scene had only been used once before, it is judged "not boring" and used as the basis for the new scene. Then the new scene is added to the current story and to episodic memory.

Now episodic memory contains two scenes in which a knight fights a

---

[3]Currently, MINSTREL considers a solution boring if it has been used twice previously. The threshold can be set to other values by the user.

dragon. The next time MINSTREL creates a scene in which a knight fights a dragon (perhaps again to solve the "build a scene in which a knight is endangered" problem), the boredom assessment will reject the scene. "Knights fighting dragons" has become boring, and MINSTREL will be driven to create a new way in which a knight can be endangered, *even though problem solving succeeded in finding a useful solution to the original problem.*

As MINSTREL tells stories and indexes them in memory, MINSTREL's storytelling behavior changes. MINSTREL may tell stories about knights fighting dragons for a while, but these soon become boring and MINSTREL moves on to other topics. Thus, the boredom assessment models the artistic drive to create. MINSTREL, like any human faced with a repetitive task, becomes bored with the "known" solutions, and is driven to create new solutions. And because of its creativity heuristics, MINSTREL can invent new solutions when it becomes bored with old ones.

MINSTREL's boredom heuristic is simple. It ignores the type of problem being solved and other constraints that might realistically affect an artist's determination of whether a concept or solution should be reused. A storyteller, for example, will not want to create new solutions for every character action in a story. How a knight gets from place to place is probably unimportant, and any known solution will do, no matter how frequently it has been used in the past. And in other domains there will be similar considerations.

For storytelling, MINSTREL applies the boredom heuristic only when creating the story events that illustrate the plot of the story. The plot, which is the sequence of story events that illustrate the theme or most important point of the story, is the most important element of the story, and so MINSTREL strives to be creative when building the plot. Other elements of the story, such as events that were added to keep the story causally consistent, are of less importance, and so MINSTREL accepts noncreative solutions for these problems.

For any particular artistic domain, then, there will be other considerations in determining whether a concept is "boring." But the basic consideration will remain the novelty of the concept: how often that concept or a similar one has been used in the past. The basic process behind MINSTREL's boredom heuristic—using episodic memory to determine the novelty of an idea—supports this basic need and has the flexibility to be augmented into a more complete and realistic boredom assessment.

2.5 The Challenges of Creativity

By what processes are new solutions created? As Janelle's example illustrated, people invent new solutions by (1) recalling knowledge not part of the known solutions to the problem, and (2) adapting that knowledge to create a solution (Weisberg, 1986). Four factors make this a difficult task.

First, the obvious source of knowledge about the current problem—similar past problems—has been exhausted. Case-based problem solving tries to find solutions indexed under similar past problems. But the creative process begins when problem solving fails; the solutions indexed under the current problem have already been tried and rejected. To discover a new solution, the problem solver must find knowledge *not* indexed under the current problem. The difficulty is knowing where in the space of episodic memories to seek knowledge. Knowledge grabbed willy-nilly from memory will be unlikely to apply to the current problem.

New solutions require knowledge not indexed under the current problem.

Second, the problem solver may not even have any incorrect or partial solutions on which to base his problem solving efforts. If the current problem is sufficiently different from past problems, then case-based problem solving may have failed to recall any similar past problems and their associated solutions. Thus it is difficult for the creative problem solver to search for new knowledge in the solution space, because he may not have even an incorrect solution from which to start. However, he will always have his problem description, so he can search the *problem space*. In general, the problem solver must find new knowledge by searching the problem space. The problem solver must change the current problem into some new problem, in hopes of finding useful knowledge in the recalled solutions to the new problem. This casts the problem of creativity in a new light: The first step to creativity is changing the problem, not the solution.

Creativity involves recasting the problem.

Third, the complexity of adapting the discovered knowledge may overwhelm the creative effort. If Janelle had attempted to adapt her plan for the "getting to school" problem to the "spilled milk" problem, the difficulty of the adaptation task would be insurmountable. (How can knowledge about riding a school bus be applied to the problem of cleaning up spilled milk?) Trying to solve a difficult problem by substituting an impossible problem is a poor strategy. Somehow the creative process must limit the complexity of the adaptation process.

Adaptation must avoid too much complexity.

Finally, the creative process must be capable of discovering solutions substantially different from the original solution. There is a need to limit the creative process to simplify the search for new knowledge and the adaptation problem, but there is also a need to find the knowledge needed to created an original solution. Some mechanism must exist that will enable the creative problem solver to find necessary knowledge, even when it is conceptually distant from the original problem.

Creativity must be capable of "leaps" to new problem solutions.

The challenge of creativity research is to find a cognitive mechanism that is not crippled by these requirements. The creative process must be able to (1) find useful knowledge by searching the problem space, (2) limit the adaptation task, and (3) discover solutions substantially different from the original solution.

2.6 MINSTREL's Creativity Heuristics

The MINSTREL model of creativity is based on creativity heuristics that associate problem transformations with specific solution adaptations. To search the problem space for possible new solutions, MINSTREL begins at the original problem and applies small transformations that create new, slightly different problems. If one of these new problems can be solved, the associated solution adaptation can be used to create a new solution to the original problem.

Suppose, for example, that MINSTREL is trying to invent a method for a knight to kill a dragon. Figure 2.2 illustrates the search space for this problem. At the center is the original problem, and around it are similar problems. To discover a new solution to the original problem, MINSTREL applies a problem transformation, jumping from the original problems to one of the nearby problems. MINSTREL now tries to solve this new problem. If MINSTREL is suc-

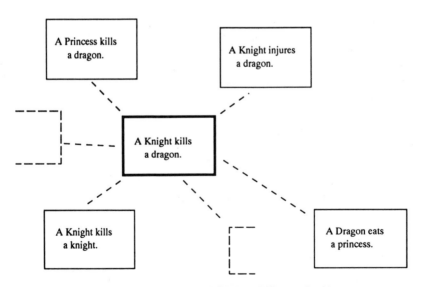

Figure 2.2 Search Space of Slightly Different Problems

cessful (by recalling a solution from episodic memory), it then tries to adapt the recalled solution to the original problem, jumping back to the center of the search space. The result is a new solution to the original problem.

The process of "Transform-Recall-Adapt" is the heart of MINSTREL's model of creative problem solving. In the Transform step, MINSTREL takes a problem description and changes it into a slightly different problem. In the Recall step, MINSTREL takes the new problem description and tries to recall similar past situations from episodic memory, and the solutions used in those situations. In the Adapt step, MINSTREL takes the recalled solutions and adapts them to the original problem. The Transform step *searches* the problem space, the Recall step *finds* new knowledge, and the Adapt step *applies* that knowledge to the current problem.

MINSTREL implements this process in creativity heuristics called Transform-Recall-Adapt Methods, or TRAMs. Each TRAM consists of a transformation to be applied to a problem and a specific adaptation that will apply recalled solutions to the original problem. Figure 2.3 shows a simplified example of one of MINSTREL's TRAMS, TRAM:Cross-Domain-Solution. This TRAM suggests that a new solution to a problem can be found by (1) translating the problem into a new domain [Transform], (2) solving the problem in that domain [Recall], and (3) translating the solution back into the original domain [Adapt]. MINSTREL uses TRAM:Cross-Domain-Solution to create the following story scene (from "Richard and Lancelot"):

> One day while out riding, Lancelot's horse went into the woods. Lancelot could not control the horse. The horse took him deeper into the woods. The horse stopped. Lancelot saw Andrea, a Lady of the Court, who was out picking berries.

The original specification for this problem is "create a scene in which a knight accidently meets a princess." TRAM:Cross-Domain-Solution transforms

TRAM:Cross-Domain-Solution

Transform Strategy

> Find a new problem domain with similar actions and actors, and map the original problem into this new domain. Retain the mapping for use in the Adapt step.

Adapt Strategy

> Map any discovered solutions back to the original domain by reversing the mapping used in the Adapt step.

Figure 2.3 TRAM:Cross-Domain-Solution

this problem specification by mapping it into the modern domain. Elements of the original problem specification are mapped to corresponding elements in the new domain. "A knight" becomes "a businessman" and "a princess" becomes "a friend." The new problem specification is "a businessman accidently meets a friend" and recalls this story:

Walking The Dog

John was sitting at home one evening when his dog began acting strange. The dog was scratching at the door and whining for a walk. Finally, John decided to take the dog for a walk. While they were out, John ran across his old friend Pete, whom he hadn't seen in many years.

This story is adapted to the original problem by mapping the story back into the King Arthur domain, creating the scene in which Lancelot's horse leads him to Andrea. The resulting scene is creative—novel and useful—because TRAM:Cross-Domain enabled the problem solver to (1) discover knowledge previously unconnected to the original problem, and (2) apply that knowledge to create a new solution.

2.7   The MINSTREL Model of Creative Problem Solving

Figure 2.4 illustrates how TRAMs are integrated into the case-based problem solving model. The Recall and Adapt steps of the basic problem solving model are augmented with a pool of TRAMs. During problem solving, a TRAM is selected from this pool and applied to the original problem. If the TRAM succeeds in discovering a solution and adapting it to the original problem, then problem solving succeeds. If problem solving fails, then the current TRAM is discarded, another selected from the pool of available TRAMs, and the cycle repeats.

2.7.1   Transform

The first step of the augmented problem solving model is to transform the original problem. In this step, the Transform portion of one of MINSTREL's TRAMs is applied to the original problem description, changing it into a new problem. This step is a new addition to the model of case-based problem solving. It is this transformation that permits MINSTREL to search the problem space for new knowledge, a capability that normal problem solving lacks.

Of course, a problem solver needs to be creative only if problem solving fails. So before applying a transformation to the original problem specification, the problem solver should try to solve the original problem.

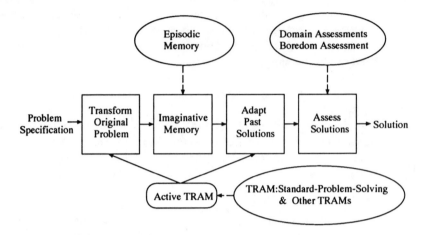

Figure 2.4 Model of Problem Solving with TRAMs

This is accomplished by a special creativity heuristic called "TRAM:Standard-Problem-Solving." TRAM:Standard-Problem-Solving is the null creativity heuristic: It applies no transformation to the problem description and applies no adaptation to any recalled solutions. So when TRAM:Standard-Problem-Solving is the Active TRAM, MINSTREL performs standard case-based problem solving. TRAM:Standard-Problem-Solving thus implements standard case-based problem solving within the framework of creativity. TRAM:Standard-Problem-Solving is illustrated in Figure 2.5.

TRAM:Standard-Problem-Solving is always the first TRAM selected from the pool of available TRAMs. This ensures that the first effort of MINSTREL's creative problem solving will be to find a known solution. By selecting TRAM:Standard-Problem-Solving first from the pool of TRAMs, MINSTREL will always use an old, known solution if available and acceptable to the solution assessments.

TRAM:Standard-Problem-Solving

Transform Strategy

Do not transform the problem description.

Adapt Strategy

Do not adapt the recalled solution. Apply as is to the current problem.

Figure 2.5 TRAM:Standard-Problem-Solving

2.7.2 TRAM Selection

When TRAM:Standard-Problem-Solving fails to find a solution, a new TRAM must be selected from the pool of available TRAMs to begin MINSTREL's effort to create a new solution.

The TRAMs in the pool of available TRAMs are organized according to the types of problems to which they apply. Some TRAMs are general, and can modify any problem description. Other TRAMs are specific to certain types of problem descriptions. To select a TRAM for the current problem, MINSTREL uses the problem specification to select the applicable TRAMs from the pool of available TRAMs.

MINSTREL indexes the pool of available TRAMs using episodic memory. Just as episodic memory contains past problems and their associated solutions, episodic memory also contains past problems and associated TRAMs. Finding the TRAMs that apply to a particular problem thus becomes a matter of recall. MINSTREL uses the current problem as an index to episodic memory, and finds similar past problems and their associated TRAMs. TRAMs that apply to many different types of problem are associated with very general problem descriptions; TRAMs that apply to specific types of problems are associated with more specific problem descriptions. By recalling all of the problem descriptions that match the current problem, MINSTREL gathers all the applicable TRAMs.

From the applicable TRAMs, one TRAM is selected randomly. The reason for using random choice is straightforward. Creativity heuristics search the problem space for useful knowledge to apply to the current problem. But prior to actually performing that search, the problem solver cannot know where the useful knowledge lies. In this sense, the applicable TRAMs are indistinguishable. Hence the problem solver has no reason to prefer one heuristic over another, making random selection a reasonable algorithm.

Another possible algorithm for selecting between competing TRAMs is to use past creativity experience to guide TRAM selection. For example, the problem solver might want to use TRAMs according to how frequently they've been successful in past problem solving situations. Or, since that might lead to repetition, the problem solver might want to try heuristics that haven't been frequently used. Or the problem solver might want to try the most recently successful heuristic again, to reinforce the value of newly learned heuristics. All of these are interesting strategies.

Although MINSTREL does not currently use past creativity experience to guide TRAM selection, the use of episodic memory to organize TRAMs provides support for these types of strategies. As TRAMs are used and indexed into episodic memory, the problem solver retains knowledge about the usage of creativity. However, what form a cognitively valid record of creativity would take remains an open question.

2.7.3 Recall

The second step in the MINSTREL model of creative problem solving is recall of similar past problems. If similar past problems can be recalled, the associated solutions are passed on to the adaptation step. The index for recall is the problem specification. For this reason, episodic memory must be organized by past problems, and the recall process must be able to take a possibly incomplete problem specification and recall similar past problems.

MINSTREL's model of episodic memory is based on the "context plus index" model (Kolodner, 1984; Reiser, 1986; Schank, 1982). Context plus index models of memory organizes a specific episode according to its general context (i.e., a plane trip) and the distinguishing features of the episode (i.e., taking Pan-Am, flying to Central America). In the MINSTREL model, problem types correspond to different contexts, and the specific features of each problem are used as indexing features. This permits MINSTREL to organize memory according to past problems, and to recall matching problems when given a problem specification.

2.7.4 Adaptation

The third step of MINSTREL's creative process is adaptation. Past solutions to problems are passed to the adaptation step, where the Adapt portion of the controlling TRAM modifies them for use on the current problem.

In general, the problem of adapting knowledge—even useful knowledge—to a new problem is very difficult. Consider what a problem solver must do to adapt the story "Walking the Dog" to the problem of "Lancelot meets Guinevere unexpectedly."

Walking The Dog

> John was sitting at home one evening when his dog began acting strange. The dog was scratching at the door and whining for a walk. Finally, John decided to take the dog for a walk. While they were out, John ran across his old friend Pete, whom he hadn't seen in many years.

The problem solver must first fully understand this story, so that he can recognize that it is also an unexpected meeting. Then he must determine what its relationship is to the original problem, to know how to apply this knowledge to it. He must realize that it is in another problem domain, and determine what that domain is. Finally, he must build a mapping from this domain to the original problem domain and translate the story.

In MINSTREL, though, the problem of adaptation is greatly simplified by associating adaptations with specific problem transformations. Because each adaptation is applied only to problem solutions that arose from a particular problem transformation, there is no need to fully understand the problem solution and determine its relation to the original problem. The relation of the recalled solution to the original problem is fixed by the Transform portion of the TRAM. Instead, the adapt portion of each TRAM needs only do the final work of adaptation—to make the necessary changes to the recalled solution.

For example, in TRAM:Cross-Domain-Solution the Adapt step need only apply the cross domain mapping generated during the Transform step in reverse upon the problem solution. This translates the recalled solution back into the original problem domain, making it suitable for the original problem. The Adapt step does have to understand the recalled solution, or determine its relationship to the original problem.

2.7.5   Assessment

The fourth step of MINSTREL's creative process is assessment. The purpose of the assessment step is to evaluate a proposed solution in light of acceptance criteria specific to a particular domain. For example, a mechanical engineer might evaluate his designs in terms of their efficiency, what kinds of materials they use, and so on. Although the problem solving process tries to create solutions that fit the original problem specification, it may inadvertently fail (see the discussion of "Creativity Errors" in this chapter), or there may be additional criteria that cannot be easily expressed in the problem specification. In these cases, domain assessments can be used to catch faulty solutions.

A special assessment for artistic problem domains is the boredom assessment. The boredom assessment rejects solutions that are too similar to previous solutions, and models the drive for originality in the arts. The boredom assessment is an example of an assessment that embodies a criteria that is difficult to express in the original problem specification—namely, that the solution be original.

When a proposed solution fails a domain assessment, problem solving fails, the active TRAM and the proposed solution are discarded, and another TRAM is selected. The problem solving process then repeats under the control of the new TRAM.

One shortcoming of this algorithm is that it discards the proposed solution, which may be almost entirely correct. Re-inventing the correct parts of that solution may take a great deal of effort. An alternative possibility is to "repair" proposed solutions which fail a domain assessment.

For example, if a domain assessment for mechanical invention notices that a device has a redundant component, it can repair that design by removing the redundant component. Another possibility is to use problem solving recursively to repair a faulty solution. If a domain assessment in mechanical invention notices that a device lacks a power source, it can repair this problem by recursively using problem solving to invent a power source.

MINSTREL is capable of both these types of repair. Domain assessments can directly manipulate the proposed solutions or call problem solving to create a correction. Whether a proposed solution should be rejected or repaired depends both upon the cost and efficacy of the repair technique.

First, repair should be undertaken only when it provides a cost savings over rejecting the faulty solution and finding a new solution. Repairing a solution with major faults may be much more expensive and time-consuming than simply throwing out the faulty solution and finding an entirely new one. For a mechanical device lacking a power source, inventing a power source may be a very difficult problem that would take more time and effort than simply finding a different solution to the original problem. If this is the case, it would be better to reject the proposed solution rather than repair it.

Efficacy of repair can also be a factor. Consider the earlier example in which a repair removes a redundant piece from a mechanical device. Is that always a correct and safe change to the design? Only insofar as the repair understands the device design. Perhaps the redundant pieces was added to the design by problem solving in order to balance the weight of the device. In general, a repair heuristic will not be as knowledgeable and powerful as problem solving, and so will sometimes make errors.

Deciding the likely costs of repair vs. rejection, or determining whether a repair will be efficient without introducing more serious faults are difficult issues. Currently MINSTREL's boredom assessment uses rejection, while the two assessments used in mechanical invention use repair, but these are simply design choices that are not founded on any deep understanding of the issues of repair vs. rejection. For further discussion of the role of repair in planning, see Hammond (1988).

2.8 Summary of Creativity Model

Earlier we identified the three challenges of creativity as: (1) finding useful knowledge by searching the problem space, (2) limiting the adaptation task, and (3) discovering solutions substantially different from the original solution. The MINSTREL model of creativity answers these challenges by associating problem transformations with corresponding solution adaptations. Problem transformations permit MINSTREL to search the problem space, and because each problem transformation has an associated, specific solution adaptation, the complexity of adaptation is eliminated. And this adaptation of knowledge from other problems leads to the creation of new solutions with substantial differences from previous solutions.

2.9   Leaps of Creativity

TRAMs find new solutions to problems by making *small* changes in the problem description and corresponding small adaptations to any discovered solutions. In light of the definition of creativity as a solution with a "substantial" difference from past solutions, this may seem counterintuitive. Why not use creativity heuristics that make large changes to the problem descriptions? There are several reasons, which are founded in our current understanding of human cognition.

First, MINSTREL is an integrated model of problem solving and creativity, in which creativity is an extension of problem solving. In most problem solving situations, there is no need for powerful creativity. Most problems are solved using standard solutions or past solutions that have been only slightly adapted. It is only in rare cases that a problem solver must invent a solution substantially different from a past solution.

Consequently we expect creativity heuristics to be very efficient at discovering small adaptations while still capable of larger adaptations. By using heuristics that make small adaptations, MINSTREL is efficient at the types of simple problem solving and creativity that make up the bulk of problem solving situations. (The question of whether MINSTREL is capable of larger adaptations is discussed below.) But there are other reasons to use small adaptations as a basis for creativity.

One advantage of creativity heuristics that make only small changes to a problem description is that they are more likely to find useful knowledge. Slightly different problems are good sources of useful knowledge because they share many of the same constraints as the original problem, and their solutions are likely to have some applicability to the original problem. Examining slightly different problems constrains the search task to an area of the problem space that is localized and fertile.

A second advantage is that small adaptations are easier and more likely to be successful than large adaptations. Adapting a very different solution to a new problem (i.e., adapting the "getting to school" solution to the "spilled milk" problem) requires a great deal of knowledge and effort and is likely to fail no matter what the expenditure. Adapting a solution that has only small differences (i.e., adapting the "spilled juice" solution to the "spilled milk" problem) requires less knowledge and effort and is more likely to succeed.

So there are several reasons to use small adaptations. But are small adaptations capable of discovering more creative solutions?

Sometimes even simple heuristics are capable of discovering unique solutions. Consider the heuristic to "substitute an agent" which Janelle used to create a solution involving a kitten. Although the heuristic itself is simple and commonplace, in this case the solution it discovers is surprisingly creative.

But even if creativity heuristics taken singly are not capable of major discoveries, they can be when taken *in combination*. The strategy of small problem transformations tends to find solutions with small differences from the original problem. But if a single heuristic does not find a new solution, transformations can be repeatedly applied until substantially different solutions are discovered. And because the adaptation of the created solution is done in many small, simple steps, the process of adaptation remains simple.

Leaps in creativity result from combinations of small modifications.

How can several creativity heuristics be applied to a single problem? In MINSTREL, this is achieved through a mechanism called *imaginative memory*.

2.9.1 Imaginative Memory

The central step of MINSTREL's creative problem solving model is recalling a solution from episodic memory. But recall *itself* can be viewed as a kind of "problem solving." What happens if creative problem solving is used to solve the "recall problem"?

To do this requires replacing the Recall step of creative problem solving with a recursive call to creative problem solving with the problem specification "Find something in episodic memory that matches these features." Of course, this could lead to endless recursion: at each level of problem solving, the Recall step calls problem solving again. To terminate this endless recursion, TRAM:Standard-Problem-Solving is modified so that it will continue to use episodic memory for recall. Since TRAM:Standard-Problem-Solving is always the first TRAM used by creative problem solving, this means that the first attempt at recall at each level of recursion will use episodic memory instead of recursing to another level of problem solving. The result is that creative problem solving first tries to recall a solution from episodic memory. If that fails, it recursively calls creative problem solving to solve the "recall" problem. This process is illustrated in Figure 2.6.

Now when a problem solver needs to recall something, TRAM:Standard-Problem-Solving is the first TRAM used, and passes the recall features unchanged to episodic memory. If an episode that matches the recall features is found, problem solving succeeds. Because TRAM:Standard-Problem-Solving is always the first TRAM used and continues to use episodic memory normally, recall behaves as expected when an episode exists that matches the recall features.

Something more interesting happens when the Recall step of TRAM:Standard-Problem-Solving fails. If TRAM:Standard-Problem-Solving cannot find an episode in memory that matches the recall features, problem solving fails and a new TRAM is selected. This TRAM modifies the recall features and recursively calls the problem solving process with the new recall features.

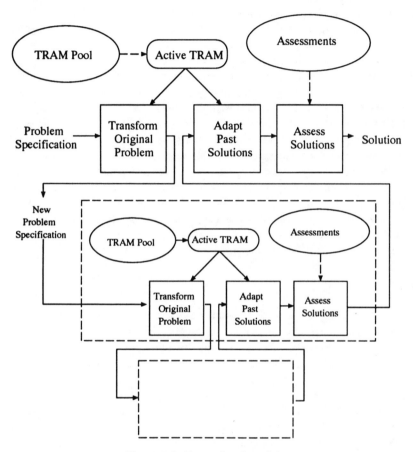

Figure 2.6 Recursive Creativity

The first TRAM used on the recursive call is TRAM:Standard-Problem-Solving. If the new features recall an episode, the episode is returned to the previous recursion of problem solving, where it is adapted to the original problem by the previous TRAM, and recall succeeds. *But because the recalled episode was changed by the Adapt portion of the previous TRAM, it is no longer the episode that was found in memory.*

Recall has succeeded in a strange way: by recalling an episode that does not exist in episodic memory. Episodic memory has become imaginative. When an appropriate episode exists, it is recalled. When no appropriate episode exists, recall uses creativity heuristics to "imagine" an appropriate episode.

Treating recall as problem solving also enables the problem solver to apply multiple TRAMs to a problem. Each time recall fails the recursive use of creative problem solving will apply another TRAM to the recall features. In this way, a number of TRAMs can be successively applied to a problem. Each TRAM changes the problem in only a small way, but the cumulative effect may be large, enabling the creative problem solver to discover new solutions significantly different from known solutions.

There are two advantages to imaginative memory.

First, it provides a simple and powerful mechanism for the repeated applications of creativity heuristics to a problem. Each time the Recall step of problem solving fails, imaginative memory will recurse and apply a new creativity heuristic. If no useful knowledge can be found in the problem space near the original problem, repeated problem transformations will move the creative problem solver into more distant areas of the problem space.

More importantly, imaginative memory implements creativity at a low cognitive level. By embedding creative problem solving in the recall process, imaginative memory makes creativity transparently available to *any* cognitive mechanism that uses episodic memory for reasoning. By integrating creativity into the foundation of the cognitive process, imaginative memory increases the reasoning power of all cognitive mechanisms.

2.10   Integrated Model

Figure 2.7 illustrates how the boredom assessment, Transform-Recall-Adapt Methods and imaginative memory are integrated with case-based reasoning to form a complete model of creative problem solving. The three steps of case-based reasoning (Recall, Adapt, Assess) have been augmented with a Transform step. An active TRAM controls the Transform and Adapt steps. Initially this is TRAM:Standard-Problem Solving, which is simply the strategy of recalling a similar past problem and using the solution from that problem. The Assess step applies a pool of assessments to proposed solutions. In creative domains, this includes the boredom assessment, which rejects solutions that are too similar to past solutions. The Recall step uses imaginative memory (a recursive call to problem solving) except when controlled by TRAM:Standard-Problem Solving.

The problem solving cycle begins when a problem description enters the recall step. Initially TRAM:Standard-Problem Solving is in control. The original problem description is used to recall similar problem solving situations from episodic memory. If recall succeeds, the recalled situations are passed to the Adapt step. Under TRAM:Standard-Problem Solving, no adaptation is needed because the recalled solutions are very similar to the original problem, so the recalled solutions are passed along to the Assess step. In the Assess step, all active assessments are applied to the recalled solutions, and if a solution passes all the assessments, it is output as a solution to the original problem. This is the normal problem solving cycle.

If TRAM:Standard-Problem Solving fails, either because no solutions were recalled or because the recalled solutions failed some assessment,

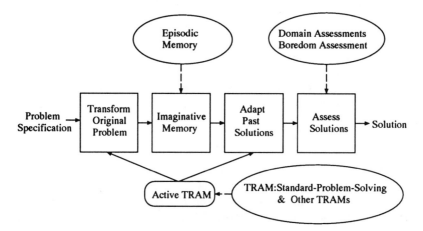

Figure 2.7 MINSTREL's Process Model of Creativity

TRAM:Standard-Problem Solving is discarded and a new TRAM selected. The selection of a TRAM is based on the type of problem being solved and the TRAMs previously used.

The selected TRAM transforms the original problem specification, creating a new problem specification. The new problem specification is passed to imaginative memory. If recall succeeds, the recalled solutions are passed to the adapt step, where the active TRAM applies a specific adaptation which reverses the problem transformation. If recall fails, then imaginative memory recursively applies a second TRAM, and creative problem solving repeats.

Figure 2.6 illustrates the recursive use of creativity problem solving. When recall from episodic memory fails, imaginative memory resolves to a recursive use of problem solving. This continues until recall from episodic memory succeeds (or a processing limit is reached). The solution from each level is passed back to the previous level, where it is adapted, assessed, and passed up again. Eventually the solution reaches the top level, at which point it has been adapted to the original problem.

At each step, adapted solutions are assessed by domain assessments and, if appropriate, the boredom assessment. If a solution passes all assessments, problem solving succeeds. If all solutions fail, the active TRAM is discarded, a new TRAM selected, and the Recall-Adapt-Assess cycle repeats.

2.11   Examples of Creativity

The model of creative problem solving presented in this chapter has been implemented in a computer program called MINSTREL. The next two sections show
how MINSTREL uses creative problem solving to discover new solutions for a
simple planning problem in the domain of King Arthur, and to create a scene for
a story. These examples should give the reader a better understanding of the
TRAM model of creativity.

2.11.1   Suicide Example

In this example, MINSTREL is trying to discover a way for a knight to commit
suicide. Initially, MINSTREL knows nothing about suicide, but does know
about killing dragons and drinking a potion to become ill. Using this knowledge
and creative problem solving, MINSTREL discovers three methods of suicide
and invents[4] the notion of "poison."

2.11.1.1   Representation

MINSTREL uses a schema-based representation language called RHAPSODY
Turner (1985). Goals, actions, and states of the world are represented as
schemas; instances of these schemas make up the episodes in MINSTREL's
memory and the elements of the stories MINSTREL tells. Each schema has
named slots which contain schema information. Goal schemas, for example,
have slots for the type of the goal and the actor of the goal. Schemas can also
have named links to other schemas. Goal schemas typically have links to plans,
and to the states that achieve the goals. Schema names begin with an ampersand
(&) and schema instances are given either descriptive names (such as
&KNIGHT-FIGHT) or generated names based on the schema type (such as
&GOAL.112). For a more complete discussion of MINSTREL's representation,
see (Turner, 1985).

2.11.1.2   The Problem

Figure 2.8 illustrates MINSTREL's representation of the suicide problem.
&HUMAN.12 is an instance of the human schema which represents the knight.
The type slot of a human instance indicates the character's major role in the
King Arthur world, and illustrates how MINSTREL uses schema slots to instan-
tiate particular schema instances. The knight has a goal (&GOAL.11) which
will be achieved by the knight being dead (&STATE.8). The plan for this goal
(&ACT.4) is currently uninstantiated. MINSTREL's goal in this example is to

---

[4] I use the term *invent* to indicate a concept that is new to MINSTREL, if not necessarily
new to the reader.

instantiate &ACT.4 as an action or series of actions that will achieve the knight's goal of committing suicide.

2.11.1.3   Initial State of Episodic Memory

All of MINSTREL's knowledge of the King Arthur domain is contained in episodic memory. MINSTREL's creativity heuristics have general knowledge about goals, plans, and states of the world, but specific knowledge about the goals, plans, and actions of characters in the King Arthur domain is deduced from the contents of episodic memory.

At the beginning of this example, MINSTREL knows nothing about how a knight might kill himself. Initially, MINSTREL's episodic memory contains only these two episodes:

Knight Fight

A knight fights a troll with his sword, killing the troll and being injured in the process.

The Princess and the Potion

A lady of the court drank a potion to make herself ill.

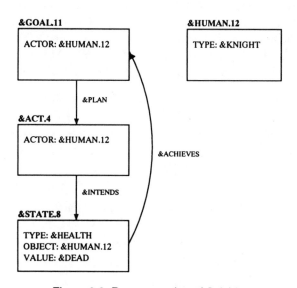

Figure 2.8 Representation of Suicide

Figure 2.9 shows the schema representation of "The Princess and the Potion." &ACT.14 represents the action of Lady Andrea quaffing a potion. &STATE.17 represents the intentional outcome of that action—Lady Andrea becoming ill.

2.11.1.4   Trace

Figure 2.10 shows a trace of MINSTREL inventing three different methods of suicide. In this example, MINSTREL has been configured to exhaustively invent solutions to the suicide problem and present them in English as created. Normally MINSTREL generates copious debugging and tracing output. To spare the reader, the trace shown in Figure 2.10 has been edited to improve readability. Uninteresting portions of the trace and reasoning dead-ends have been deleted. These deletions have been marked in the trace with "[...]." Except for this editing, the trace appears exactly as generated by MINSTREL. The level of indentation of the trace reflects the level of recursive problem solving.

MINSTREL begins the example shown in Figure 2.10 by generating the initial problem specification in English: "A knight named John did something. John died." This is an English description of the schema representation shown in Figure 2.7. MINSTREL's English descriptions of schemas are produced by a phrasal generator (Reeves, 1989; Zernik, 1987).

The problem specification is followed by a trace of the problem solving cycle. As each new TRAM is applied, the name of the TRAM (i.e., TRAM:GENERALIZE-CONSTRAINT) is printed out. When TRAM:Standard-Problem Solving is used to attempt recall from episodic memory, a message is printed out showing the recall index and what was recalled. The very first part of the trace shows TRAM:EXAGGERATE-SCALED-VALUE being applied to this problem and failing when nothing (i.e., NIL) is recalled from episodic memory.

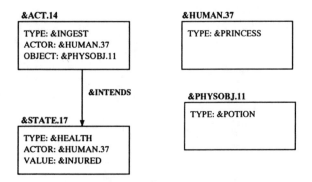

Figure 2.9   Representation of "The Princess and the Potion"

```
==================================================
            MINSTREL Invention
==================================================
Initial specification is &ACT.105:
(A KNIGHT NAMED JOHN DID SOMETHING *PERIOD*
JOHN DIED *PERIOD*)

Problem Solving Cycle: &ACT.105.
Executing TRAM:EXAGGERATE-SCALED-VALUE.
  Recalling &ACT.105: NIL.
  ...TRAM fails.
[...]
Executing TRAM:GENERALIZE-CONSTRAINT.
  Generalizing :OBJECT on &STATE.112.
  Recalling &ACT.118: &KNIGHT-FIGHT.
TRAM succeeds: (&ACT.405).

Minstrel invented this solution:
(A KNIGHT NAMED JOHN FOUGHT HIMSELF BY MOVING
HIS SWORD TO HIMSELF IN ORDER TO KILL HIMSELF
*PERIOD* JOHN DIED *PERIOD*)

[...]
Executing TRAM:SIMILAR-OUTCOMES-PARTIAL-CHANGE.
  Recalling &ACT.136: NIL.
  [TRAM Recursion: &ACT.136.]
    Executing TRAM:GENERALIZE-CONSTRAINT.
    Generalizing :ACTOR on &ACT.138.
      Recalling &ACT.138: &PRINCESS-POTION.
    ...TRAM succeeds: (&ACT.447).
  ...TRAM succeeds: (&ACT.447).

Minstrel invented this solution:
(A KNIGHT NAMED JOHN DRANK A POTION IN ORDER
TO KILL HIMSELF *PERIOD* JOHN DIED *PERIOD*)

[...]
Executing TRAM:INTENTION-SWITCH.
  Recalling &ACT.174: NIL.
  [TRAM Recursion: &ACT.174.]
    Executing TRAM:SIMILAR-OUTCOMES-PARTIAL-CHANGE.
    Recalling &ACT.178: &KNIGHT-FIGHT.
    ...TRAM succeeds: (&ACT.588).
  ...TRAM succeeds: (&ACT.588).

Minstrel invented this solution:
(A KNIGHT NAMED JOHN FOUGHT A DRAGON BY MOVING
HIS SWORD TO IT IN ORDER TO KILL HIMSELF
*PERIOD* JOHN DIED *PERIOD*)
```

Figure 2.10 Suicide Trace

When a solution is discovered, MINSTREL prints a message to that effect and generates an English language description of the solution.

2.11.1.5 TRAM:Generalize-Constraint

The first TRAM that succeeds in discovering a solution to the suicide problem is TRAM:Generalize-Constraint. This TRAM suggests that a new solution to a problem can be found by removing a solution constraint, solving the new problem, and then adding the constraint back to the new solution. Figure 2.11 shows an informal outline of this heuristic.

In the suicide problem, the constraints available for generalization are the schema slot fillers of the problem specification (Figure 2.7): (1) the actor is a knight, (2) the object of the state is the actor, (3) the type of the state is health, and (4) the value of the state is dead. TRAM:Generalize-Constraint suggests recalling scenes in which one of these constraints has been generalized.

In this example, MINSTREL generalizes constraint (2). The original problem specification is "a knight kills himself." TRAM:Generalize-Constraint generalizes this specification by removing the constraint that the knight kill himself and replacing it with the more general constraint that the knight kill *something*. This is indicated by the message "Generalizing :OBJECT on &STATE.112." printed in the trace. The new problem specification is "a knight kills something." This generalization recalls the "Knight Fight" episode:

TRAM:Generalize-Constraint

Transform

1. Select and generalize a feature (call it $generalized-feature) of the scene specification. Use this new scene specification as an index for imaginative recall.

Adapt

1. Adapt the recalled solution to the current problem by adding $generalized-feature back to the recalled scene.

Figure 2.11 Informal Outline of TRAM:Generalize-Constraint

```
[...]
Executing TRAM:GENERALIZE-CONSTRAINT.
Generalizing :OBJECT on &STATE.112.
Recalling &ACT.118: &KNIGHT-FIGHT.
Adapting by replacing &MONSTER.15 with &HUMAN.12.
TRAM succeeds: (&ACT.405).
```

In "Knight Fight," a knight kills a troll by hitting it with his sword. This episode is adapted to the original suicide problem by reversing the original transformation. The troll corresponds to the generalized constraint that a knight kills "something." To adapt this solution to the original problem, this more general constraint must be replaced with the original constraint—that the knight kill himself. Therefore the Adapt portion of TRAM:Generalize-Constraint replaces the troll with the knight, creating a scene in which a knight kills himself by hitting himself with his sword:

```
Minstrel invented this solution:
(A KNIGHT NAMED JOHN FOUGHT HIMSELF BY MOVING
 HIS SWORD TO HIMSELF IN ORDER TO KILL HIMSELF
 *PERIOD* JOHN DIED *PERIOD*)
```

TRAM:Generalize-Constraint has used previous knowledge about how knights kill monsters to create a scene in which a knight kills himself. This process is shown graphically in Figure 2.12.

Three issues that must be addressed in TRAM:Generalize-Constraint are (1) how features are selected for generalization, (2) how the selected feature is generalized, and (3) how the selected feature is added back into the created scene.

To maximize the success of the recall step of TRAM:Generalize-Constraint, the feature chosen for generalization should be likely to lead to the recall of a scene. To achieve this, MINSTREL makes a broad generalization of each feature in the representation and attempts recall using the generalized episode. Every generalization that results in recall is added to a pool, and the problem constraint to be generalized is selected randomly from this pool.

MINSTREL uses two methods to generalize a feature. First, the feature can be completely removed from the problem specification. This is the broadest possible generalization, and is used when selecting the candidate pool. And while this method provides a good, quick indication of whether generalizing a particular feature is useful, it is so broad that it often leads to the recall of scenes which are difficult to adapt to the original problem.

For example, suppose that MINSTREL is creating a scene in which "a knight gives a princess something that makes her happy" and chooses to generalize the "princess" feature by removing it altogether from the problem specification. The new problem specification—"A knight gives somebody something that makes him happy"—can recall *any* episode in memory in which a knight

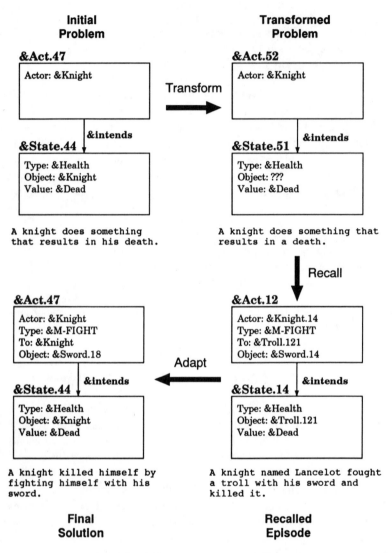

Figure 2.12 Invention of Suicide Example

gives something. If this recalls a scene in which a knight makes a troll happy by giving him a hunk of raw meat, it leads to a scene in which the knight pleases the princess by giving her a hunk of raw meat!

This type of mistake occurs because there is little similarity between the original feature ("princess") and the instantiation of its generalization ("troll"). A better generalization would ensure some similarity between the original feature and the instantiations of the generalization. One such generalization is based on *class hierarchies*.

Classes group concepts that have many similarities. The "People" class groups a variety of characters—princesses, knights, kings, and hermits—that have many similar features. There can be many class hierarchies, and objects can belong to several classes. Knights, for example, are members of both the "People" class and the "Violent Characters" class. By generalizing problem features within classes, MINSTREL is more likely to find a useful reminding.

For this reason, MINSTREL's implementation of TRAM:Generalize-Constraint uses class generalizations. In the suicide example, the "knight" feature is generalized to "a Violent Character." This recalls the "Knight Fight" episode, in which a knight fights a troll in order to kill the troll, because trolls are also members of the "Violent Character" class. If this generalization had failed, MINSTREL would have generalized to the superclass ("Actors"), and if that generalization failed, TRAM:Generalize-Constraint would have failed. A portion of MINSTREL's class hierarchy is shown in Figure 2.13.

The final step in TRAM:Generalize-Constraint is to adapt the recalled episode to the original specification. This is achieved by replacing the generalized feature value with the original feature value throughout the recalled episode. In the suicide example, the troll in "Knight Fight" is replaced by the knight throughout the recalled episode, resulting in a scene in which a knight kills himself by fighting himself with his sword.

Figure 2.14 illustrates TRAM:Generalize-Constraint as implemented in the current version of MINSTREL.

2.11.1.6   TRAM:Similar-Outcomes

MINSTREL discovers a second method for committing suicide by using both TRAM:Generalize-Constraint and a new heuristic, TRAM:Similar-Outcomes-Partial-Change. TRAM:Similar-Outcomes-Partial-Change suggests that if an action results in a particular outcome, it might also result in other, similar outcomes. For example, if MINSTREL doesn't know anything about riding horses except that a knight once rode one to a castle, MINSTREL can use TRAM:Similar-Outcomes to guess that a knight might also ride a horse to some other destination.

In the suicide example, TRAM:Similar-Outcomes-Partial-Change recognizes that being killed is similar to being injured, and transforms the problem description from "a knight purposely kills himself" to "a knight purposely injures himself." If MINSTREL can recall an action in which a knight purposely injures himself, it will be adapted to the current problem by replacing the injury with death. In essence, TRAM:Similar-Outcomes-Partial-Change "guesses" that an

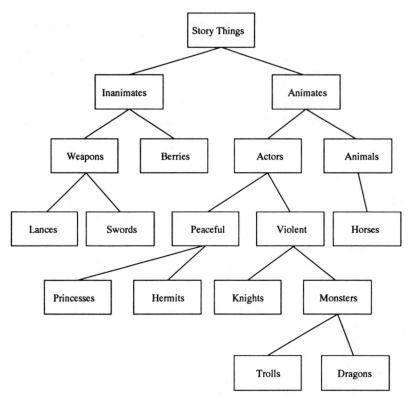

Figure 2.13 A Portion of MINSTREL's Class Hierarchy

action that is known to result in injury might also result in death. MINSTREL then tries to recall a scene in which "a knight purposely injures himself":

```
[...]
  Executing TRAM:SIMILAR-OUTCOMES-PARTIAL-CHANGE.
    Transforming &DEATH to &WOUND.
    Recalling &ACT.136: NIL.
```

However, this does not recall either of the episodes in MINSTREL's episodic memory (as indicated by "Recalling &ACT.136: NIL."). "Knight Fight" is not recalled because the knight does not intentionally injure himself;

TRAM:Generalize-Constraint

Transform Strategy

1. For each feature in the scene specification, eliminate the feature and attempt recall from episodic memory. If recall is successful, then add the feature to a pool of acceptable generalizations.

2. Randomly choose a feature from the pool of acceptable generalizations ($feature).

3. Create a generalization of $feature based on the class membership. Attempt to recall or create a scene based on that generalization. If successful, pass the recalled scene ($recall) to the adapt step.

4. Otherwise, create a generalization based on the superclass, and attempt recall.

5. Otherwise, create a generalization by eliminating the feature, and repeat, and attempt recall.

6. Otherwise, fail this feature and attempt another feature from the pool of possible generalizations.

Adapt Strategy

1. Build a correspondence between the original scene specification ($original) and $recall by matching all the features in $original with the same features in $recall.

2. Add to this correspondence a mapping from the selected feature ($feature) to the instantiation of that feature in $recall.

3. Copy features that are present in $recall but missing in $original from $recall to $original, translating through the correspondence.

Figure 2.14 TRAM:Generalize-Constraint

"Princess and the Potion" is not recalled because the actor is not a knight. Since recall fails, imaginative memory recurses and applies a new TRAM:

```
[...]
Executing TRAM:SIMILAR-OUTCOMES-PARTIAL-CHANGE.
  Transforming &DEATH to &WOUND.
  Recalling &ACT.136: NIL.
  [TRAM Recursion: &ACT.136.]
    Executing TRAM:GENERALIZE-CONSTRAINT.
    Generalizing :ACTOR on &ACT.138.
      Recalling: &PRINCESS-POTION.
    ...TRAM succeeds: (&ACT.447).
  ...TRAM succeeds: (&ACT.447).

Minstrel invented this solution:
(A KNIGHT NAMED JOHN DRANK A POTION IN ORDER
TO KILL HIMSELF *PERIOD* JOHN DIED *PERIOD*)
```

At this new level, MINSTREL applies TRAM:Generalize-Constraint to the description "a knight purposely injures himself" and generalizes the "knight" feature. "Knight" is generalized to "anyone," which results in the new problem specification "Someone does something to purposely injure himself." Note that this problem specification has been modified twice from the original specification, once by TRAM:Similar-Outcomes-Partial-Change, and once by TRAM:Generalize-Constraint.

The new problem description recalls "The Princess and the Potion" in which a lady of the court drinks a potion to make herself ill. The Adapt portion of TRAM:Generalize-Constraint then adapts this scene by replacing "lady of the court" (the generalized constraint) with "a knight" (the original constraint). This results in a scene in which a knight makes himself ill by drinking a potion.

The adapted scene is returned to the previous problem solving level, where TRAM:Similar-Outcomes-Partial-Change also adapts the scene, by replacing the illness with death. The adaptation reverses the transformation that turned "death" into "illness." This results in a scene in which a knight kills himself by drinking a potion, filling the original description "a knight kills himself." Note that in the course of inventing this scene, MINSTREL has also invented the idea of poison—a potion that kills (vs. just making one ill).

(In fact, MINSTREL has invented the more narrow notion of "a potion which will kill a knight." To apply this to other animate beings, MINSTREL will have to use creativity again to generalize about the actor of this action. MINSTREL does this by applying TRAM:Generalize-Constraint again.)

The main issue in TRAM:Similar-Outcomes is determining when two outcomes are interchangeable. MINSTREL has two methods for deciding this question. These are implemented as separate TRAMs called TRAM:Similar-Outcomes-Partial-Change and TRAM:Similar-Outcomes-Implicit.

TRAM:Similar-Outcomes-Partial-Change reasons that if an action can result in a partial relative change of a state then the action can also result in a complete change of the state. TRAM:Similar-Outcomes-Partial-Change is shown in

Figure 2.15. In this example, TRAM:Similar-Outcomes-Partial-Change reasons that something that makes someone ill (a partial negative change in health) might also kill them (a complete negative change in health).

Like many of MINSTREL's creativity heuristics, TRAM:Similar-Outcomes-Partial-Change is a "common-sense" rule that captures reasoning that is often useful but not always correct. For example, extending a partial state change could be used to reason that because a man can lift a book in one hand he would also be able to lift an automobile in one hand. There are two things to be said about this type of error.

First, this type of error points out the value of simple, constrained TRAMs that make only small changes in problem descriptions. By making only small extensions to a problem solver's knowledge, a TRAM is less likely to make an error in its extrapolation. In fact, MINSTREL's version of TRAM:Similar-Outcomes-Partial-Change only extends state changes one additional "step" in a known direction. If state of health is represented by the scale "Excellent Good Normal Ill Dead," and MINSTREL knows an action that changed a man's health from Normal to Ill, then TRAM:Similar-Outcomes-Partial-Change can only extrapolate that to an action that changes a man's health from Normal to Dead. TRAM:Similar-Outcomes-Partial-Change cannot extrapolate to an action that would take a man's health from Ill to Excellent, or even from Excellent to Dead. Similar limits can be applied to states which do not have discrete representations, although MINSTREL does not currently handle this. By using simple, constrained creativity heuristics, MINSTREL reduces the number of reasoning errors it makes.

Incremental imaginative steps reduces errors in reasoning.

Second, even with restricted TRAMs, MINSTREL can still make reasoning errors of this sort. But this is to be expected: A creative problem solver *should* make errors. MINSTREL uses creativity to actively extend its knowledge. By

TRAM:Similar-Outcomes-Partial-Change

Transform Strategy

If the problem specification has an act that results in a partial relative change of a state in some direction, create a new specification in which the relative change is extended in the same direction.

Adapt Strategy

Replace the change of state in the recalled episode with a relative change of state copied from the original problem specification.

Figure 2.15 TRAM:Similar-Outcomes-Partial-Change

making good use of what it already knows, MINSTREL can often make accurate guesses about what it doesn't know. But sometimes it will err. The challenge faced by a creative problem solver is to find creativity heuristics that are productive without an inordinate number of reasoning errors. The issue of creativity errors is discussed in more detail in Chapter 8.

Imaginative reasoning will sometimes produce errors.

The second TRAM MINSTREL uses to determine when two outcomes are interchangeable is TRAM:Similar-Outcomes-Implicit. TRAM:Similar-Outcomes-Implicit reasons that two outcomes are interchangeable in *every* situation if it can recall *any* situation in which they are interchangeable. For example, if MINSTREL can recall a scene in which a knight fought and killed a troll, and another scene in which a knight fought and killed a dragon, MINSTREL can use this knowledge to guess that trolls and dragons are generally interchangeable. TRAM:Generalize-Constraint used a class hierarchy—an explicit representation of object similarities—to substitute one feature for another. TRAM:Similar-Outcomes uses an implicit representation of similarities to substitute one outcome for another.

Like TRAM:Similar-Outcomes-Partial-Change, TRAM:Similar-Outcomes-Implicit is a heuristics that can sometimes err. Again, this is a direct consequence of its function as an extrapolator of knowledge, and is to be expected in a creative problem solver.

TRAM:Similar-Outcomes-Implicit

Transform Strategy

1. Create a new problem specification: An uninstantiated act that results in the state from the original problem specification. Use this to recall different acts which can cause the result from the original problem.

2. Use episodic memory to recall other possible results of the actions collected in (1). Build a pool of these alternate results.

3. Create a new problem specification in which the act from the original problem specification results in a randomly-selected alternate result. Use this new specification for recall.

Adapt Strategy

1. Replace the alternate result of the recalled episode with the result copied from the original problem specification.

Figure 2.16 TRAM:Similar-Outcomes-Implicit

2.11.1.7 TRAM:Intention-Switch

MINSTREL's final plan for suicide is discovered using TRAM:Intention-Switch. This heuristic suggests that if the effect of an action was intentional it might just as well have been unintentional. TRAM:Intention-Switch is illustrated in Figure 2.17.

In the suicide example, TRAM:Intention-Switch transforms the original specification from "a knight purposely kills himself" to a "knight accidently kills himself." Recall on this new specification (&ACT.174) fails, because MINSTREL's episodic memory does not contain any episodes in which a knight accidently kills himself:

```
[...]
  Executing TRAM:INTENTION-SWITCH.
    Recalling &ACT.174: NIL.
    [TRAM Recursion: &ACT.174.]
        Executing TRAM:SIMILAR-OUTCOMES-PARTIAL-CHANGE.
          Recalling &ACT.178: &KNIGHT-FIGHT.
        ...TRAM succeeds: (&ACT.588).
  ...TRAM succeeds: (&ACT.588).

Minstrel invented this solution:
  (A KNIGHT NAMED JOHN FOUGHT A DRAGON BY MOVING
   HIS SWORD TO IT IN ORDER TO KILL HIMSELF
   *PERIOD* JOHN DIED *PERIOD*)
```

Problem solving is used recursively, and TRAM:Similar-Outcomes-Partial-Change modifies the current problem description "a knight accidently kills himself" by changing "kills himself" into something similar: "injures himself." The new problem description is "a knight "accidently injures himself." This recalls "Knight Fight", in which a knight is injured while killing a troll.

TRAM:Intention-Switch

Transform Strategy

If an action in the problem specification intends a result, create a new problem specification in which the same action unintentionally achieves the result.

Adapt Strategy

Replace the unintentional result of the recalled episode with a similar intentional result.

Figure 2.17 TRAM:Intention-Switch

Both TRAM:Similar-Outcomes-Partial-Change and TRAM:Intention-Switch adapt this recalled scene. TRAM:Similar-Outcomes-Partial-Change replaces "injures himself" with "kills himself," and TRAM:Intention-Switch replaces "accidently" with "purposely," resulting in a scene in which a knight commits suicide by intentionally losing a fight with a troll.

Three things are interesting about this particular invention. First, although this particular TRAM is very simple, it results in a very novel and interesting plan—a knight purposely losing a fight to a dangerous opponent. This demonstrates that simple, limited TRAMs applicable to a wide variety of problems still have the power to invent new solutions to problems.

Second, it is interesting to note that MINSTREL has invented two different methods of suicide from the same episodic memory. Using TRAM:Generalize-Constraint, MINSTREL transformed the "Knight Fight" episode into a plan in which a knight fights himself. Using TRAM:Intention-Switch and TRAM:Similar-Outcomes-Partial-Change, MINSTREL transforms the same episode into a plan in which a knight purposely loses a fight to a dangerous opponent. The ability to invent several solutions from a single episode shows the flexibility and power of MINSTREL's creativity process.

Third, unlike TRAM:Similar-Outcomes-Implicit and TRAM:Similar-Outcomes-Partial-Change, TRAM:Intention-Switch will never make a creativity error. Any action which can be done intentionally can be done unintentionally, and vice versa. Unlike the Similar-Outcome TRAMs, which extrapolate the problem solver's knowledge into new areas, TRAM:Intention-Switch redirects the problem solver into a little-used area of his knowledge. Intentionally doing things accidently (a seemingly self-contradictory idea) is a reasoning strategy that is seldom useful to a problem solver, so episodic memory is unlikely to contain general plans of this sort. Instead, TRAM:Intention-Switch redirects the problem solver to this strategy for the restricted type of problems in which it might be useful.

2.11.1.8 Summary

The suicide example demonstrates two points about the MINSTREL model of creativity. First, it demonstrates that MINSTREL's creativity process has operational validity; MINSTREL *can* invent novel solutions to a problem. Second, it demonstrates the power of Transform-Recall-Adapt Methods. Using only two episodic memories and three TRAMs, MINSTREL invents three different methods of suicide and the notion of poison.

2.11.2   Storytelling Example

We now look at how MINSTREL's creativity functions in the context of a larger task: storytelling.

To tell stories, MINSTREL must select a theme, instantiate the events of the theme (the plot), assure that the events of the story are consistent, achieve literary goals such as building suspense, and so on. Many of these tasks can be achieved without creativity. MINSTREL knows that knights ride hoses, and hence doesn't have to invent a way for knights to travel from place to place. But sometimes MINSTREL encounters a new problem in the course of storytelling, or becomes bored with a particular story development. In these cases, creative problem solving is used to invent a solution.

This example presents a specific task MINSTREL encountered in telling *The Vengeful Princess*:[5]

The Vengeful Princess

Once upon a time there was a lady of the court named Jennifer. Jennifer loved a knight named Grunfeld. Grunfeld loved Jennifer.

Jennifer wanted revenge on a lady of the court named Darlene because she had the berries which she picked in the woods and Jennifer wanted to have the berries. Jennifer wanted to scare Darlene. Jennifer wanted a dragon to move towards Darlene so that Darlene believed it would eat her. Jennifer wanted to appear to be a dragon so that a dragon would move towards Darlene. Jennifer drank a magic potion. Jennifer transformed into a dragon. A dragon move towards Darlene. A dragon was near Darlene.

Grunfeld wanted to impress the king. Grunfeld wanted to move towards the woods so that he could fight a dragon. Grunfeld moved towards the woods. Grunfeld was near the woods. Grunfeld fought a dragon. The dragon died. The dragon was Jennifer. Jennifer wanted to live. Jennifer tried to drink a magic potion but failed. Grunfeld was filled with grief.

Jennifer was buried in the woods. Grunfeld became a hermit.

MORAL: Deception is a weapon difficult to aim.

---

[5]Titles for MINSTREL's stories were provided by the author. Throughout this dissertation, MINSTREL's stories are presented exactly as produced, except for typography.

The particular portion of *The Vengeful Princess* this example focuses on is the creation of Jennifer's reason for wanting revenge on Darlene:

```
... Jennifer wanted revenge on a lady of the court named
Darlene because Darlene had the berries which she picked
in the woods and Jennifer wanted to have the berries.
```

When telling this story, MINSTREL knew nothing about what kinds of goal conflicts might lead a lady of the court to want revenge on another lady. This example shows how MINSTREL invents a conflict over possession of berries as a reason for wanting revenge.

2.11.2.1   The Problem

This example looks at how MINSTREL invents a reason for Jennifer to want revenge on Darlene. MINSTREL's representation of this problem is shown in Figure 2.18. Jennifer's goal of wanting revenge (&GOAL.1751) is motivated by a state of the world (&STATE.992) that achieves Darlene's goal (&GOAL.3029) at the expense of Jennifer's goal (&GOAL.2112). (One of the interesting storytelling aspects of this story is that MINSTREL knows that Jennifer wants revenge before it knows why Jennifer wants revenge. This is a consequence of how MINSTREL develops stories from the theme outward.)

When this example begins, MINSTREL has three goals: (1) to instantiate the state that causes Jennifer to want revenge (&STATE.992), (2) to instantiate Darlene's goal achieved by this state (&GOAL.3029), and (3) to instantiate Jennifer's thwarted goal (&GOAL.2112).

2.11.2.2   Episodic Memory

For storytelling, MINSTREL's episodic memory contains 10 story fragments from the King Arthur domain. For this example, the only relevant episode is "Picking Berries":

Picking Berries

A lady named Guinevere who wanted berries went to the woods and picked some.

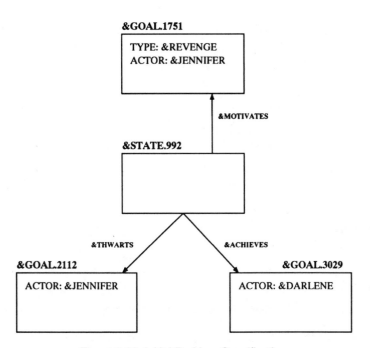

Figure 2.18 Initial Problem Specification

2.11.2.3 Standard Problem Solving During Storytelling

MINSTREL uses creative problem solving to instantiate Jennifer's thwarted goal (&GOAL.2112 in Figure 2.18). But before MINSTREL does this, it instantiates the state which thwarts this goal (&STATE.992 in Figure 2.18). To instantiate this state, MINSTREL uses standard case-based problem solving.

TRAM:Standard-Problem Solving is a TRAM that implements standard case-based problem solving. Given a problem description, TRAM:Standard-Problem Solving tries to recall from episodic memory an exactly similar problem. If it can, it uses the solution from that previous problem to solve the current problem. TRAM:Standard-Problem Solving is illustrated in Figure 2.5.

In this case, the problem description is &STATE.992: "Something happens which fulfills a princess's goal." Without transformation, this recalls a similar episode from memory: the "Picking Berries" story fragment. This scene is used to fill in as much of &STATE.992 and surrounding schemas as possible. The scene development at this point is shown in Figure 2.19. Notice that this has also resulted in the addition of a new schema to the story, &ACT.1178. This new schema represents Darlene's action in picking the berries.

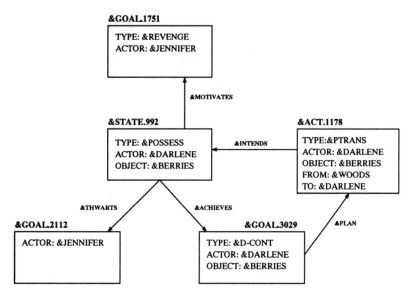

Figure 2.19 Intermediate Scene State

This example illustrates how standard case-based problem solving occurs in MINSTREL. TRAM:Standard-Problem Solving recalls an episode from memory and applies it without modification to the current problem. What happens when TRAM:Standard-Problem Solving cannot recall an appropriate episode?

2.11.2.4 Creative Problem Solving During Storytelling

MINSTREL now tries to instantiate Jennifer's thwarted goal. To do this, MINSTREL must show how Darlene's possession of the berries could thwart one of Jennifer's goals. MINSTREL's author-level representation of this goal is &GOAL.3067, and Figure 2.20 shows a trace of MINSTREL achieving this goal.

The first part of this trace shows MINSTREL recalling author-level plans for instantiating a story scene. MINSTREL recalls 4 plans. The first, ALP:Dont-Instantiate, fails. The second, ALP:General-Instantiate, succeeds. ALP:General-Instantiate tries to instantiate a story scene by using creative problem solving at the character level. The second portion of the trace (beginning with "TRAM Cycle: &GOAL.2112") shows creative problem solving being used to instantiate the scene.

ALP:General-Instantiate passes the story scene to be instantiated to problem solving. TRAM:Standard-Problem Solving is tried but fails, because MINSTREL does not have any scenes in episodic memory in which a lady's goal is

```
Author-level goal &INSTANTIATE applied to &GOAL.2112.
Recalling plans for &INSTANTIATE: 4 plans.
Trying author-level plan ALP:DONT-INSTANTIATE.
...plan fails.
Trying author-level plan ALP:GENERAL-INSTANTIATE.
TRAM Cycle: &GOAL.2112.
    Executing TRAM:STANDARD-PROBLEM SOLVING.
      Recalling:    NIL.
    ...TRAM failed.
    Executing TRAM:OPPOSITE-STATE-ACHIEVES.
      Recalling:    (&GOAL-BERRIES).
    ...TRAM succeeds: (&GOAL.3155).
TRAM Cycle succeeds: (&GOAL.3155).
Found a reminding in ALP:GENERAL-INSTANTIATE:
Author-level planning succeeded.
```

(JENNIFER WANTED TO HAVE THE BERRIES *PERIOD*)

Figure 2.20 MINSTREL Trace of Story-Level Creativity

thwarted by someone else possessing some berries. (In fact, MINSTREL's memory does not contain *any* scenes in which a lady's goal is thwarted.)

TRAM:Standard-Problem Solving fails, so it is discarded. The next TRAM used is TRAM:Opposite-State-Achieves. This TRAM suggests that the opposite of a state that achieves a goal will thwart the goal, and vice versa. If being healthy achieves the goal of protecting your health, then being dead will likely thwart the goal of protecting your health, and so on. So to invent a thwarted goal, you can recall an achieved goal and reverse it.

In this case, the opposite of the thwarting state (Darlene's possession of the berries) is Darlene not possessing the berries (i.e., someone else possessing the berries). TRAM:Opposite-State-Achieves changes the problem specification from "A princess's goal is thwarted by Darlene possessing some berries" to "A princess's goal is *achieved* by *someone* possessing some berries." If TRAM:Opposite-State-Achieves can recall something similar to this new specification, it can be used in the original problem by reversing the recalled scene from achievement to thwarting.

MINSTREL constructs this opposite state and tries to recall goals from episodic memory that are achieved by this new state. This recalls &GOAL-BERRIES, which is Guinevere's goal of wanting to possess berries from the "Picking Berries" episode: "Guinevere's goal of possessing berries is achieved by Guinevere possessing the berries."

The recalled episode can be adapted to the original problem by filling Jennifer and Darlene into the correct roles and "reversing" the outcome. This is achieved in three steps: (1) replacing the actor of the goal with Jennifer (i.e., "Jennifer's goal of possessing the berries is achieved by Guinevere possessing the berries"), (2) replacing the possessor of the berries with Darlene (i.e., "Jennifer's goal of possessing the berries is achieved by Darlene possessing the berries"), and (3) by replacing the achievement with thwarting (i.e., "Jennifer's goal of possessing the berries is thwarted by Darlene possessing the berries")

The adapted solution can now be used to fill in the original scene. The result is shown in Figure 2.21. In English, the scene shown in Figure 2.21 is expressed:

> ... Jennifer wanted revenge on a lady of the court named Darlene because Darlene had the berries which she picked in the woods and Jennifer wanted to have the berries.

Notice what has happened during the creation of this thwarted goal. Prior to creating this goal, MINSTREL had no explicit knowledge about conflicts of possession, or of the idea that one person's possession of an object prevents another person from also possessing the object. By using a very simple story episode and a general creativity heuristic, MINSTREL was able to invent these concepts and apply them to a specific problem. And as these concepts are invented they are indexed into episodic memory, where they are available for future problem solving, or as a basis for additional creativity. In this way, MINSTREL uses creativity to constantly expand its knowledge, and avoids having to reinvent the same concepts over and over.

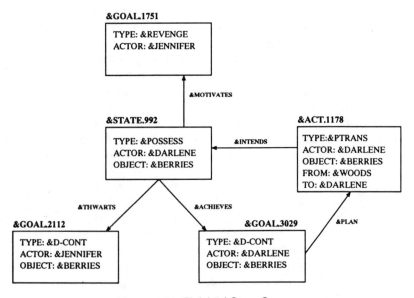

Figure 2.21 Finished Story Scene

2.11.2.5 Summary

This example demonstrates MINSTREL's use of problem solving and creativity during storytelling. By using TRAM:Opposite-State-Achieves, MINSTREL solves a problem it cannot solve during standard problem solving. In solving this goal, MINSTREL discovers the idea of conflict over possession of an object. This is a concept not explicitly known to MINSTREL before its invention in *The Vengeful Princess*, and illustrates how MINSTREL's creativity can extend its knowledge.

2.12 Issues in Creativity

This chapter has no doubt raised in the reader's mind a number of issues about creativity and MINSTREL's model of the creative process. This section addresses the more common questions about MINSTREL's creativity model.

2.12.1 Errors in Creativity

The previous section showed how MINSTREL used creativity to invent a scene in which Jennifer wants revenge on Darlene because Darlene has some berries that Jennifer wants. Readers of this scene sometimes complain that possession of berries is insufficient motive for revenge. MINSTREL's creative problem solving has invented an incorrect solution, at least according to some readers. How did this happen, and what does it say about the creative process?

When MINSTREL begins telling *The Lady's Revenge*, it has only minimal knowledge about revenge. MINSTREL knows that revenge can be motivated by a thwarted goal, but it does not have any specific examples of revenge in the King Arthur domain in memory, and neither does it have any examples of thwarted goals in the King Arthur domain. Creativity must be used to extend MINSTREL's knowledge about both thwarted goals and revenge.

MINSTREL's creativity heuristics correctly extend its knowledge about possession of objects and thwarted goals. The scene in which Darlene takes the berries that Jennifer wants was created by TRAM:Opposite-State-Achieves from a scene that contained no thwarted goals. Initially MINSTREL knows that possessing an object can achieve a person's goal of controlling an object. After telling *The Lady's Revenge*, MINSTREL has discovered that possessing an object can also thwart another person's goal of controlling an object.

The same creativity heuristic is less successful in extending MINSTREL's knowledge about revenge. The thwarted possession of berries is invented as motivation for a revenge goal, but as most people recognize, that is probably insufficient motivation. Revenge is only plausible if the retribution is commensurate with the offense, or if the character seeking revenge is evil and likely to seek revenge out of proportion with the offense.

Creativity extends a problem solver's knowledge. By making good use of what he already knows, a problem solver can often make accurate guesses about what he doesn't know. But sometimes he'll be wrong. That is the nature of creativity. Unlike first-order predicate logic and standard problem solving, creativity is a heuristic activity that trades infallibility for power. Creativity is able to discover many solutions that standard problem solving cannot because it take risks. In this case, MINSTREL makes a reasonable guess about how the world operates—that possession of an object prevents possession by another, and that thwarting a possession goal is reason for revenge – but the guess is not completely correct.

Of course, this particular error could be easily corrected. MINSTREL could be given additional knowledge about revenge or possession of objects, and hence avoid this error. As this points out, creativity alone cannot extend a problem solver's knowledge indefinitely or without error. The problem solver must also be able to learn directly from outside experience. In a complete cognitive model, creativity must act in concert with noncreative learning to correctly extend a problem solver's knowledge of the world.

But no matter how much knowledge a problem solver has, creativity will extend beyond the borders of that knowledge, and errors of this type will continue to occur. The challenge is to find a model of creativity that will limit errors while still providing the power to discover novel, useful ideas.

MINSTREL's model of creativity limits errors by using creativity heuristics that make specific, small problem transformations. By limiting the changes made to a problem specification, MINSTREL increases the likelihood that any solution it discovers will apply correctly to the original problem. The success of this strategy is apparent even in MINSTREL's failures. "Possessing berries" may be a poor reason for revenge, but not an *unreasonable* one. The reader may judge it insufficient motivation, but he does at least understand the reasoning.

It is worth noting that in a complete cognitive system, errors in creativity would lead to learning experiences. If MINSTREL were able to learn from criticism, the reader's comments about the possession of berries being insufficient motivation for revenge would be an opportunity for MINSTREL to refine its knowledge about revenge and possession of objects, and avoid similar mistakes in the future. Creativity can thus be seen as a motivator and director of noncreative learning. At this time, however, MINSTREL has no ability to learn from criticism.

2.12.2   Learning in MINSTREL

Although MINSTREL does not have the ability to learn from criticism, it is able to do a simple sort of learning from creativity. When MINSTREL invents a new solution to a problem, the solution is indexed in episodic memory according to the problem it solves. So when MINSTREL discovers that a conflict over possession of berries is a reason for revenge, that new knowledge is stored in episodic memory, where it can be used in future problem solving. This serves several purposes.

First, it permanently extends MINSTREL's knowledge. If MINSTREL did not remember its past inventions, it would always begin its creative problem solving from the same base of knowledge, and would always explore the same area around the edges of its knowledge. But if a useful new solution is discovered and incorporated into MINSTREL's knowledge base, the new solution becomes an island from which MINSTREL can continue its creative exploration. By saving its creative successes, MINSTREL increases its ability to discover new solutions. The larger MINSTREL's episodic memory, the vaster its experience, the more powerful and effective its creativity.

Second, saving successful new solutions improves MINSTREL's efficiency as a problem solver. Standard case-based problem solving is very efficient, because it finds solutions that apply immediately and with a minimum of effort. Creativity is less efficient, because it must search the problem space and apply solution adaptations. By remembering past solutions, MINSTREL avoids having to reinvent them, and this improves MINSTREL's efficiency.

Both these benefits require MINSTREL to save *successful* solutions. Saving solutions that are wrong or even doubtful (like the "possession of berries" solution) can be counterproductive, because it will lead to MINSTREL repeating its past mistakes. It should be obvious, then, that criticism is an important element to a creative problem solver that learns from its creativity. Although MINSTREL does not currently address this issue, it is an area for future research.

Experiments that study MINSTREL's ability to learn from creativity and the effect that has on MINSTREL's problem solving behavior are presented in Chapter 8.

2.12.3   MINSTREL's Efficiency

Saving invented solutions improves MINSTREL's efficiency in the long run because it allows standard problem solving to solve problems that would otherwise require creativity. But how can we characterize the efficiency of creativity in the short run, that is, for a particular problem solving effort?

To begin with, creativity does not become inefficient as episodic memory grows. Retrieval from episodic memory is proportional to the number of significant features in the problem description, not upon the number of episodes in memory.[6] Episodic memory is organized as a tree based on the values of significant features of the indexed episodes (Kolodner, 1984; Reiser, 1986; Schank, 1982). Retrieval involves comparing the significant features of the recall description with the branches of this tree (i.e., traversing a multibranched tree). Since there is one comparison for each feature of the recall description, the time efficiency of recall is characterized by the number of features.

In fact, creativity tends to become *more* efficient as episodic memory grows. As memory grows, the likelihood that a transformed problem description will recall a solution increases, and so the likelihood of creativity succeeding also increases. There is no easy way to characterize this trend, because creativity does not search memory in an orderly fashion, and memory does not grow in an orderly fashion. But in general, the more the knowledge captured in episodic memory, the more likely it is that creativity will discover a solution. Some studies of how MINSTREL's behavior changes as episodic memory changes are discussed in Chapter 8.

The efficiency of creativity depends primarily upon the number of creativity heuristics that are applicable to a particular problem. If a creative problem solver has three heuristics that apply to a problem, and tries every combination of these heuristics without finding a solution, the problem solver will try 24 different combinations. In the worst case (when no solution is found), creativity is $O((n + 1)!)$, where n is the number of applicable heuristics.

In practice, a creative problem solver is likely to limit the amount of time and effort expended to find a solution. MINSTREL, for example, applies no more than three heuristics simultaneously, regardless of how many are applicable. Because combinations of heuristics search the problem space farther and farther from the original problem specification, they are correspondingly less likely to discover a solution (although if they do it is likely to be quite different from known solutions). Consequently, the problem solver soon reaches a point of diminishing return and abandons the search for a solution.

Experience with MINSTREL also indicates that because MINSTREL's creativity heuristics are very specific only a few of the available heuristics apply to any given problem. An analysis of the problems solved by MINSTREL in telling stories based on four different story themes revealed that of MINSTREL's 24 creativity heuristics, on average only 1.4 TRAMs applied to any particular problem. This indicates that MINSTREL's strategy of specific problem transformations not only increases the likelihood of discovering a useful solution, it also limits the effort expended in searching for a solution. (For experiments and studies on MINSTREL's usage of TRAMs, see Chapter 8).

---

[6] We assume a constant-time hashing function to traverse the memory tree.

2.12.4 Randomness in MINSTREL

A common question when people first hear about MINSTREL is "How does it make up the stories? Does it just make random choices?" As should be apparent to the reader of this chapter, MINSTREL solves problems (including the problem of telling a story) by purposeful, directed use of the knowledge in episodic memory. MINSTREL does not, in general, make random selections when problem solving or being creative.

The only use of random selection in MINSTREL occurs when MINSTREL must select between equally likely alternatives. When MINSTREL has no way to distinguish two or more choices, it selects randomly between the choices. This can occur in two situations.

First, episodic memory may recall two (or more) episodes which fulfill the recall criteria. Episodic memory is organized by the significant features of episodes. Two episodes with identical significant features will therefore fall into the same category in memory, and be recalled together. (If more than a small number of episodes fall into the same category, episodic memory builds and returns a generalization based on those episodes.) When this occurs, MINSTREL selects and uses one of the episodes randomly.

Second, MINSTREL selects randomly from its available plans and creativity heuristics when there is more than one applicable plan or heuristic. For any particular author-level goal there may be several author-level plans available. Similarly, for any particular problem solving situation, there may be several applicable creativity heuristics. In these situations, MINSTREL selects the plan or heuristic to apply randomly.

It is important to note that while MINSTREL does select randomly in these situations, MINSTREL does not make random *decisions*. When MINSTREL selects between two recalled episodes, it has already decided what it needs, and both episodes will fulfill those needs. Similarly, when MINSTREL selects an author-level plan randomly from those that apply to an author-level goal, it has already decided the goal. So MINSTREL's random selections are not random decisions, merely a way to distinguish otherwise indistinguishable outcomes.

3 A Model of Storytelling

3.1 Why Tell Stories?

Authors create stories for a bewildering variety of reasons. A mother spins a fanciful bedtime tale to lull her young child asleep; a rabbi crafts an elegant anecdote to illustrate the generosity of God; a distressed young woman writes a novel to heal the grief she feels over losing her mother. And not only do authors write for many different reasons, they often pursue many goals at once in their writing. Shakespeare wrote works that both illuminate the human condition and delight the ear; Jonathan Swift wrote stories that were both entertaining adventures and biting social commentary on the England of his day. The goals and purposes of storytelling are as diverse and varied as human intellect itself.

But whatever the reasons, it is clear that human authors write *intentionally*. The stories authors create are carefully crafted to achieve particular goals. These goals and the ways they are achieved differ greatly from author to author, but every author has an explicit awareness of writing as a way to achieve some personal goals.

The importance of author goals in storytelling is best illustrated by an early model of computer storytelling called TALESPIN. TALESPIN was a computer program developed at Yale by James Meehan (Meehan, 1976). TALESPIN had knowledge about the likely goals and plans of a cast of simple woodland creatures. To tell a story, TALESPIN generated some likely goals for these creatures and then simulated their attempts to achieve those goals:

John Bear is somewhat hungry. John Bear wants to get some berries. John Bear wants to get near the blueberries. John Bear walks from a cave entrance to the bush by going through a pass through a valley through a meadow. John Bear takes the blueberries. John Bear eats the blueberries. The blueberries are gone. John Bear is not very hungry.

As this example illustrates, TALESPIN often told stories that lacked purpose. The characters act in reasonable ways and the story world is consistent and detailed, but the stories have no point or reason. TALESPIN's stories don't read like *stories*.

The reason for this is simple. TALESPIN knows about the characters in its story world, about the kinds of things they can do and the kinds of goals they can have, but TALESPIN lacks any knowledge about itself as an author. TALESPIN does not know *why* it tells stories. At best TALESPIN has an implicit understanding of storytelling as "making characters do something to achieve likely goals." But because TALESPIN focuses on character-level goals rather than author-level goals, its characters have the purpose its stories lack.

Clearly storytelling is more than creating plausible accounts of how characters might achieve their goals. Authors are not purely "simulators" of reality; they have purpose and intention in their writing. The events of a story are crafted to fulfill goals other than a mere slavish consistency with real life. To be cognitively plausible, and to create stories with purpose and direction, a model of storytelling must explicitly represent the author's goals and the process of achieving those goals.

Stories are the purposeful achievement of author goals.

Aside from its ability to be creative, MINSTREL's fundamental advancement over TALESPIN is an explicit author model. Like a human author, MINSTREL tells stories to achieve particular goals. As MINSTREL tells a story, it has an agenda of author-level goals it is trying to fulfill, such as illustrating a specific story theme, and building suspense in a particular part of the story. Because MINSTREL is a purposeful storyteller with knowledge of its goals as an author, it creates stories that are better organized, more purposeful, and more recognizable as "stories" than those created by TALESPIN.

3.2   Author Goals

If the uses of storytelling are as diverse as human intellect itself, then surely cataloging the goals of authors is a hopeless task. How then can we learn about the authoring process?

One way to begin is by identifying and defining the goals that are necessary to tell stories of a particular type. The hope is that by carefully examining the authoring process for one particular type of writing, something will be discovered about the authoring process in general. So although we may not understand everything about *why* authors write, we will learn something about *how* they write. And this knowledge will serve as a basis for further research that will lead to a deeper and more general understanding of author-level goals.

This approach has led to MINSTREL, a computer program that tells short, theme-based stories about King Arthur and his Knights of the Round Table. Narrowing the range of storytelling to a specific style, a specific length, and a specific milieu makes the storytelling problem manageable and permits MINSTREL to focus on the process of storytelling rather than the diverse "whys" of storytelling.

Restricting MINSTREL to theme-based stories limits the types of author goals MINSTREL must solve. Selecting a single, specific primary author goal—to tell a story that illustrates a particular theme—greatly narrows the range of author goals. MINSTREL does not have to tell bedtime stories, satires, or any of the other myriad types of stories. At the same time, theme-based stories are complex and rich enough to address a variety of issues in storytelling, the way certain storytelling styles—such as the stories of very young children, or mathematical story problems—would not.

Restricting the length of the stories it tells to about one page allows MINSTREL to concentrate on stories in which immediate character actions predominate. Longer works such as novels often use character interactions, interplays of moods and emotions, digressions, and complicated presentation techniques to effect their purposes. Limiting the length of MINSTREL's stories concentrates this research on how one particular tool—creating story events—can be used to achieve a variety of author-level goals.

Finally, restricting MINSTREL's storytelling to a specific milieu focuses this research on issues in storytelling rather than issues in understanding and representing knowledge about the world. The King Arthur milieu is relatively straightforward: knights love princesses and kill dragons, hermits live in the woods and heal people. Were MINSTREL to tell stories in a more complicated milieu, or in several different milieus, more effort would have had to be expended to give MINSTREL knowledge about those milieus. Although this might have led to some interesting results, the time and effort it would take to understand and represent knowledge about different milieus would have subtracted from the time available to develop a general model of storytelling and creativity. It was decided early in this research effort that the development of the general models of storytelling and creativity was of greater interest, and limiting MINSTREL to a single storytelling domain permitted a more in-depth development of this area of the storytelling model.

3.2.1 MINSTREL's Author-Level Goals

Limiting MINSTREL to telling short, theme-based stories about King Arthur revealed four important classes of author-level goals:

> (1) Thematic Goals
> (2) Drama Goals
> (3) Consistency Goals
> (4) Presentation Goals

Thematic goals are concerned with the selection and development of a story theme. Drama goals are concerned with the use of dramatic writing techniques to improve the artistic quality of a story. Consistency goals focus on creating a story that is plausible and believable. And presentation goals are concerned with how a story is presented to the reader.

To further explain these goals and illustrate how they combine to create a complete story, we look at the role each class of goals play in one of MINSTREL's stories. The story we use is called *Richard and Lancelot*. Except for typography, it is reproduced here exactly as written by MINSTREL:

Richard and Lancelot

It was the spring of 1089, and a knight named Lancelot returned to Camelot from elsewhere. Lancelot was hot tempered. Once, Lancelot lost a joust. Because he was hot tempered, Lancelot wanted to destroy his sword. Lancelot struck his sword. His sword was destroyed.

One day, a lady of the court named Andrea wanted to have some berries. Andrea went to the woods. Andrea had some berries because Andrea picked some berries. At the same time, Lancelot's horse moved Lancelot to the woods. This unexpectedly caused him to be near Andrea. Because Lancelot was near Andrea, Lancelot saw Andrea. Lancelot loved Andrea.

Some time later, Lancelot's horse moved Lancelot to the woods unintentionally, again causing him to be near Andrea. Lancelot knew that Andrea kissed with a knight named Frederick because Lancelot saw that Andrea kissed with Frederick. Lancelot

```
believed  that  Andrea  loved  Frederick.  Lancelot
loved  Andrea.  Because  Lancelot  loved  Andrea,
Lancelot wanted to be the love of Andrea.  But he
could not because Andrea loved Frederick.  Lancelot
hated Frederick.  Because Lancelot was hot tempered,
Lancelot wanted to kill Frederick.  Lancelot went to
Frederick. Lancelot fought with Frederick.  Freder-
ick was dead.
     Andrea  went  to  Frederick.  Andrea  told  Lancelot
that  Andrea  was  siblings  with  Frederick.  Lancelot
believed  that  Andrea  was  siblings  with  Frederick.
Lancelot wanted to take back that he wanted to kill
Frederick,  but  he  could  not  because  Frederick  was
dead.  Lancelot  hated  himself.  Lancelot  became  a
hermit.  Frederick was buried in the woods.  Andrea
became a nun.

     Moral: ''Done in haste is done forever.''
```

This story was selected to illustrate MINSTREL's storytelling goals because, more so than MINSTREL's other stories, this story is straightforward and obvious in achieving those goals. This is particularly apparent in the third paragraph, where MINSTREL produces a long, overly detailed explanation of the character actions and reasoning. But although this makes the story clumsy and somewhat difficult to read, it also makes it easier to follow MINSTREL's purposes in creating the story.

3.2.2 Thematic Goals

The theme of a story is the main point or purpose of the story. Because there are many possible reasons to tell a story there are many possible story themes. MINSTREL tells stories about a particular type of theme called a Planning Advice Theme, or PAT. Planning Advice Themes represent concise pieces of advice about planning, and they can often be summarized by adages, such as "A bird in the hand is worth two in the bush."

MINSTREL's author-level thematic goals are concerned with selecting and illustrating a story theme. *Richard and Lancelot* is based on a Planning Advice Theme called PAT:Hasty-Impulse-Regretted. This theme advises a planner to avoid making hasty decisions that cannot be retracted if they turn out to be incorrect. The events in a story that illustrate the theme are called the story *plot*. In *Richard and Lancelot*, the following scenes illustrate the theme of the story:

```
Lancelot knew that Andrea kissed with a knight named
Frederick  because  Lancelot  saw  that  Andrea  kissed
with  Frederick.  Lancelot  believed  that  Andrea  loved
```

> Frederick. Lancelot loved Andrea. Because Lancelot
> loved Andrea, Lancelot wanted to be the love of
> Andrea. But he could not because Andrea loved Fred-
> erick. Because Lancelot was hot tempered, Lancelot
> wanted to kill Frederick. Lancelot went to Freder-
> ick. Lancelot fought with Frederick. Frederick was
> dead.
>
> Andrea told Lancelot that Andrea was siblings with
> Frederick. Lancelot believed that Andrea was sib-
> lings with Frederick. Lancelot wanted to take back
> that he wanted to kill Frederick, but he could not
> because Frederick was dead.

These events form an example of the abstract advice represented in the story theme. By structuring the stories it tells around themes, MINSTREL assures that they will have the purpose that was missing from stories told by TALESPIN.

MINSTREL has two author-level thematic goals. The first goal is to select a theme for storytelling. The second is to create a sequence of story events that form an example of the selected theme.

Chapter 4 discusses MINSTREL's representation of story themes, MIN-STREL's thematic goals, and the plans MINSTREL uses to achieve those goals.

3.2.3 Drama Goals

Human authors use a wide variety of techniques to improve the craftsmanship and literary quality of their stories. Foreshadowing, characterization, irony, suspense, and tragedy are all examples of writing techniques that authors use to improve the quality and impact of their stories. Using these techniques is rarely the primary purpose of an author's storytelling. Instead, these are secondary writing goals that improve the artistic values of a story while supporting the theme of the story.

MINSTREL implements four drama goals: suspense, tragedy, foreshadow-ing, and characterization. Two of these techniques are used in *Richard and Lancelot*.

Foreshadowing is used to increase the impact of the scene in which Lancelot (erroneously) discovers that Andrea loves another knight by echoing parts of that scene earlier in the story:

> At the same time, Lancelot's horse moved Lancelot to
> the woods. This unexpectedly caused him to be near
> Andrea. Because Lancelot was near Andrea, Lancelot
> saw Andrea. Lancelot loved Andrea.
> [...]
> Some time later, Lancelot's horse moved Lancelot to
> the woods unintentionally, again causing him to be

```
near Andrea.  Lancelot knew that Andrea kissed with
a knight named Frederick because Lancelot saw that
Andrea kissed with Frederick.
```

Lancelot's willful horse first causes him to unexpectedly meet and fall in love with Andrea, and then later causes him to unexpectedly see Andrea kissing Frederick and fall out of love with Andrea. This juxtaposition and repetition of similar scene elements improves the impact of the story theme by echoing and strengthening the underlying pattern of the story.

Characterization is used to establish the hot temper of Lancelot, which contributes to his later hasty decision:

```
Lancelot was hot tempered.  Once, Lancelot lost a
joust.  Because he was hot tempered, Lancelot wanted
to destroy his sword.  Lancelot struck his sword.
His sword was destroyed.
```

To develop the characterization of Lancelot as hot-tempered, MINSTREL creates a story scene which shows how his hot temper affects how he reacts to events. By establishing the personality of the main character early in the story, MINSTREL improves the plausibility of later events and enhances the overall quality of the story. Chapter 5 discusses MINSTREL's use of dramatic writing techniques.

3.2.4   Consistency Goals

Another concern for authors is to tell stories that are consistent and believable. Characters should act rationally and events should happen in accordance with the author's best understanding of how the world functions. Readers expect stories to reflect and agree with what they know about the world, and so the author must take care to maintain that plausibility, and to explain it when absent or different from common understanding.

Story inconsistencies normally arise as side-effects of other author-level goals. For example, when MINSTREL creates the story events needed to illustrate a story theme, it creates *only* the events necessary for the theme. This might include a scene in which a character dies. But unless the theme happens to also include scenes explaining how the character died, who killed him, and what emotional reactions all the characters in the story had to the character's death, the resulting story will be incomplete. The reader expects explanations of how and why things happen. The purpose of MINSTREL's consistency goals is to detect these types of situations and to correct them by adding explanatory story events.

MINSTREL implements a variety of author-level goals aimed at maintaining story consistency. One class of goals checks to see that characters are shown achieving all the steps of successful plans:

```
Lancelot was hot tempered, Lancelot wanted to kill
Frederick. Lancelot went to Frederick. Lancelot
fought with Frederick. Frederick was dead.
```

In *Richard and Lancelot*, Lancelot's murder of Frederick was created to illustrate the story theme. After this scene is created, a consistency goal notices that a necessary precondition to fighting someone—being colocated with them—hasn't been fulfilled. Although Frederick's death is necessary to illustrate the story theme, an explanation of how Lancelot and Frederick came to be in the same place is not, and so MINSTREL's thematic goals did not create one. To make the story understandable, a story event is created that achieves the colocation precondition. Consistency goals "repair" the story by noticing and correcting inconsistencies left over from other author-level goals.

Another class of goals checks to be sure that characters are reacting properly to events in their world:

```
Lancelot wanted to take back that he wanted to kill
Frederick, but he could not because Frederick was
dead. Lancelot hated himself.
```

People normally have emotional reactions to the events in their lives. They feel happy when they achieve important goals, sad when a major plan fails, anxious when they are worried about their self-preservation, and so on. In this example, Lancelot discovers that he has violated a major goal because of a character flaw, but has no emotional reaction to this event. A consistency goal notices this and creates a scene describing a plausible emotional reaction. This improves the consistency of the story and the believability of the character.

The range of MINSTREL's consistency goals and the plans MINSTREL uses to achieve them are discussed in Chapter 6.

3.2.5 Presentation Goals

Presentation goals concern how the story is communicated to the reader. The author of the story must decide the order in which events in the story are presented to the reader, which events must be fully described and which can be summarized or omitted, and how each story event will be expressed in English.

Richard and Lancelot contains the following sequence of story scenes:

```
Lancelot was hot tempered. Once, Lancelot lost a
joust. Because he was hot tempered, Lancelot wanted
```

to destroy his sword. Lancelot struck his sword.
His sword was destroyed...
    Because Lancelot was hot tempered, Lancelot wanted
to kill Frederick. Lancelot went to Frederick.
Lancelot fought with Frederick. Frederick was
dead...

The first scene is created by MINSTREL to illustrate the characterization of Lancelot as hot tempered. The second scene is part of the theme, and turns upon Lancelot's hot temper. MINSTREL's presentation goals must recognize the purposes of these two scenes and use that knowledge to order them correctly.

MINSTREL's presentation goals are also concerned with selecting scenes to be in the story and with expressing story events in English. For more on MINSTREL's presentation goals and how they are achieved, see Turner (1993).

3.3 Author-Level Planning and Problem Solving

The previous sections identified four classes of important author-level goals and showed how they combined to create a complete story. Now we shift our attention to the process of how those goals arise and are achieved.

As noted earlier, authors tell stories to achieve particular goals. The process of storytelling involves selecting a goal from the author's pool of goals, trying to find a plan to achieve that goal, and executing the plan, possibly adding new goals to the agenda or deleting old ones. This continues until the author is satisfied with the story, that is, until the author has no more unsatisfied author-level goals.

MINSTREL models this using two processes. The *planning process* is concerned with the management of author-level goals. The planning process maintains the pool of author goals and when necessary, selects a goal to achieve. The *problem solving process* is concerned with solving author-level goals. It takes a goal selected by the planning process and finds, evaluates, and executes a plan to achieve that goal. These processes are illustrated in Figure 3.1.

3.3.1 Author-Level Planning

MINSTREL uses an agenda-based planning model, patterned on similar models in Lenat (1976) and Warren (1978). As goals arise they are given a priority and placed on an agenda. Priorities are represented by integer numbers on a scale of 1 to 100. At each planning cycle, the highest priority goal is selected from the agenda and passed to the problem solving process.

MINSTREL begins storytelling with an initial goal to "tell a story." This goal breaks down into subgoals including selecting a theme, illustrating a theme, applying drama goals, checking the story for consistency, and presenting the story to the reader. At each cycle, MINSTREL selects the author-level goal with

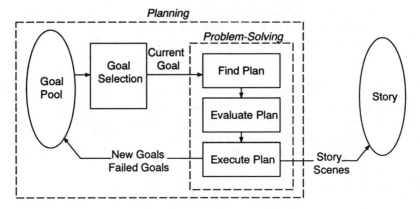

Figure 3.1 Author-Level Processes

the highest priority from the goal agenda and passes it to the problem solving process. Problem solving finds a plan for that goal and executes it.

Two important actions that MINSTREL's plans can take are to create and add new scenes to the story, and to create and add new author-level goals to the planning agenda. As new scenes are created, they are added to the current story. As new goals are created they are added to the goal agenda. Storytelling finishes when the goal agenda is empty.

One important feature of MINSTREL's planning model is that MINSTREL has the ability to requeue failed goals. When all the plans found for achieving a goal fail, the failed goal is placed back on the agenda at a lower priority. This can be repeated until the priority drops to a cut-off level, below which the goal "falls off" the agenda and is ignored.

This facility permits MINSTREL to periodically retry goals that have failed, in hopes that the achievement of some intermediate goal will have changed the problem solving situation enough to permit the failed goal to now succeed. The purpose of this is to permit MINSTREL's goals to interact with one another to synergistically find solutions that a straightforward, top-down pursuit of goals would miss.

When faced with a set of interdependent goals, it is often difficult for a problem solver to determine which goal to work on first. Tracing the dependencies between goals can be a very difficult and time-consuming task. MINSTREL's ability to re-queue goals permits MINSTREL to avoid the problem of selecting a proper starting point from amongst a collection of interdependent author-level goals. Instead, MINSTREL begins with some likely goal. If the starting point selected turns out to be unsuccessful, it is re-queued and another tried until a fruitful starting point is found.

Thus MINSTREL's ability to re-queue goals not only permits it to solve goals that a straightforward, top-down approach would not be able to solve, but it also simplifies MINSTREL's planning model by eliminating the need for a mechanism to correctly select amongst competing author-level goals.

MINSTREL's planning model, and in particular, the role that re-queuing of goals plays in MINSTREL's storytelling are further discussed in Chapter 8.

3.3.2   Author-Level Problem Solving

It's not unusual to view artists with something approaching awe. The process of making art seems very different from the kinds of prosaic tasks one tackles in day-to-day life. So few are successful at art, and what they produce is so different and interesting, that there is an automatic tendency to assume that art involves unique and special mental processes.

But although Koestler (1964), Wallas (1926), and others have argued that creative domains such as storytelling, art, and music are somehow fundamentally different from more mundane problem domains, most psychological evidence suggests the opposite (Weisberg, 1986). People solve problems in creative domains in much the same way they solve problems in more traditional problem solving domains. In art as in day-to-day life, people have goals, find or create plans to achieve those goals, apply the plans, evaluate the results, and so on. We are not used to thinking of artistic endeavors such as painting and music in terms of problem solving, but at a general process level there is little to distinguish between creating and playing a musical piece and creating and writing a thank-you note.

MINSTREL's author-level model of problem solving is shown in Figure 3.2. Author-level goals are input at the left side, where they are used to recall similar past storytelling situations. The author-level plans used in these past situations are then adapted and applied to the current goal. Finally, the adapted plan is assessed to determine if it meets domain-specific considerations (i.e., if you are telling a realistic story you might reject a plan that would be acceptable for a fantasy). Although this model is being applied to author-level problems, it is the same case-based model used for all problem solving processes in MINSTREL. The portion of this model within the dotted lines is the same model described in Chapter 2. All that has been changed is the types of goals being solved.

In MINSTREL, a single problem solving model is used for all problem domains, artistic and otherwise. MINSTREL's author-level storytelling goals are solved by the same process used to solve character-level goals in the King Arthur domain and to invent devices in the mechanical invention domain. Uniformity of the problem solving process is a fundamental tenet of this research.

The process of problem solving is invariant across problem domains.

One interesting consequence of MINSTREL's uniform model of problem solving

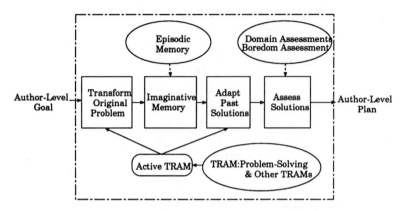

Figure 3.2 A Case-Based Model of Problem Solving

is that the same creative process used to invent new story scenes and new solutions to problems in the King Arthur domain is also active in problem solving at the author level. But before we can look at the role of creativity in solving author-level goals, it is necessary to digress momentarily to discuss the representation of author-level goals and plans.

3.3.2.1 Representation of Author-Level Goals And Plans

Character-level goals in MINSTREL's stories are represented using goal schemas. For example, Lancelot's goal to kill a dragon is represented as a &GOAL schema with appropriate values for the TYPE, ACTOR, and OBJECT slots. An example of a character-level goal is shown in Figure 3.3. MINSTREL's author-level goals are also represented using goal schemas. Each of MINSTREL's goals in telling a story is represented using a &GOAL schema and appropriate values for the TYPE, ACTOR, and OBJECT slots. Figure 3.4 shows an example of an author-level goal to check the consistency in a particular story scene. Note that the actor of this goal is &MINSTREL, a symbol that MINSTREL uses to refer to itself, and that the object of this goal is an event in the story being told. This example author-level goal represents MINSTREL's desire to check the schema pointed to by the OBJECT slot (&State.99) for consistency.

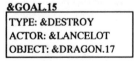

Figure 3.3 Example Character-Level Goal Schema

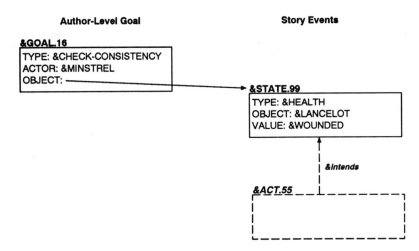

Figure 3.4   Example Author-Level Goal Schema

This consistent representation permits MINSTREL to treat character-level and author-level goals identically. The same processes can be used to store, recall, and manipulate both types of goals.

Unlike the representation of goals, MINSTREL's representation of plans is *not* consistent across the character and author levels. Character-level plans in MINSTREL are represented as interconnected collections of goal, act, and state schemas. Figure 3.5 shows the representation for a knight's plan to achieve the goal of destroying a dragon. This plan is represented as a goal (destroy a dragon, &Goal.15), a plan to achieve that goal (fight the dragon, &Act.17), and the result of executing that plan (the dragon is dead, &State.7).

Although the same type of representation could be used for MINSTREL's author-level plans, it would be clumsy and time consuming. Schemas for complicated computational actions such as looping, recursion, and so on would have to be defined and an interpreter built to perform those actions. Fortunately, MINSTREL is built upon a representation for computation—Lisp. Rather than reinvent the wheel, MINSTREL uses Lisp to represent its author-level plans and uses the Lisp interpreter to execute those plans.

Each of MINSTREL's author-level plans (ALPs) is a structured, independent block of Lisp code. Each ALP contains a test that determines when the plan is applicable and a body that executes the plan. Because Lisp code can be difficult to understand, the author-level plans presented in this text are shown in a structured English format. An example of this format appears in Figure 3.6. The author plan shown in Figure 3.6 is one of the plans MINSTREL uses to check the consistency of a story. This plan assures that characters who are injured react

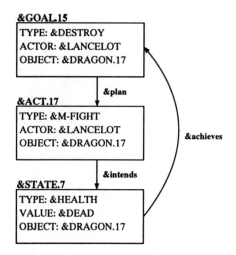

Figure 3.5 Example Character-Level Goal Schema

Name:	ALP:Make-Consistent-P-Health
Goal Type:	&Check-Consistency
Object:	*AL-OBJ*
Test:	*AL-OBJ* is a state schema that represents a character being wounded, and it is not motivating a goal by that character to protect his health.
Body:	1. Create a &P-Health (health protection) goal for the character being wounded in *AL-OBJ*.
	2. Add the new goal to the story by creating a &THWARTS link from *AL-OBJ* to the new goal (i.e., being wounded thwarts a character's goal of protecting his health).
	3. Create author-level goals to make sure the new goal is consistent and fully instantiated.

Figure 3.6 ALP:Make-Consistent-P-Health

properly by having a goal to protect their health. This plan would apply to the author-level goal shown in Figure 3.4.

There are five components to each of MINSTREL's Author-Level Plans (ALPs). The **Name** identifies the plan. The **Goal Type** specifies the type of author-level goal to which the plan applies. The type of an author-level goal is the value of the TYPE slot of the &GOAL schema. The **Object** is a symbol by which the value of the OBJECT slot of the author-level goal can be referenced when this plan is applied. The **Test** determines whether this plan applies to a particular instance of a goal. Finally, the **Body** of the ALP is the series of actions required to execute the plan.

3.3.3   Creativity in Author-Level Problem Solving

MINSTREL has a consistent representation for goals and a single model of problem solving that is used to solve problems at both the character and author levels. This model of problem solving includes creativity—the ability to invent new problem solutions when needed. Consequently, when MINSTREL cannot solve an author-level goal, creativity heuristics will be applied to try to invent a new plan for solving that goal, just as happens when MINSTREL cannot solve a character-level goal.

There are three steps to the creative problem solving process:

(1) Transform the original problem specification.
(2) Recall a similar past problem situation.
(3) Adapt the associated plan to the original problem.

Because MINSTREL has a consistent representation for both author-level and character-level goals, and a single model of episodic memory, the first two steps of creative problem solving are the same for both author-level and character-level problem solving. The primary difference between character-level and author-level creativity lies in the third step: adapting the associated plan.

MINSTREL's character-level plans are represented by act and state schemas, and MINSTREL's creativity heuristics (TRAMs) know how to modify and adapt this representation. But MINSTREL's author-level plans are represented as structures of Lisp code, and MINSTREL's TRAMs do not know how to adapt Lisp code. MINSTREL's author-level plans are opaque and nonadaptable, and so MINSTREL *cannot* adapt author-level plans. This limits the creativity heuristics (TRAMs) that MINSTREL can apply when problem solving at the author level.

In case-based problem solving, plans to solve problems are found by recalling similar past problems. Creativity requires recalling plans from past problems different from the current problem and adapting them to the current problem. But because MINSTREL cannot adapt plans at the author-level (because they are opaque blocks of Lisp code) MINSTREL cannot apply any creativity heuristics which involve plan adaptation. However, there are a few types of creativity that do not require plan adaptation.

Consider, for example, a problem solver finding his way home from a newly built shopping mall. The problem solver has never come home from this mall before, so standard problem solving will not recall any ready-made plans. But if he recalls that the shopping mall stands on the site of a former restaurant he frequented, then he can recall a route for driving home from the restaurant and use it without change. The problem solver has invented a solution to a problem by making use of an old solution *without adaptation.*

We call this type of creativity "nonadaptive creativity," because it hinges upon finding a solution that can be applied to a new problem without having to change the solution.

At the character-level, we have already seen some examples of creativity heuristics that do not require adaptation. One of these is TRAM:Recall-Act. TRAM:Recall-Act suggests that if you are trying to find an act that fits some particular set of constraints, then you can probably ignore all the constraints except the goal the act is intended to fulfill and the intended effects of the action. By ignoring the other constraints, TRAM:Recall-Act permits the problem solver to recall solutions which he would not have otherwise recalled, because they would not fulfill the extraneous constraints. And because the extra problem constraints are extraneous, the recalled solution—even though it does not fill those constraints—does not need adaptation.

TRAM:Recall-Act illustrates the central feature of nonadaptive creativity: redirecting recall to a new area of memory where immediately useful plans are likely to be found. TRAM:Recall-Act finds new solutions to a problem by redirecting recall to solutions that lack the extraneous constraints.

So although MINSTREL cannot use all types of creativity at the author-level, it can use nonadaptive creativity. To understand MINSTREL's author-level nonadaptive creativity works, it is first necessary to understand how MINSTREL's author-level episodic memory is organized.

MINSTREL's author-level plans are indexed in episodic memory according to specific past goals they have solved, just as character-level plans are indexed according to past goals they have solved. So, for example, the author-level plan ALP:Make-Consistent-P-Health is indexed under a goal of type &Check-Consistency applied to a &State schema. A portion of MINSTREL's author-level episodic memory illustrating this organization is shown in Figure 3.7. Episodic memory is organized as a tree of (feature, value) pairs. &Goal.16 is an author-level goal from a past instance of storytelling in which MINSTREL's goal to check the consistency of a particular state in a story (&State.99) was achieved by ALP:Make-Consistent-P-Health. This is organized in episodic memory by the features and values of &Goal.16, including the object of the goal, &State.99. If a new goal is encountered with similar features, ALP:Make-Consistent-P-Health will be recalled.

MINSTREL also has generalized author-level plans. These are plans that can apply to a number of different objects. Generalized author-level plans have a null Object and are indexed accordingly. Figure 3.7 shows the indexing for a generalized author-level plan called ALP:Default-Consistent. ALP:Default-Consistent is a simple plan that recognizes a schema as consistent if it has had its Type slot filled in.

When MINSTREL has a goal to the check the consistency of a state schema,

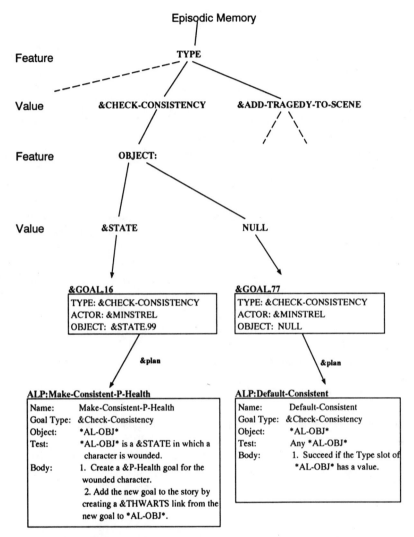

Figure 3.7 Example Organization of Author-Level Memory

the goal will be used as an index to memory and because its features and values match those of &GOAL.16, MINSTREL will find &GOAL.16 and its associated plan, ALP:Make-Consistent-P-Health. This is standard problem solving—recalling a similar past problem and using the solution to that problem for the current problem.

Nonadaptive creativity comes into play when this fails. When an author-level goal does not recall a similar past goal and its associated solution, or if all the recalled solutions fail, then MINSTREL must look elsewhere in author-level episodic memory for an author-level plan that can be applied to the current goal without adaptation. There is one place that such a plan can be found: a generalized author-level plan.

Generalized author-level plans will not be found by standard problem solving because the Object slot of the current goal will not match the null slot under which the generalized plans are indexed. But precisely because these plans are generalized we know that they can be applied without adaptation to any goal of the proper type. What is needed is a creativity heuristic that will find these plans by looking in the appropriate place, that is, a nonadaptive creativity heuristic.

MINSTREL's TRAM for achieving this is called TRAM:Generalized-AL-Plans. This TRAM finds generalized plans to apply to a specific author-level goal by eliminating the Object slot from the current goal and returning without adaptation whatever plans it finds. TRAM:Generalized-AL-Plans is shown in Figure 3.8. When TRAM:Generalized-AL-Plans is applied to the author-level goal illustrated in Figure 3.4, it eliminates the Object slot and uses the transformed goal as an index to memory. This recalls ALP:Default-Consistent, which is then applied to achieve the original goal.

Because MINSTREL's TRAMs cannot adapt MINSTREL's author-level plans, creativity at the author-level is limited to nonadaptive creativity. Although nonadaptive creativity is not as powerful as other types of creativity, it does illustrate the invariance of MINSTREL's model of problem solving and demonstrate that the same creative problem solving process used to solve character-level goals can also solve author-level goals.

3.3.4 Achieving Author-Level Plans

Our examination of the authoring process began with the identification of author goals. For the particular type of stories that MINSTREL tells, we identified four important classes of author-level goals. Then we looked at the processes of planning and problem solving: How author goals were managed, and how plans to

TRAM:Generalized-AL-Plans

Transform Strategy

Remove the Object slot of the author-level goal.

Adapt Strategy

Do not adapt the recalled solution. Apply it as is to the current problem.

Figure 3.8 TRAM:Generalized-AL-Plans

solve author-level goals were found or created. The last step is to look at the contents of author-level plans: What they do to achieve author-level goals.

The following chapters will discuss in detail each of MINSTREL's author-level plans, identifying what goal each plan applies to, and describing how the plan achieves that type of goal. But before we turn to the details of MINSTREL's author-level plans, we should like to examine this problem in more general terms. What does an author do to illustrate a theme, use a dramatic technique, or correct a causal inconsistency?

Consider a hypothetical author writing a short story about Lancelot, with a goal to portray Lancelot as deceptive. He achieves this goal in two steps.

First, the author uses his knowledge of the goal he is trying to achieve and his knowledge of how stories are told to specify his goal as an abstract description of story events which, if part of the story, would achieve his goal. In this case, the author knows that "deception" is a character trait and that character traits are reflected in character actions. From this he realizes that his goal of portraying Lancelot as deceptive will be achieved if the story contained some scenes in which Lancelot used a deception plan. Note that the author hasn't yet achieved his goal. He has only further specified it as a particular, abstract description of story events which would achieve the goal.

The abstract specification the author arrives at will depend on his knowledge of storytelling. From reading and writing stories, he will have built up a library of author-level plans that translate author-level goals into story specifications. Illustrating a character trait by including a story event demonstrating the trait might be a plan the author learned through conscious study, or by reading many stories that used this technique.

Next, the author tries to create story elements to fulfill this abstract specification. Using his knowledge of the genre of the story, the goals of the story, and the already-completed portions of the story, the author tries to invent scenes to fit the abstract specification. Thinking about one person deceiving another may remind the author of a time when a coworker fooled him with a falsified memo from their boss. Being reminded of this scene, the author may decide to use it as the basis for the Lancelot story scene. But to make that reminding work in his story, the author must make some adaptations. Lancelot will have to take the coworker's place, the memo will have to be replaced with something appropriate to the King Arthur milieu—perhaps a note from the king—and so on. The end result is a scene in which Lancelot fools Guinevere by forging a note from the King.

We call this process of taking an abstract specification and general story constraints and inventing scenes to fit the specification *instantiation*.

1. Define an abstract specification of a needed story element.
2. Create a specific story element to match the abstract specification.

The claim of this research is that this two-step process of specification and instantiation is the fundamental process by which author-level goals are achieved. Not all author-level goals are achieved by this process: Goals may be achieved by creating subgoals, reordering events in the story, creating English language sentences, and so on. But the process of specification and instantiation is a pervasive and fundamental element of storytelling.

3.3.5 The Role of Episodic Memory in Storytelling

How is instantiation achieved? In the foregoing example, the author instantiated his abstract specification by a process of transform, recall, and adapt, which the reader will recognize as creative case-based problem solving. In fact, instantiating an abstract concept description can be viewed as a special form of creative case-based problem solving. But instantiation differs from normal problem solving in an important way. In normal problem solving, the problem solver uses a complete problem description to recall similar past problems, so that the problem solver can use the associated plans. But in instantiation, the problem solver uses an incomplete description to recall a complete description, without any interest in the associated plans.

The product of normal problem solving is a plan for the current problem. Suppose, for example, that a knight finds himself threatened by a dragon and wants to save himself. The knight recalls a past situation in which he was threatened by a troll. He'd solved that by charging the troll on his horse, so he decides to apply that same plan to the dragon. By recalling a similar past problem solving situation, the knight has found a plan to solve his current problem.

In instantiation, though, the product of problem solving is the *recalled problem situation*, not the associated solution. Suppose, for example, that an author is creating a scene in which "Lancelot, a knight, is endangered." This abstract description is passed to case-based problem solving and recalls a past situation in which a knight was threatened by a troll and consequently killed the troll by charging it on his horse. The author can now use the recalled problem situation to fill in or instantiate the current scene. The associated plan (charging the monster on horseback) may or may not be used, depending on the author's particular storytelling needs. In fact, the scene being instantiated could be a belief, an emotion, or some other type of story element that does not have a plan associated with it at all.

Because there is not necessarily an associated problem solution, and because instantiation may not make use of the problem solution even if it exists, there is no need to perform the second and third steps of problem solving: adapting the recalled solution and assessing the result. Instantiation requires only the recall of a similar past scene, and not the rest of the problem solving effort.

However, a problem arises when the author cannot recall a similar past scene. In this case, recall alone is not sufficient, because the author needs to create a story scene to fit his abstract scene description.

The solution is to use *imaginative memory*. Imaginative memory incorporates creativity into the recall process, permitting episodic memory to invent a memory to match a set of recall indices. If the recall indices are the features of an abstract scene specification, then imaginative memory will either recall or invent the specific story scene needed to instantiate the scene specification. Instantiation is thus simply the process of imagination—using creativity and the knowledge in episodic memory to imagine scenes to fit a particular criteria.

Instantiation is achieved through imaginative memory.

It's a common intuition to link imagination with storytelling. By explicitly representing instantiation as a fundamental process in storytelling and showing how instantiation can be achieved by imaginative memory, MINSTREL identifies and defines the link between imagination and storytelling. And by showing how creativity can be incorporated into the recall process, MINSTREL demonstrates the link between creating new problem solutions and the ability to imagine plausible new situations and ideas.

3.3.6 Planning With Many Constraints

One reason storytelling is a difficult task for humans and computers alike is that it requires the storyteller to solve a large number of interdependent goals simultaneously. In a successful story, the events of a story fulfill a range of goals. They illustrate the theme of the story, develop the literary value of the story, maintain the story consistency, and so on. But it is difficult for humans to solve planning situations that involve a number of simultaneous goals (Flower & Hayes, 1980). Each added goal increases the complexity of the planning task, until it may be nearly impossible. "The act of writing is best described as the act of juggling a number of simultaneous constraints." (Flower & Hayes, 1980, p. 31).

One solution to planning with many constraints which is often applied to the storytelling problem is to partition the problem into semiindependent subproblems (Flower & Hayes, 1980). Rather than try to solve all the problems involved in creating a story at once, the author breaks the writing process down into a sequence of goals, that is, theme, drama, consistency, presentation.

The technique of delaying constraints is often sounded in writing handbooks:

...begin by doing some "free writing". This simply means writing down whatever comes into your mind about a subject... this is not the time to think about spelling, punctuation, or the correct choice of words... What you'll produce is generally called the first or "rough" draft, and it will probably need some revisions and changes.... (Tchudi & Tchudi, 1984, pp. 21-24)

Delaying constraints or partitioning the storytelling problem into semiindependent subproblems permits the author to solve problems that would otherwise be too complex. But one consequence of this strategy is that solving one subproblem may violate another. For example, MINSTREL creates the following story scene in order to illustrate the theme "Done in haste is oft regretted":

```
One    day,   Lancelot   wanted   to   kill   Frederick.
Lancelot fought with Frederick.  Frederick was dead.
```

This scene does serve to illustrate the theme (by showing Lancelot performing a hasty action he will later regret). But it is otherwise incomplete. It does not explain why Lancelot wants to kill Frederick, or how Lancelot came to be in the same location as Frederick. The goal to illustrate the theme has been achieved, but other goals have not.

Human authors have the same difficulties when they partition complex problems. Problem constraints may be violated or even forgotten. An article on revising that appeared in *Writer's Digest* includes a "Tactical Analysis Checklist" of mistakes of this sort:

> • Look at the motives of your major story characters. Have you included sufficient information about their past lives to make it credible that they want what they want, feel what they feel, think as they think, act as they act, or have the skills they call on in your plot? (Bickham, 1992, p. 28)

For both human and computer authors, breaking a complex problem with many constraints into simpler, semiindependent subproblems is a valuable writing strategy. But because a story is an integrated whole, no subproblem can be truly independent of the other subproblems. So the author must be prepared to detect and correct constraint violations during the writing process. In MINSTREL, this is achieved through opportunistic goals.

3.3.7 Active Versus Opportunistic Goals

At any time during the storytelling process, MINSTREL has a number of goals that it is actively trying to achieve. Each of these goals is present on the goal agenda and the active goal with the highest priority is being achieved. Initially, the active goals include the goals (1) to tell a story illustrating a particular theme, and (2) to present the story to the reader in English. These goals are achieved via author-level plans that may create additional active goals (i.e., subgoals).

In addition to the active goals, storytelling conditions can cause *opportunistic goals* to arise. An opportunistic goal is an author-level goal that becomes active whenever a specified storytelling situation arises. For example, MINSTREL has an opportunistic goal that arises whenever a story scene is created that contains inconsistencies. When an inconsistent story scene is created an opportunistic goal to correct the inconsistency is triggered. Similarly, MINSTREL has opportunistic author-level goals to achieve various dramatic writing purposes, such as building suspense. When a story scene is created that is suitable for suspense (such as a character's life being threatened), an opportunistic goal arises to consider building suspense in that scene.

Opportunistic goals serve two purposes in MINSTREL. First, opportunistic goals provide a mechanism for detecting and correcting constraint violations. As described earlier, MINSTREL reduces the difficulty of the storytelling problem by breaking it into a sequence of semiindependent subgoals. Opportunistic goals provide a mechanism for detecting when the solution of one subgoal violates the constraints of another subgoal, as for example when a scene created to illustrate the theme of a story contains causal inconsistencies.

Second, opportunistic goals are used to represent secondary author goals. In general, we suppose that any author has a variety of goals when telling a story, some which are primary and some which are secondary. These two categories represent a sharp, qualitative divide in author priority. The author's primary goals are those which the author considers essential to the telling of the current story. If the author cannot achieve his or her primary goals, then the storytelling process has failed. For MINSTREL, the primary goals are (1) to tell a story concerning a particular theme, (2) to make the story consistent and believable, and (3) to present the story in English. If any of these goals fail, then the storytelling process itself has failed.

Secondary goals, on the other hand, represent goals that are desirable but not essential to the storytelling process. The author is pleased if he or she can achieve these goals, because it means that the story is better than it might otherwise be. But if the opportunities do not arise, the story is not a failure. MINSTREL's goals to use literary techniques are secondary goals. If they succeed, they add additional quality and complexity to the stories MINSTREL tells, but the story can succeed even if they fail. (Although it will likely have less literary value.)

Of course, how an author categorizes his or her goals varies from author to author, and from story to story. For a writer of mystery stories, building suspense is probably an essential goal in the writing process. But for the writer of romantic fantasies, it is a secondary goal, and for the writer of comedy it may be actively avoided. And even for a single author, goal priorities will vary from story to story.

In terms of the storytelling process, primary and secondary goals differ primarily in how they arise. Primary goals are self-directed, while secondary goals are reactive. In MINSTREL, primary goals arise directly from MINSTREL's initial storytelling goal. MINSTREL's initial goal ("tell a story") creates subgoals to tell a story about a particular theme, to tell a consistent and believable story, and to tell the story in English, that is, all of MINSTREL's primary goals. The secondary goals, on the other hand, arise in reaction to the developing story. In MINSTREL, each secondary goal is represented by an opportunistic goal. If the opportunity arises to achieve a secondary goal, then the opportunistic goal triggers. Thus primary goals are guaranteed to arise and be attempted, while secondary goals may or may not arise, depending on the story development.

It is also interesting to note that author-level plans used to achieve a primary goal are generally not suitable for achieving that same goal opportunistically, and vice versa. For example, MINSTREL has an author-level plan to add suspense to a story scene by having a character attempt an escape from a dangerous situation. This plan cannot be used actively, because it depends on the prior existence of a dangerous situation. In general, plans to achieve primary goals must be able to create the story events necessary to achieve the goal from scratch, while opportunistic goals can be achieved by plans that modify or augment existing story scenes.

3.4   Conclusions

MINSTREL has three major advancements over previous models of storytelling.

First, MINSTREL demonstrates the importance of an explicit author model in storytelling. The particular author-level goals and plans MINSTREL uses to tell stories are of great interest, and are fully discussed in the following chapters. But as important is MINSTREL's architecture as a storyteller with an explicit knowledge of its own goals.

Second, MINSTREL models storytelling as problem solving. By this, MINSTREL clarifies the relationship between achievements in artistic domains such as storytelling and achievements in traditional problem solving domains such as mechanical repair. MINSTREL demonstrates the fundamental similarities between artistic endeavors and traditional problem solving, and MINSTREL is *prima facie* evidence that artistic ability can be explained in terms of problem solving, and that no further or different cognitive process need be stipulated.

Third, MINSTREL explicitly models instantiation as a fundamental storytelling process. By recognizing the importance of instantiation, MINSTREL is able to clarify and define a process that has previously been unrecognized and unilluminated. And by implementing instantiation using imaginative memory, MINSTREL further defines the links between creativity, memory, and problem solving.

4

Thematic Goals in Storytelling

4.1 Introduction

When MINSTREL tells a story, its primary goal is to illustrate a particular story theme. MINSTREL's story themes are stereotypical planning situations, which can often be summarized by an adage such as "A bird in the hand is worth two in the bush" or "Deception serves the devil." To understand the role of story themes in MINSTREL's storytelling process, there are five issues that must be addressed:

1. What is a theme?
2. How is a theme represented?
3. What themes does MINSTREL know?
4. What author-level thematic goals does MINSTREL have?
5. What plans does MINSTREL have to achieve these goals?

4.2 What Is a Theme?

Webster's New Collegiate Dictionary defines a theme as "the subject or topic of discourse or of artistic expression"; Roget's Thesaurus lists synonyms for themes that include "point," "motif," "topic," "pattern," and "design." The theme of a story is the underlying concept or topic that organizes the story into a coherent whole; it is the theme that gives rise to a story's organization and structure.

But stories are told for a wide variety of purposes. People use stories as teaching devices, for amusement, and to illustrate human nature. Consequently themes are as varied as stories themselves.

Fortunately, it isn't necessary to have a precise definition or classification of story themes in order to investigate the processes and knowledge involved in storytelling. Instead, we can restrict our study to specific themes or classes of themes and look at how stories are told about those themes. The hope is that what we learn about a specific type of theme will give us insight and understanding about themes in general.

One type of story theme is characterized by the tales in "Aesop's Fables." Each fable presents a stereotypical planning situation and shows the consequence of a particular planning decision. An example of an Aesop's Fable, "The Fox and the Crow," is shown in Figure 4.1.

"The Fox and the Crow" illustrates the consequences of listening to false praise. The themes of Aesop's Fables are captured by simple adages or morals, such as "Pride goes before a fall." Because these themes give advice about how a planner should act, we call this type of story theme a "Planning Advice Theme." Examples of other Planning Advice Themes are shown in Figure 4.2.

Planning Advice Themes are suitable for computer storytelling for several reasons. They are simple, easy to understand and recognize, and yet interesting enough to appear in a wide range of literature. MINSTREL uses Planning Advice Themes from Aesop's Fables, Hollywood movies, and *Romeo and Juliet.*

A crow who had stolen some meat,
  Came down in a tree
Where a fox who wanted the treat
  Could look up and see.

So the clever fox started to sing
  The bird's praises. "Our choice,"
He said, "you would be for King,
  If you had a good voice."

To show him, the crow dropped the meat
  And raised a loud croaking,
While the fox ate the meat at his feet
  So fast he was choking.

But he managed these words to the crow,
  Who now felt rather small:
"Kings need lots of things, you know,
  But good sense most of all!"

Figure 4.1 The Fox and the Crow (Rees, 1966)

Adage	Meaning
A bird in the hand is worth two in the bush.	*Don't abandon an achieved goal to achieve another goal, because you may end up with neither.*
Pride goes before a fall.	*Don't use pride as a justification for an action.*
Honesty is the best policy.	*Don't use plans which call for lying.*
The early bird catches the worm.	*Initiate plans to achieve goals in a timely fashion.*

Figure 4.2 Example Planning Advice Themes

By limiting MINSTREL to Planning Advice Themes, we are able to address many of the issues in telling theme-based stories without the need to create a general theory of themes.

4.3   Representing Planning Advice Themes

Story themes have been of interest to researchers in artificial intelligence for some time, and many different representations for story themes have been proposed. These include Thematic Organization Packets (Hammond, 1990; Schank, 1982), story points (Wilensky, 1982), and plot units (Lehnert, 1982). Although each of these representations captures some type of story abstraction, none of them looked specifically at planning advice themes, or sought to explicitly represent themes as planning advice.

One representation that did capture the planning advice aspect of themes was Thematic Abstraction Units, or TAUs (Dyer, 1983). TAUs were used in program called BORIS that read and developed an in-depth understanding of narratives. BORIS used TAUs to guide its understanding of stories in which unexpected events occurred. An example TAU (TAU-POST-HOC) is shown in Figure 4.3.

TAU-POST-HOC represents a specific type of planning situation, in which a planner tries to recover from a goal failure by executing a prevention plan after the goal failure. This is represented as a sequence of abstracted planning actions. When BORIS encountered a story scene that matched one of the actions in a TAU, it could use the TAU to predict possible future story events, or to understand past story events.

For example, upon reading the story fragment:

The hired hand always wanted a raise, but the farmer would not grant it. Finally, the hired hand got an offer to work at a neighboring farm.

TAU-POST-HOC

(1) x has preservation goal G active since enablement condition C is unsatisfied.

(2) x knows a plan P that will keep G from failing by satisfying C.

(3) x does not execute P and G fails. x attempts to recover from the failure of G by executing P. P fails since P is effective for C, but not in recovering from G's failure.

(4) In the future, x must execute P when G is active and C is not satisfied.

Adage: "Closing the barn door after the horse is gone."

Figure 4.3 TAU-POST-HOC

BORIS could use TAU-POST-HOC to expect a story event in which the farmer belatedly offers a raise, and this fails to retain the hired hand.

A TAU consists of an abstracted sequence of planning actions. This sequence of planning actions can be used to anticipate or expect future events, or used to retroactively understand confusing past events. But although TAUs capture abstract planning situations, and can be used to index recovery or avoidance plans (as in [4] in Figure 4.3), they do not explicitly structure this knowledge as advice. TAU-POST-HOC does not identify what the planner's decision was, what part of the planning process the decision applied to, what the bad consequence of the decision was, in what contexts the decision is bad, and so on. To find and apply this knowledge, a planner must reason from the goal/plan structure of TAU-POST-HOC. In general, this may be difficult and inefficient.

For example, in TAU-POST-HOC, a reasoner looking for advice might find either of two bits of planning advice. One is captured by (4) in Figure 4.3, namely "One should execute a preventive plan when an enablement condition is unsatisfied," and the other is "One should not execute a preventive plan when the goal failure has already occurred." These two pieces of advice apply to different parts of the planning process (the first applies to goal activation, the second to plan selection), in different contexts, and so on. Extracting this knowledge from the goal/plan structure of TAU-POST-HOC, identifying its structure as advice, and resolving any ambiguities is a difficult task.

MINSTREL has addressed this problem by expanding TAUs to explicitly represent the advice aspect of planning advice themes. To the representation of TAUs as abstract goal/plan networks MINSTREL adds a structuring of the network as advice. Making the advice aspect of story themes explicit (1) identifies unambiguously the advice content of a story theme, (2) permits efficient use of this knowledge, and (3) more accurately defines a class of story themes.

What is needed in a representation of planning advice? Planning advice tells a planner what decision to make in a particular planning situation.

Consequently, a representation of planning advice must capture three things: (1) the planning decision, (2) a value judgment about the planning decision, and (3) a justification for the value judgment.

The *planning decision* represents the decision the planner is making as well as the context in which the decision is being made.

The *value judgment* indicates whether the planning decision was good or bad.

The *justification* is the reason or explanation for the value judgment. If the judgment is positive, the reason explains why the planning decision is a good decision. If the judgment is negative, the reason explains why the planning decision is a bad one.

The two pieces of advice implicit in TAU-POST-HOC are:

(1)   *Planning Decision*   Planner chooses not to activate a goal to alleviate an unsatisfied enablement condition.
     Judgment   Negative
     Justification   The unsatisfied enablement condition will cause a goal failure.

(2)   *Planning Decision*   Planner selects a prevention plan P to recover from a goal failure.
     Judgment   Negative
     Justification   Prevention plans cannot be used to recover from goal failures.

MINSTREL represents themes as schemas called Planning Advice Themes (or PATs). Figure 4.4 lists the parts of a PAT and gives a simple textual example of a Planning Advice Theme, PAT:Violent-Plans. PAT:Violent-Plans advises a planner to avoid plans that involve violence, because the violence might backfire, that is, "Live by the sword, die by the sword."

The first part of the PAT identifies the type and value of the planning advice:

Type identifies the decision point in the planning process to which the advice applies. MINSTREL currently knows about two decision points in the planning process: Plan Selection and Goal Activation. Plan Selection occurs when a planner selects a plan to achieve a goal. PATs about Plan Selection either encourage or discourage the use of particular plans in particular situations. Goal Activation occurs when a plan activates a goal in response to a change in the state of the world. PATs about Goal Activation either encourage or discourage activating particular goals in particular situations. Other decision points in the planning process include Goal Selection (which goal to attempt to achieve from a collection of goals) and Goal Abandon (when to quit pursuing a goal), but MINSTREL does not currently represent any themes based on these planning decision points.

Type of Advice	Explanation	PAT-Violent-Plan
Decision Point	The planning decision type this advice applies to.	*Plan Selection*
Value	Is this positive or negative advice?	*Negative*
Advice		
Decision	An abstract, stereotypical representation of a planning decision.	*Planner chooses a violent plan to achieve a goal.*
Consequence	An abstract, stereotypical representation of the consequence of the decision.	*The violent act backfires, and Planner is hurt.*
Connection	The causal connection between the decision and its consequence.	*The violent plan intends a violent action.*
Object	The goal, plan, or action to which the decision applies.	*The violent plan.*
Planner	Who the decision-maker is.	*"Planner"*
Context		
Active Goals	A description of the relevant goals in the planner's goal tree at the time he makes the decision.	*The goal Planner is trying to achieve.*
Current Goal	The planner's current goal.	*The goal Planner is trying to achieve.*
Current Plan	The planner's current plan.	*The violent plan.*
World Facts	Context in which to apply this advice.	

Figure 4.4 Representation of Planning Advice Themes

PAT:Violent-Plan is a PAT of Type "Plan Selection" because it advises one not to select a plan that involves violence to achieve a goal. An example of a Goal Activation PAT is "A bird in the hand is worth two in the bush." This theme advises a planner not to activate a goal that could cause the thwarting of another, already achieved goal.

Value determines whether a PAT is positive or negative advice. Positive advice encourages a planner to do something; negative advice informs him of a planning failure to avoid. For PAT:Violent-Plans, the Value is Negative, because PAT:Violent-Plans is advising the planner to *avoid* selecting a plan that involves violence.

The second portion of the PAT represents the advice itself:

Decision is an abstract schema-based representation of the planning choice identified by Type.

A Plan Selection decision is represented by a goal and the plan selected to achieve that goal. The details of the goal and the plan represented depend on the advice being represented. For PAT:Violent-Plans, the goal is any goal, and the plan is any violent plan. Thus, the Decision for PAT:Violent-Plans represents a planner's decision to use a violent plan to achieve a goal.

Consequence is an abstract, schema-based representation of the consequence of the Decision. The Consequence of a PAT represents the reason why Decision should be made (if the PAT is Positive advice) or avoided (if the PAT is Negative advice).

The Consequence of a Negative PAT (a theme which advises against some planning decision) generally involves a failed goal for the planner. In Positive PATs, the Consequence typically includes an achieved goal for the planner.

In PAT:Violent-Plan, the Consequence is a representation of the plan backfiring, causing the planner, rather than some other person, to be hurt. Since this PAT is negative advice, the Consequence involves a goal failure (loss of health) for the planner. This bad result is the reason to avoid the planning decision represented in the Decision part of the PAT.

Connection identifies the causal link between the Decision and the Consequence. Typically, this is the chain of events that leads from the planning decision to the achieved or failed goal in the Consequence. In PAT:Violent-Plan, the connection between the Decision and the Consequence is that the violent plan intends a violent action (which subsequently backfires).

Object identifies the specific schema within the Decision to which the advice applies. This is necessary because the representation of the Decision may have many different plans, goals, actions, and actors. In PAT:Violent-Plan, the Decision has only one representation of a Plan Selection, so identifying the planning decision to which the advice applies is trivial. But in general, a PAT may have a complex network of goals and plans in the Decision, so Object is necessary to identify the specific decision point to which the advice applies.

Planner identifies the actor to which the advice applies, in a way similar to Object. The Decision, Consequence, and Connection may involve many different actors. Planner identifies the actor to which the PAT applies.

The third portion of the PAT represents the context in which this advice applies. The context has two parts: knowledge about the world and knowledge about the planning process. Context knowledge is used to determine when advice is applicable. For example, there may be advice that applies only when the planner's life is in danger (knowledge about the world) or when the planner is trying to achieve two mutually incompatible goals (knowledge about the planning process).

Current Goal represents the planner's current goal. The current goal is the goal associated with the planning decision of this PAT.

Current Plan represents the plan, if any, associated with the planning decision of this PAT.

Active Goals represents the planner's active goals, which affect whether or not this advice should apply. A planner is assumed to have a prioritized list of goals that he is trying to achieve; Active Goals is a list of goals that must be present in this goal tree for this advice to apply.

For PAT:Violent-Plan, the goal the planner is trying to achieve by using a violent plan is the only relevant goal. The current goal will always be in the Goal Tree part of a PAT. For some planning advice, other goals may also be relevant.

Consider, for example, the advice "Save yourself first." This adage advises a planner to achieve a goal of saving himself from some harm before attempting to achieve a goal to save someone else from harm. In this case, the relevant goals from the planner's goal tree are the goal to save himself and the goal to save another.

World Facts represent facts about the world which must be true in order to apply the advice represented by this PAT. As a simple example, the advice "Save yourself first" would apply only if it were true that the planner's life was in danger. In MINSTREL, facts about the world are represented by state schemas.

The primary advantage of MINSTREL's Planning Advice Themes is that they explicitly organize thematic goal/plan structures as advice. Previous representations of story themes (TOPS Hammond, 1990; Schank, 1982), story points (Wilensky, 1982), TAUs (Dyer, 1983) have concentrated on representing and categorizing the goal/plan structures that appear as story themes. To this representation PATs add a secondary structure as advice. PATs add indices into goal/plan representations of story themes that identify parts of the themes as parts of an advice structure.

The purpose of representing story themes as both goal/plan structures and as advice structures has been to permit MINSTREL to use the secondary organization of the theme as advice to guide the use of the theme in creating stories. This knowledge is used in a number of ways by MINSTREL. For example, because MINSTREL knows that the World Facts of a PAT are preconditions for applying the advice of the theme, it knows to present the story scenes that correspond to the World Facts *before* presenting the rest of the theme. Similarly, because it is easier to create the result of an action once the action is known, and MINSTREL knows from the PAT that the Consequence is a causal result of the Decision, MINSTREL knows to create the story scenes corresponding to the Decision before creating the story scenes corresponding to the Consequence.

A secondary reason to develop a combined representation of story themes and advice is to clarify, simplify, and consolidate these two different types of representation. Advice is often given in the form of stories; and stories can often be seen as advice. Creating a unified representation for story themes and advice may help us better understand the underlying connections between these two topics. One question that MINSTREL's representation of themes as advice raises is: Are there common story themes that *cannot* be represented as advice?

If not, this would suggest that story themes and advice share an underlying representation. If there are, it would advance our understanding of the types and forms of story themes. MINSTREL does not address these questions directly, but hopefully MINSTREL's representation of story themes as PATs will provide the basis for investigating these and similar questions in the future.

4.4 MINSTREL's Plan Advice Themes

In MINSTREL, Plan Advice Themes have been used to represent six different story themes: two themes from *Romeo and Juliet*, a theme from the Frank Capra movie *It's a Wonderful Life*, and three themes based on adages. Unlike PAT:Violent-Plans, these themes have been fully represented using a schema-based representation system.

The following two sections describe the themes PAT:Good-Deeds-Rewarded and PAT:Hasty-Impulse-Regretted in detail. Full descriptions of the remainder of MINSTREL's themes can be found in Turner (1993).

4.4.1 PAT:Good-Deeds-Rewarded

PAT:Good-Deeds-Rewarded is based on a theme from the movie *It's a Wonderful Life*. *It's a Wonderful Life* stars Jimmy Stewart as George Bailey, a good, unselfish man who constantly turns away from his dreams in order to do good deeds for others. When it appears that the town tyrant is going to take the Bailey Savings and Loan away from George he despairs and wishes that he had never been born. An angel shows George what the lives of his friends and family would have been like if he had never been born and that experience restores his spirit. At the end of the film, the people he has helped all his life band together to help him save the bank. One of the central themes of this movie is that one should be kindly and help others when possible, because someday that kindness may be returned. PAT:Good-Deeds-Rewarded represents this theme.

PAT:Good-Deeds-Rewarded is a Goal Activation theme. This PAT advises a planner to activate the goal to help others under any circumstances (i.e., there is no restricting context). The Consequence that justifies this advice is that someday the favor will be returned.

Figure 4.5 illustrates MINSTREL's representation of PAT:Good-Deeds-Rewarded. The Value of PAT:Good-Deeds-Rewarded is &POSITIVE, because it advises a planner to do something (activate a goal). The Decision Point is &Goal-Activation, because it applies to the point in the planning process in which a planner is deciding whether or not to activate a goal.

The Decision, Connection, and Consequence portions of this PAT all point to abstract schema representations. These schemas involve two characters, &Planner and &Other. As indicated by the Planner slot of PAT:Good-Deeds-

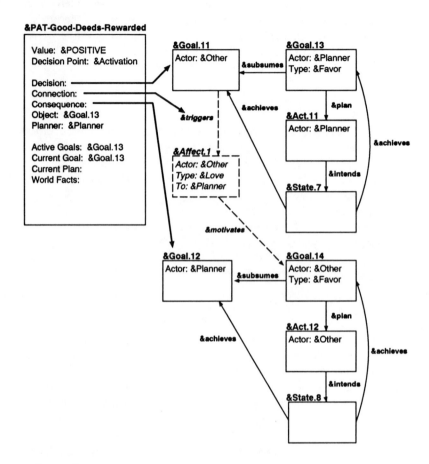

&PAT-Good-Deeds-Rewarded

Value: &POSITIVE
Decision Point: &Activation

Decision: ————
Connection: ————
Consequence: ————
Object: &Goal.13
Planner: &Planner

Active Goals: &Goal.13
Current Goal: &Goal.13
Current Plan:
World Facts:

&Goal.11
Actor: &Other

&Goal.13
Actor: &Planner
Type: &Favor

&subsumes

&achieves

&triggers

&Act.11
Actor: &Planner

&plan

&Affect.1
Actor: &Other
Type: &Love
To: &Planner

&achieves

&State.7

&intends

&motivates

&Goal.12
Actor: &Planner

&Goal.14
Actor: &Other
Type: &Favor

&subsumes

&plan

&Act.12
Actor: &Other

&achieves

&achieves

&intends

&State.8

Summaries

Decision: &Planner does a favor for &Other, helping him achieve a
                 goal.
Connection: &Other loves &Planner for his good deed.
Consequence: &Other returns &Planner's good deed.

Figure 4.5 PAT:Good-Deeds-Rewarded

Rewarded, the character to whom this planning advice applies is &Planner. The actual goal the planner is advised to activate is indicated by the Object slot, which points to &Goal.13.

The schema representation pointed to by the Decision slot represents &Planner doing a favor for &Other. A favor happens when one character intentionally helps another character achieve a goal without achieving any goals of his own. (The help must be intentional to distinguish a favor from a happy accident; the help must not achieve one of the planner's own goals to distinguish from self-interest such as acting as a paid agent.) MINSTREL represents favors as a &FAVOR goal of the planner, which subsumes the other character's goal. In PAT:Good-Deeds-Rewarded, &Goal.13 represents the &Planner's goal to help &Other. &Act.11 represents &Planner's actions to achieve both the favor goal and the subsumed goal.

The schemas pointed to by the Connection slot (which are shown dotted) represent &Other's emotional response to &Planner's favor. &Other has a positive emotional response to &Planner (&Love) as a result of the favor. This emotional response later motivates &Other to return the favor. The Connection explains the causal events that lead from a planning decision (Decision) to eventual good or bad consequences of that decision (Consequence).

In PAT:Good-Deeds-Rewarded, Consequence points to another favor, this time with &Other acting to help &Planner.

In English, PAT:Good-Deeds-Rewarded can be summarized as: A planner should do favors for others, because if he does, he'll make the other person love him, and that will later lead to the favor being returned.

4.4.2 PAT:Hasty-Impulse-Regretted

In the final act of Romeo and Juliet, when Romeo discovers Juliet's body, he is moved by his love of Juliet to kill himself. This is a tragic error, for if had waited but a moment longer he would have seen Juliet awaken.

PAT:Hasty-Impulse-Regretted captures Romeo's planning error: "Do not do in haste what you cannot undo." PAT:Hasty-Impulse-Regretted is a Plan Selection theme that advises a planner not to use irreversible plans to achieve goals motivated by a hasty deduction about the world, because the deduction might prove to be incorrect. PAT:Hasty-Impulse-Regretted is a complex theme that involves both beliefs and character traits. MINSTREL's representation of PAT:Hasty-Impulse-Regretted is shown in Figure 4.6.

MINSTREL represents deductions about the world as a type of belief. In the Decision part of PAT:Hasty-Impulse-Regretted, &Belief.1 represents the planner's initial, hasty deduction about the world. The type of the belief is &Deductive, to indicate that it represents a deduction about the world. (MINSTREL also uses predictive beliefs, which represent character beliefs about things that may occur in the future, as when a character believes he will be eaten by a dragon.) The &Evidence link of a &Deductive belief points from the belief to the state of the world that is evidence for the belief. The evidence is the state of the world from which another state was deduced. The &Mental-Event link of a &Deductive belief points to the deduced state of the world.

In the actual story of *Romeo and Juliet*, the Decision portion of PAT:Hasty-Impulse-Regretted is instantiated by Romeo's deduction from Juliet's still and unresponsive form (the &Evidence) that she is dead (the &Mental-Event).

&PAT-Hasty-Impulse-Regretted

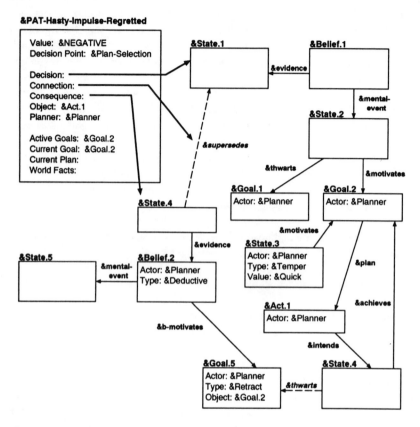

Summaries

Decision: &Romeo believes something (&Belief.1) that causes a goal failure for him (&Goal.1). This and his hasty disposition motivate him to do something irreversible (&Act.1).

Connection: &Romeo learns something new (&State.4) that supersedes the evidence for his earlier belief (&Belief.1).

Consequence: &Romeo now has a different belief, which motivates him to retract his earlier goal (&Goal.2) but he cannot, because his earlier action (&Act.1) is irreversible.

Figure 4.6 PAT:Hasty-Impulse-Regretted

In the Decision part of PAT:Hasty-Impulse-Regretted, the &Mental-Event of the planner's belief (&State.2) thwarts one of the planner's goals (&Goal.1) and motivates another goal (&Goal.2). The motivated goal, which is also motivated by the planner's quick temper, is achieved by &Act.1 and &State.4.

The Consequence of PAT:Hasty-Impulse-Regretted involves a second deductive belief. New evidence (&State.4) leads the planner to a new deduction (&State.5) and motivates him to retract his previous, hasty goal (&Goal.2). But this is thwarted by the irreversible nature of the state that achieved that goal.

Interestingly enough, the Consequence of PAT:Hasty-Impulse-Regretted is not instantiated in *Romeo and Juliet*. In *Romeo and Juliet*, Romeo's hasty action is killing himself, and this prevents him from later realizing that his belief was in error. However, the reader of *Romeo and Juliet* can still recognize the theme by empathic reasoning. Placing himself in Romeo's shoes, the reader can reason "I made a mistake by killing myself, because Juliet is really still alive."

This reliance on the reader to mentally extend the events of the story to understand the theme of the story is a literary technique MINSTREL is not currently capable of using. However, it is interesting to note that in this case the omitted portions of the theme correspond exactly to the Consequence of the theme, suggesting that the advice representation of story themes might be used as a basis for determining what parts of a theme could be omitted.

4.5 Using Themes in Storytelling

As the previous sections showed, Planning Advice Themes can be used to represent a variety of common story themes. To make use of these story themes to tell new stories, MINSTREL must perform two tasks:

1. Select a theme.
2. Create story scenes to illustrate the theme.

4.5.1 Selecting a Theme

MINSTREL has two methods for selecting a theme.

First, the user can select a theme from amongst the PATs that MINSTREL knows, and ask MINSTREL to tell a story about the selected theme. This permits testing and demonstration of MINSTREL's storytelling abilities.

Second, MINSTREL can select a theme for storytelling by being reminded of one of the themes it already knows, in the same way a human author might be reminded of a theme and decide to tell a story based on the reminded theme.

Human authors are reminded of stories they've read and episodes from their lives by clues from their environment, both physical and mental. A human author who passes a mailman on the staircase might recall Ellison's "The Man Who Wasn't There" and be motivated to write a similar story. Autobiographical memories of this sort may be recalled involuntarily when cued by events in a person's environment (reminding), may be deliberately sought and retrieved, or may arise by a combination of reminding and deliberate retrieval (Cohen, 1989).

Although one can imagine a robot writer who was able to move through the world and receive inputs from his environment, MINSTREL is only a computer program running on a workstation. Input from the environment must be simulated, by asking the user to provide clues as if they came from MINSTREL's environment.

When MINSTREL is asked to find a story theme, it makes use of a pool of representation fragments (provided by the user) as initial indices into memory. For example, this pool may contain representations for "a woman" and the scene "someone does a favor for someone," as if MINSTREL had just seen a woman do a favor. These fragments are used as indices to episodic memory. If these indices can be used to recall an episode that was part of a story theme, then the associated theme can be used as the basis for a new story.

For example, the indices "a woman" and "someone does a favor for someone" might recall a scene in which a knight saves a princess, which itself is part of a story that illustrates PAT:Bird-In-Hand. MINSTREL will then use PAT:Bird-In-Hand as a basis for a new story.

This reminding process involves recall from episodic memory. Since MINSTREL's episodic memory is imaginative, these indices do not have to match a memory episode exactly. MINSTREL can use creativity heuristics to find episodes quite different from the initial clues. This is an example of how embedding creativity in the recall process makes it available to other cognitive processes.

MINSTREL's author-level plan for selecting a theme is shown in Figure 4.7.

ALP:Find-Story-Theme

Goal: &Tell-Story

Input: *AL-OBJ*, a list of story fragments such as "a woman" and "someone does a favor for someone," to be used as indices to memory.

Body: 1. Use *AL-OBJ* as an index for recall from imaginative memory.
2. If the recalled episode has an associated story theme, use that as the theme for a new story. Create a new author-level goal to &Tell-Story using the new theme.
3. Otherwise, this plan fails.

Figure 4.7 ALP:Find-Story-Theme

4.5.2 Illustrating a Theme

How can an author write a story that will communicate a theme to a reader? One way is to include story events that illustrate the theme—story events that act as an instance or example of the theme. In *Romeo and Juliet,* Juliet's use of a potion to appear dead, Romeo's mistaken belief that Juliet is dead, and the consequent tragedy are the story events that illustrate the theme PAT:Juliet. From the particular instance of the theme that appears in the story the reader can deduce the general, abstract theme. The story events that illustrate a theme are called the *plot* of that theme.

Although there are other ways that a story can communicate a theme, most rely on creating an example of the theme. For example, one character can repeat an adage corresponding to the theme to another character, but if this not supported with an example, or reflected in the second character's behavior in the story, the impact of the adage is lost. Similarly, a theme can be repeated in a story to improve its impact, but this depends on creating multiple examples of the theme. Consequently, the focus in MINSTREL has been on how an author can take an abstract, general principle like a Planning Advice Theme and create story events that illustrate that principle.

Planning Advice Themes can be illustrated by creating specific story events that correspond to each part of the theme: the Decision, Connection, Consequence, and Context parts of the PAT. To create a story that illustrates PAT:Juliet, MINSTREL must create story events in which a character uses a deception plan (the Decision), in which the deception fools some unintended character (the Connection), and in which the fooled character does something to thwart one of the main character's goals (the Consequence). These concrete story events, in which the abstract actors, goals, and other features from the theme have been replaced with specific values, illustrate the theme by presenting the reader with a particular example of the theme. In general, an author can incorporate an abstraction into a story by creating story events that act as a particular example of the abstraction. As previously discussed, this process is called instantiation. The problem of illustrating a theme—creating the plot of a story—is thus the problem of instantiating the schemas that make up the theme. MINSTREL's plan to illustrate the theme is then simply to instantiate the parts of the theme (Figure 4.8).

Once these instantiations have been achieved, MINSTREL is finished with the thematic level of the story. A theme has been chosen and story scenes created to illustrate that theme.

ALP:Tell-Story

Goal: &Tell-Story

Input: An uninstantiated instance of a Planning Advice Theme, *AL-OBJ*.

Body: 1. Create an author-level goal to instantiate the Decision of *AL-OBJ*.
2. Create an author-level goal to instantiate the Connection of *AL-OBJ*.
3. Create an author-level goal to instantiate the Consequence of *AL-OBJ*.
4. Create an author-level goal to instantiate the context of *AL-OBJ*.

Figure 4.8 ALP:Tell-Story

4.5.3 MINSTREL Example

Let's look now at an example of MINSTREL selecting and illustrating a story theme. This example looks at how the story theme for "Richard and Lancelot"[6] was chosen:

Richard and Lancelot

It was the spring of 1089, and a knight named Lancelot returned to Camelot from elsewhere. Lancelot was hot tempered. Once, Lancelot lost a joust. Because he was hot tempered, Lancelot wanted to destroy his sword. Lancelot struck his sword. His sword was destroyed.

One day, a lady of the court named Andrea wanted to have some berries. Andrea went to the woods. Andrea had some berries because Andrea picked some berries. At the same time, Lancelot's horse moved Lancelot to the woods. This unexpectedly caused him to be near Andrea. Because Lancelot was near Andrea, Lancelot saw Andrea. Lancelot loved Andrea.

Some time later, Lancelot's horse moved Lancelot to the woods unintentionally, again causing him to be near Andrea. Lancelot knew that Andrea kissed with a knight named Frederick because Lancelot saw that Andrea kissed with Frederick. Lancelot believed that Andrea loved Frederick. Lancelot loved Andrea. Because Lancelot loved Andrea, Lancelot wanted to be the love of Andrea. But he could not because Andrea loved Frederick. Lancelot hated Frederick. Because Lancelot was hot tempered, Lancelot wanted to kill

---

[6] Except for typography, "Richard and Lancelot" appears here exactly as output by MINSTREL.

Frederick. Lancelot went to Frederick. Lancelot fought with Frederick. Frederick was dead.

Andrea went to Frederick. Andrea told Lancelot that Andrea was siblings with Frederick. Lancelot believed that Andrea was siblings with Frederick. Lancelot wanted to take back that he wanted to kill Frederick. but he could not because Frederick was dead. Lancelot hated himself. Lancelot became a hermit. Frederick was buried in the woods. Andrea became a nun.

Moral: ''Done in haste is done forever.''

MINSTREL begins storytelling by selecting a story theme. This is done by using a set of initial story fragments provided by the user as indices to episodic memory. These initial story fragments represent chance remindings or clues from the environment that might remind MINSTREL of a theme about which to write a story. In telling "Richard and Lancelot," MINSTREL is given a single story fragment to use as an index. This fragment is "A man has a thwarted goal" (see Figure 4.9). Figure 4.10 illustrates the top level of MINSTREL's episodic memory of goals in the King Arthur domain. ALP:Find-Story-Theme uses the story fragment shown in Figure 4.9 (&Goal.216) as an index into this memory. If the story fragment recalls an episode with an associated story theme, then MINSTREL will tell a story about that theme.

In this case, the context of the story fragment (a Goal schema) and a single feature (the goal was thwarted) are sufficient to recall an episode from memory. The value of the "&thwarted-by" link in the story fragment (&State.118) matches the value of the only branch of the "&thwarted-by" portion of the episodic memory tree (&State.52), and &Goal.143 is recalled.

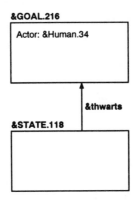

Figure 4.9 Example Index

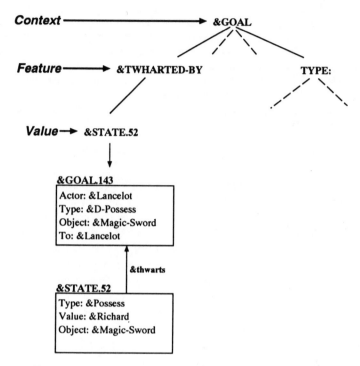

Figure 4.10 A Portion of MINSTREL's Episodic Memory

Generally, episodic memory will have many levels, and each feature will have several possible values. If the story fragment provided to ALP:Find-Story-Theme does not possess sufficient features to recall a particular episode, additional features are elaborated by methods similar in function to those described in Kolodner (1984). Feature elaboration adds new features to a recall index that are likely to result in the recall of an episode. For this example, the new feature "the actor of the goal is a knight" might be added, because it is likely that story episodes in the King Arthur domain involve knights. In this way, episodic memory can recall episodes even when the recall index is underspecified.

If feature elaboration also fails to recall an episode, then creativity heuristics are applied. Creativity heuristics can change the recall index in more elaborate ways than feature adaptation, and can adapt any recalled episodes to match the original recall index.

It is important to note that in MINSTREL, both feature elaboration and the use of creativity heuristics are the normal processes of imaginative memory; no special mechanisms are needed to be reminded of a story theme.

If, despite feature elaboration and creativity, the story fragment provided by the user fails to remind MINSTREL of an episode in memory with an associated story theme, then ALP:Find-Story-Theme fails. The "clues from the environment" that might have reminded MINSTREL of a story theme and inspired it to tell a story have not, and so storytelling fails.

In this case, however, reminding succeeds. The initial clue "a man has a thwarted goal" reminds MINSTREL of a scene in which "Lancelot fails to possess a magic sword because Richard already possesses it" (&Goal.143). &Goal.143 is part of a larger story that illustrates the theme PAT:Hasty-Impulse-Regretted. As shown in Figure 4.11, &Goal.143 is part of the Decision of an instance of PAT:Hasty-Impulse-Regretted. &Goal.143 and &State.52 are also connected to a number of other schemas representing the rest of the story of Lancelot, Richard, and the magic sword. These schemas are shown in dotted outline, because they do not enter this discussion.

When ALP:Find-Story-Theme recalls &Goal.143, it notices the associated theme (&PAT.2) and makes a copy as the basis for a new story. This copy of the theme is uninstantiated. That is, the new theme has none of the elements of &Goal.143 or any other specific story scenes. It is a blank, abstract specification of the theme PAT:Hasty-Impulse-Regretted, as shown earlier in Figure 4.9. Note that &Goal.143 will have no further role in the telling of this story unless MINSTREL is independently reminded of it later in the storytelling process. The following is a trace of MINSTREL's output as ALP:Find-Story-Theme takes the

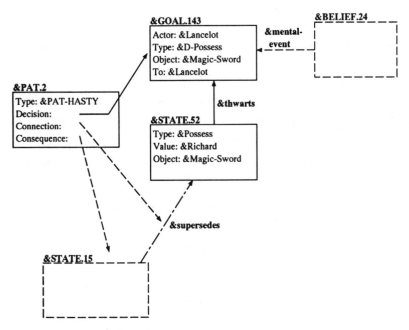

Figure 4.11 Recalled Episode

story fragment &Goal.216, uses it to recall &Goal.143, and makes a copy of PAT:Hasty-Impulse-Regretted for use in telling a new story:

```
++++++++++++++++++++++++++++++++++++++++++++++++++++++++++++++++++++++
Author-level goal &TELL-STORY applied to &GOAL.216.
Trying author-level plan ALP:TELL-STORY.
Trying author-level plan ALP:FIND-STORY-THEME.
Recalling &GOAL.216: (&GOAL.143).
Created theme: &PAT.8.
Created author-level goal to &TELL-STORY with &PAT.8.
Author-level planning succeeded.
++++++++++++++++++++++++++++++++++++++++++++++++++++++++++++++++++++++
```

Of note in this trace is that MINSTREL first tried the author-level plan ALP:Tell-Story. At this point in MINSTREL's storytelling the theme of the story has not yet been selected, so ALP:Tell-Story cannot be applied. MINSTREL next tries ALP:Find-Story-Theme, which succeeds and creates the new story theme &PAT.8, which is an instance of PAT:Hasty-Impulse-Regretted.

This new goal is achieved by the author-level plan ALP:Tell-Story, which now succeeds because a theme has been selected. ALP:Tell-Story achieves the goal of telling a story about &PAT.8 by creating a number of author-level goals to instantiate the various parts of &PAT.8. The following is a trace of MINSTREL achieving this goal:

```
++++++++++++++++++++++++++++++++++++++++++++++++++++++++++++++++++++
Author-level goal &TELL-STORY applied to &PAT.8.
Trying author-level plan ALP:TELL-STORY.
Created author-level goal to &INSTANTIATE with &BELIEF.28.
Created author-level goal to &INSTANTIATE with &STATE.202.
Created author-level goal to &INSTANTIATE with &STATE.201
Created author-level goal to &INSTANTIATE with &GOAL.225.
Created author-level goal to &INSTANTIATE with &STATE.206.
Created author-level goal to &INSTANTIATE with &BELIEF.29.
Created author-level goal to &INSTANTIATE with &GOAL.22.
[...]
Author-level planning succeeded.
++++++++++++++++++++++++++++++++++++++++++++++++++++++++++++++++++++
```

&BELIEF.28, &STATE.202, &STATE.201, &GOAL.225, &STATE.206, &BELIEF.29, and &GOAL.22 are all parts of the theme &PAT.8 that must be instantiated to create the plot of the new story. These schemas represent the portions of the story that will illustrate the theme "Do not do in haste what you cannot undo." (In the edited portion of the trace indicated by "[...]," MINSTREL creates a number of goals to fulfill other storytelling goals, such as creating suspense. These goals are unrelated to the theme of the story, and so they are not discussed here, but we return to these goals in following chapters.)

The schemas that make up the instantiation of &PAT:Hasty-Impulse-Regretted in this story are instantiated by a variety of author-level plans and creativity heuristics. MINSTREL's model of instantiation, and the various plans it uses to instantiate story scenes are fully discussed in Turner (1993). For the purposes of this discussion, it is sufficient to say that MINSTREL is able to create the story scenes it needs to illustrate PAT:Hasty-Impulse-Regretted, and to look instead at the results of the instantiations and the role these scenes play in the final story.

The first part of theme to be instantiated is the Decision. In PAT:Hasty-Impulse-Regretted, the Decision is a complicated sequence of story scenes in which the main character (the planner to whom the advice of the theme applies) makes a false deduction about the state of the world and this motivates a hasty action. MINSTREL instantiates this as a sequence of scenes in which a knight thinks his love is stolen. MINSTREL expresses these scenes in English as follows:

> Lancelot knew that Andrea kissed with a knight named Frederick because Lancelot saw that Andrea kissed with Frederick. Lancelot believed that Andrea loved Frederick. Lancelot loved Andrea. Because Lancelot loved Andrea, Lancelot wanted to be the love of Andrea. But he could not because Andrea loved Frederick. Because Lancelot was hot-tempered, he wanted to kill Frederick. Lancelot went to Frederick. Lancelot fought with Frederick. Frederick was dead.

Here the main character is Lancelot. He sees Frederick kissing Andrea and makes a hasty deduction: Andrea loves Frederick. This thwarts Lancelot's goal of having Andrea love him. Spurred on by his hot temper, Lancelot slays Frederick.

It's important to note that although these scenes fulfill the requirements of the story theme - that is, they describe a hasty decision that cannot be undone - they do not themselves form a complete story. Among other things, they lack any explanation of why Lancelot loves Andrea, how he came to see her kissing Frederick, and other features that would make the story understandable and complete. At this stage of storytelling, MINSTREL is only trying to create the scenes necessary to illustrate the story theme. Other goals—such as making the story coherent—will be achieved later.

The next portion of the story theme to be instantiated is the Connection. In

PAT:Hasty-Impulse-Regretted, the Connection is a state of the world that shows the planner (Lancelot) that his earlier belief was incorrect:

```
Andrea told Lancelot that Andrea was siblings
with Frederick.
```

That Andrea and Frederick are siblings is an alternative explanation of what Lancelot had believed earlier, and will cause him to change his belief about Andrea loving Frederick romantically.

The final portion of the PAT to be instantiated is the Consequence. In PAT:Hasty-Impulse-Regretted, the Consequence is the planner's change of belief based on the new evidence, and his regret for his earlier action:

```
Lancelot believed that Andrea was siblings with
Frederick.  Lancelot wanted to take back that he
wanted to kill Frederick.  But he could not
because Frederick was dead.
```

Here Lancelot has superseded his earlier belief with a new belief, and wants to retract his earlier, hasty actions. But that is not possible.

The final part of the theme to be instantiated is the context. But PAT:Hasty-Impulse-Regretted has no context, so nothing is created.

MINSTREL has now completed its thematic-level development of this story. Using clues provided by the user, it has selected a story theme and instantiated the parts of that theme as a sequence of story events that illustrate the theme.

4.6   The Role of Theme in Storytelling

MINSTREL's primary purpose in storytelling is to tell a story that illustrates a particular story theme. In light of this, it is interesting to examine one of MINSTREL's stories to see how big a role the scenes that illustrate the theme play in the finished story. In the following version of *Richard and Lancelot*, the portions of the story that illustrate the theme are shown in bold:

```
              Richard and Lancelot

    It was the spring of 1089, and a knight named
Lancelot  returned  to  Camelot  from  elsewhere.
Lancelot was hot tempered.  Once, Lancelot lost a
joust.  Because he was hot tempered, Lancelot wanted
to destroy his sword.  Lancelot struck his sword.
His sword was destroyed.
    One day, a lady of the court named Andrea wanted to
have some berries.  Andrea went to the woods.  Andrea
had some berries because Andrea picked some berries.
```

At the same time, Lancelot's horse moved Lancelot to the woods. This unexpectedly caused him to be near Andrea. Because Lancelot was near Andrea, Lancelot saw Andrea. Lancelot loved Andrea.

Some time later, Lancelot's horse moved Lancelot to the woods unintentionally, again causing him to be near Andrea. **Lancelot knew that Andrea kissed with a knight named Frederick because Lancelot saw that Andrea kissed with Frederick. Lancelot believed that Andrea loved Frederick. Lancelot loved Andrea. Because Lancelot loved Andrea, Lancelot wanted to be the love of Andrea. But he could not because Andrea loved Frederick. Lancelot hated Frederick. Because Lancelot was hot tempered, Lancelot wanted to kill Frederick. Lancelot went to Frederick. Lancelot fought with Frederick. Frederick was dead.**

Andrea went to Frederick. **Andrea told Lancelot that Andrea was siblings with Frederick. Lancelot believed that Andrea was siblings with Frederick. Lancelot wanted to take back that he wanted to kill Frederick, but he could not because Frederick was dead. Lancelot hated himself. Lancelot became a hermit.** Frederick was buried in the woods. Andrea became a nun.

Moral: ''Done in haste is done forever.''

The portions of the story that illustrate the theme make up less than half the story. But what these scenes lack in bulk they make up in importance. The highlighted portions of *Richard and Lancelot* are clearly more story-like than the remainder. Like a human author, MINSTREL uses theme to define "the underlying concept or topic that organizes the story into a coherent whole."

4.7 Limitations of Planning Advice Themes

MINSTREL's Planning Advice Themes capture a specific type of planning advice. PATs represent advice in which (1) a planning decision is judged as either beneficial or harmful to the planner, and (2) that judgment is justified by a single causal outcome of the planning decision. As we have shown, this type of advice can represent many of the themes present in stories such as Aesop's fables and Shakespeare. There are, however, some limitations of Planning Advice Themes as both story themes and advice.

First, PATs are only able to capture themes about the planning process. Themes about how the world works, human emotions, and many other categories are difficult or impossible to represent using PATs. Any abstract principle that does not impinge directly on the planning process cannot be represented: "There is life after death," "Behold the wonders of nature," and so on.

Of course, this is by design. As noted early in this chapter, themes like stories themselves have infinite variety. By focusing on a particular class of themes, it has been our hope that MINSTREL will illuminate larger issues. Still, it behooves us to be aware of the limitations of PATs, and not to stretch our conclusions too far.

A second limitation of PATs is in the representation of the Consequence. The Consequence is the justification or explanation of the advice encapsulated in the Value judgment (i.e., Positive or Negative) of the planning decision captured in the Decision. The Consequence can only represent abstracted, stereotypical planning situations. So while it is easy to represent a justification such as "the decision is bad because the violent act will unexpectedly hurt the planner," it is difficult to represent a justification such as "the decision is bad because the plan is inelegant." The first reason can be easily represented as a planning situation, but the second reason corresponds to a plan evaluation metric, that cannot be easily represented within the PAT framework. Further, the Consequence is a single justification, which means that PATs cannot represent a theme which has two or more reasons to support its advice. These shortcomings limit the range of advice that PATs can represent.

A possible solution to the first of these problems is to incorporate plan metrics, such as those proposed in Dyer (1983). Plan metrics are evaluations used to select between competing plans, and include measures such as cost, efficacy, risk and availability. Although Dyer (1983) used plan metrics to categorize story themes, plan metrics could also be used to capture justifications for planning decisions that cannot be easily represented solely by the goal/plan structures used by MINSTREL.

A possible solution to the second of these problems is to explicitly represent the Consequence of a PAT as a series of one or more argument-style justifications, such as those presented in Alvarado (1989). Explicitly representing the justifications has several benefits: (1) It will permit more than one justification per theme, (2) It will make PATs more useful in other reasoning tasks, such as argumentation, (3) It may help identify common elements of tasks such as storytelling and argumentation, and (4) explicitly identifying the type of justification will permit MINSTREL to use that information to more fully develop the stories it tells.

4.8 Inventing New Story Themes

The six themes MINSTREL knows were represented and hand-coded by the author. How could MINSTREL learn new story themes?

One possibility is to learn new story themes from stories or a teacher. We can imagine a system that would read a story, analyze the actions of the characters in each story, and posit new story themes. A storytelling program that could also read stories could expand its knowledge of themes by reading.

Dolan (1988) presents a system called AESOP that learns new themes by reading. AESOP reads examples from "Aesop's Fables" and tries to recognize and learn new story themes. Connecting a program like AESOP to MINSTREL would allow MINSTREL to learn new themes by reading, but no work has been done yet on this possibility.

Another possibility is to learn new themes by inventing them. Using creativity to extend MINSTREL's knowledge about storytelling is an intriguing idea. What kinds of creativity heuristics would be needed to transform and adapt known story themes to create new story themes?

MINSTREL's existing themes hint at some possibilities. The observant reader may have noticed that PAT:Spite-Face and PAT:Good-Deeds-Rewarded have parallel structures. The Decision portion of each theme involves the &Planner subsuming another character's goal. PAT:Good-Deeds-Rewarded is positive advice about activating a &Favor goal, while PAT:Spite-Face is negative advice about what kinds of plans to use to achieve &Anti-Favor goals. The almost-opposite nature of these themes suggests that new themes might be invented by applying transformations to old themes.

In previous chapters we presented a model of problem solving that explains how problem transformations can be applied to invent new problem solutions. Rather than describe in detail how this architecture could be applied to inventing new themes, we concentrate instead on identifying problem transformations which are potentially useful for inventing new story themes. Four transformations that we have identified are:

1. Generalization
2. Specialization
3. Mutation
4. Recombination

One way to create new story themes is to use *generalization and specialization* on existing story themes. The idea in this transformation is to examine existing themes to see if two or more of them are specializations of a more general theme. If they are, we can deduce the generalization of these themes, and then use creative problem solving to create a new specialization of the general theme (i.e., create an *instantiation* of the general theme).

For example, suppose a storyteller knew the two themes "A fool rushes in where angels fear to tread" and "A fool and his money are soon parted." The first theme advises that a fool does not take care in selecting his planning situations; the second that a fool does not take care in selecting plans that involve money. These two themes are specializations of a more general theme about the planning abilities of fools, namely, "Fools make poor planning selections." A creative problem solver can use this generalization to create new story themes involving fools and new types of planning selections. This might lead to a specialization concerning selecting goals to abandon: "A fool never knows when to quit" or "Only a fool quits with the end in sight."

Another useful type of transformation is *mutation*. In mutation, a specific limited change in structure is applied to an existing theme to create a new theme. One interesting type of mutation is suggested by an old adage: "The opposite of a great truth is another great truth." This suggests that the opposite of any piece of advice might also be good advice.

If we apply this transformation to PAT:Good-Deeds-Rewarded ("Good deeds do not go unrewarded") by reversing the Consequence and Value of the PAT, we get a new theme in which a planner does good deeds for people and when he finds himself in need, does *not* get repaid. This might be summarized as "A wise man helps himself" or "Do not sow where you cannot reap." Similarly, reversing PAT:Spite-Face ("Do not cut off your nose to spite your face") produces "No price too great for revenge."

Finally, new themes can also be formed by *recombination*. The idea behind this transformation is to combine parts from different themes to create a new theme. MINSTREL's planning advice themes are structured as advice, so it is simple to break themes down into their components as advice: Decision, Connection, and Consequence. If two themes have similar Connections, the Decision of one theme can be connected to the Consequence of the other, and vice versa.

For example, PAT:Bird-In-Hand and PAT:Juliet ("Deception is a weapon difficult to aim") have similar Connections. In PAT:Bird-In-Hand a state in the Decision thwarts a goal in the Consequence. In PAT:Juliet, a state in the decision motivates a goal in the Consequence. By substituting the Consequence of one into the other, we can invent two new themes.

If the Consequence of PAT:Juliet is substituted into PAT:Bird-In-Hand, the result is a new PAT in which catching a bird motivates someone else to get revenge on the bird-catcher. This does not correspond directly to a common adage, but might be best summarized by "Don't make enemies by your actions."

Substituting the Consequence of PAT:Bird-In-Hand into PAT:Juliet results in a PAT which advises not to use deception plans because the deception might cause a goal failure for the planner. This is the vacuous theme: "Avoid deception plans because you might deceive yourself."

As this last theme suggests, a critical activity in inventing new story themes is in distinguishing between good themes and boring themes. One possibility for measuring the "interestingness" of a theme is to determine how useful it is as an abstraction of known stories and life episodes. If an author invents a story theme and can see immediately how it applies to many things in his life, that is some indication that the theme is interesting. Another possibility is to compare an invented theme with known themes, to see if they share components or structure. A theme similar to past themes is also likely to be interesting.

MINSTREL does not currently invent new story themes, nor does MINSTREL implement any methods for determining the "interestingness" of a theme. But these transformations and their similarities to creativity heuristics that MINSTREL does use suggest that inventing new themes is both possible and an interesting topic for further research.

4.9 Conclusions

MINSTREL's Planning Advice Themes are a knowledge structure that captures aspects of both story themes and planning advice. PATs are a structured representation of (1) a planning decision, (2) a value judgment of that decision, and (3) a justification for that judgment. MINSTREL has used PATs to represent a variety of story themes, and to tell new stories based on those themes. MINSTREL has also taken a preliminary look at how new story themes can be created.

5 | Dramatic Writing Goals

5.1 Introduction

The primary concern of MINSTREL is to tell a story that illustrates a particular story theme. The previous chapter illustrated how MINSTREL selects a theme and actively plans to tell a story based on that theme.

But authoring involves more than just the bald statement of the events that illustrate the story theme. Good authors make use of a variety of techniques to improve the literary quality of their stories: pacing, characterization, dialogue, suspense, foreshadowing, description, and many others. These flourishes "dress up" the story, adding literary appeal to the story's basic message. A very good author uses these techniques not only to create literary value, but also to support the theme of his story.

Human authors have many literary writing techniques. A look at the creative writing section of any bookstore will reveal that there are as many writing techniques as there are authors to expound them. Every human author develops a combination of literary writing goals and techniques that create a particular writing style.

It would be impossible to model all these techniques and their myriad combinations in MINSTREL. Instead, we have chosen to select and implement a few representative techniques: suspense, tragedy, characterization, and foreshadowing. This particular combination of techniques represents, if you will, MINSTREL's writing style. More importantly, these techniques demonstrate that the MINSTREL model is capable of capturing the knowledge and processes needed to implement typical literary writing techniques.

The remainder of this chapter is divided into four sections: suspense, tragedy, foreshadowing, and characterization. Each section contains a brief discussion of the writing technique, an example of how MINSTREL used the writing technique in a finished story, and a description of the author-level goals and plans used to implement the writing technique. The final section of the chapter summarizes the lessons learned in implementing these techniques.

5.2   Suspense

The Random House Dictionary of the English Language defines suspense as "a state or condition of mental uncertainty or excitement, as from awaiting a decision or outcome." Building suspense—that is, inducing this feeling in the reader—is a key element of good writing in adventure and mystery stories. By prolonging the resolution of an uncertain outcome, the author emphasizes the eventual resolution. And human readers find the feeling of suspense followed by relief pleasurable, even when taken to great extremes, as in horror films.

5.2.1   Suspense in *The Hermit and the Knight*

In *The Hermit and the Knight*, MINSTREL has the author-level goal to build suspense in a scene in which a hermit is threatened by a dragon:

The Hermit and the Knight

> Once upon a time, there was a hermit named Bebe and a knight named Cedric. One day, Cedric was wounded when he was attacked by a dragon. Bebe, who was in the woods picking berries, healed Cedric. Cedric was grateful and vowed to return the favor.
> Later, Bebe believed that he would die because he saw a dragon moving towards him and believed it would eat him. *Bebe was very scared. Bebe tried to run away but failed!...*

In the second paragraph of this story, Bebe the hermit is endangered by a dragon. Because Bebe is a sympathetic character, the reader does not want to see Bebe harmed. This tension is the basis of suspense. MINSTREL recognizes this and attempts to increase the suspense in this situation by inventing story scenes that demonstrate Bebe's fear and in which Bebe attempts to escape his fate but fails.

As with all writing techniques, there are two fundamental questions to ask about the use of suspense in writing: (1) When is it appropriate to use this writing technique? and (2) How can this writing technique be achieved?

5.2.2   When is Suspense Appropriate?

In *The Hermit and the Knight*, MINSTREL decides to build suspense in the scene in which Bebe is threatened by the dragon. Why did MINSTREL choose to build suspense here and not, say, in the scene in which Bebe was picking berries? More interestingly, why didn't MINSTREL also choose to build suspense in the scene in which Cedric was attacked by a dragon—a scene that shares many features with the Bebe scene?

According to the dictionary, suspense can result from any undetermined decision or outcome. In reality, people feel suspense in proportion to the importance of the decision or outcome. Whether or not a character will die is inherently more suspenseful than whether or not he will have to walk to the castle, because preserving one's life is a more important goal that preserving one's feet. It is apparent, then, that suspense is most appropriate for story scenes that involve important goals.

There have been various efforts to classify common human goals according to their importance. Schank (1979) suggested that goals are interesting in proportion to their importance, and other authors have made similar suggestions or rankings of common goals. What is important to an author is not the precise ranking of goals—which will undoubtedly vary from person to person—but that he understand that the appropriateness of suspense is proportional to the importance of the goal involved, so that he can correctly identify appropriate uses of suspense. This is the first principle of suspense:

Scenes are appropriate for suspense in proportion to the importance of the character-level goals involved.

MINSTREL has a simple ranking of character goals it uses to determine when suspense is reasonable. Only one goal is important enough to warrant suspense: the goal to preserve one's life. When MINSTREL looks at story scenes to determine if they are reasonable candidates for suspense, it accepts only scenes involving the possible loss of a character's life.

Beyond the question of whether it is *reasonable* to build suspense in a scene is the question of whether it is *desirable*. As noted earlier, suspense focuses the reader's attention on the outcome of the undecided situation. Consequently, the author should use suspense only in scenes he or she wants the reader to focus upon. Consider, for example, the following story fragment:

John knew that he had to get to the hospital if he wanted to save his little brother's life. He jumped onto his bicycle and pedaled down the hill as fast as he could. The trees of his neighborhood flew by on either side as he sped down the hill towards the hospital.

At the bottom of the hill, John rode passed the city park. As he passed the park, John saw a young woman being attacked by a mugger. She tried to run away, but the mugger jumped a bush and grabbed her again. She struggled and screamed, but no one heard her. Finally she got loose and ran towards the front of the park, where she collided with a patrolman. The mugger, seeing this, darted off into the bushes.

John continued pedaling past the park, turning onto the narrow side street that led to the hospital. He risked a glance at his watch. Now he had only five minutes left! He pedaled even harder, his chest pounding with the effort...

Most readers find the part of this story concerning the mugger and the young lady distracting and irritating. Although suspenseful, it turns the reader's attention away from the main focus of the story: John's effort to save his little brother. By using suspense in a secondary scene, the author has distracted the reader from the main point or purpose of the story, and consequently weakened his story rather than strengthened it. This is the second principle of suspense:

Scenes are appropriate for suspense in proportion
to their importance to the story.

The main purpose of the stories MINSTREL tells are to illustrate a particular Planning Advice Theme (PAT). Consequently, MINSTREL limits suspense to scenes that directly illustrate the theme of the story. Thus MINSTREL is assured that the reader's attention will be focused on the main point of the story.

These two principle explain why MINSTREL chose to build suspense in the scene in which Bebe was being threatened by the dragon. The scene in which Bebe picks berries isn't suitable for suspense because the goal of the involved character is unimportant; the scene in which Cedric is injured is not suitable for suspense because it does not directly illustrate the theme of the story. The two principles of suspense focus MINSTREL's attempts to build suspense where they will be most successful and most effective. MINSTREL's author-level plan for determining whether to build suspense in a scene is shown in Figure 5.1.

Name:	ALP:Check-Scene-For-Suspense
Goal Type:	&Check-Scene-For-Suspense
Object:	*AL-OBJ*
Test:	1. Is *AL-OBJ* a &P-HEALTH or &C-HEALTH goal?
	2. Is *AL-OBJ* part of the plot of the story?
	3. If yes to both questions, succeed.
Body:	1. Create an author-level goal to &Add-Suspense-to-Scene to *AL-OBJ*.

Figure 5.1 ALP:Check-Scene-For-Suspense

5.2.3 Writing Techniques for Building Suspense

How does an author make a scene suspenseful? There are many methods, and inventive writers are always discovering more. L. Sprague De Camp (1975), advising writers on how to write imaginative literature, suggested:

> *Suspense is effected by strong emotions on the part of the characters, by threats to their well-being, by bits of atmospheric description slyly dropped into the action... (p. 147)*

MINSTREL implements two methods to build suspense. The first corresponds to De Camp's first suggestion of having the story characters display strong emotions. The second is a technique often seen in modern horror films, which we call the Horror Film Principle.

5.2.3.1 ALP:Add-Suspense-Via-Character-Emotion

MINSTREL's first author-level plan for adding suspense to a scene is to have the character whose life is threatened react by being scared. This is implemented by the author-level plan ALP:Add-Suspense-Via-Character-Emotion. This plan was used in the telling of *The Hermit and the Knight*, in the scene in which the hermit is threatened by a dragon:

```
Later, Bebe believed that he would die because
he saw a dragon moving towards him and believed
it would eat him. Bebe was very scared. Bebe
tried to run away but failed! ...
```

ALP:Add-Suspense-Via-Character-Emotion examines the scene to which suspense is being added and determines the character whose life is being threatened. ALP:Add-Suspense-Via-Character-Emotion then changes the story so that the event that motivates the character's goal to protect his life also motivates the character to be scared. ALP:Add-Suspense-Via-Character-Emotion is shown in Figure 5.2.

5.2.3.2 ALP:Add-Suspense-Via-Failed-Escape

A technique for building suspense that is commonly used in horror films is the failed escape. The young heroine, menaced by a masked, knife-wielding maniac, runs down a hallway towards a door and certain escape, only to discover at the last moment that the door is locked. The reader's tension is redoubled when the apparent resolution is reversed.

MINSTREL implements this technique in ALP:Add-Suspense-Via-Failed-Escape. This author-level plan tries to increase the suspense in a story scene in which a character's life is threatened by constructing a plan by which the threatened character can avoid dying. This plan is then executed, only to fail in the final step. ALP:Add-Suspense-Via-Failed-Escape is shown in Figure 5.3.

This plan was used in *The Knight and the Hermit* to increase the suspense in the scene in which the hermit's life is threatened by the dragon:

> Later, Bebe believed that he would die because he saw a dragon moving towards him and believed it would eat him. Bebe was very scared. *Bebe tried to run away but failed! ...*

In this case, MINSTREL finds a plan to avoid being eaten by running away. This is added to the story and the final step of this plan is marked as a failure.

Name:	ALP:Add-Suspense-Via-Character-Emotion
Goal Type:	&Add-Suspense-to-Scene
Object:	*AL-OBJ*
Test:	None.

Body:
1. Determine the actor of *AL-OBJ*, Actor. Determine the event motivating *AL-OBJ*, Motivation.
2. Create a new state representing Actor being fearful:
   a. Make a new, uninstantiated state schema.
   b. Set the Type feature of the new state to &Affect.
   c. Set the Object feature of the new state to the Actor.
   d. Set the Value feature of the new state to &Neg (negative).
   e. Set the Scale feature of the new state to &Normal.
   f. Connect the new state (representing Actor's fear) to the event that caused the fear by a &motivates link.

Figure 5.2 ALP:Add-Suspense-Via-Character-Emotion

Name: ALP:Add-Suspense-Via-Failed-Escape
Goal Type: &Add-Suspense-to-Scene
Object: *AL-OBJ*
Test: Use if the character doesn't already have a plan to avoid dying.
Body:
1. Create a plan to avoid dying:
   a. Make a new, uninstantiated act schema.
   b. Set the Actor feature of the new act to the threatened character.
   c. Connect the new act to the threatened character's &P-Health goal by a &plan link (i.e., the new act is a plan to achieve the &P-Health goal).
   d. Use author-level planning recursively to instantiate the new act.
2. Mark the final step of the plan as failed.

Figure 5.3 ALP:Add-Suspense-Via-Failed-Escape

(In this case, the plan has only one step, fleeing, so that is marked as the failure.) The result is a scene in which Bebe tries to flee but fails to outrun the dragon.

5.2.3.3 Summary

MINSTREL's use of suspense is rudimentary, but it does demonstrate the general architecture of author-level knowledge: plans to detect when to apply a writing technique, and plans to achieve that technique. The following sections show how tragedy, characterization, and foreshadowing can also be captured by this architecture.

5.3 Tragedy

Like suspense, tragedy depends on creating an emotion in the reader. To create suspense, the writer evokes anticipation. To create tragedy, the writer evokes pity and regret.

As expounded by Aristotle, the classical basis for tragedy is the character flaw: a single weakness such as pride or envy in an otherwise empathetic character which leads inevitably to downfall or destruction (Muller, 1956). From his omnipotent third-person viewpoint, the reader can recognize the character flaw and see how it leads inevitably to disaster. It is this knowledge, combined with the helplessness of the reader to affect events in the story, that makes the story events "tragic" and leads to the reader's feelings of pity and regret.

Since Aristotle, the tragedy motif has been developed and expanded in many ways. Muller (1956) follows the development of tragedy through the ages with sections such as "Greek Tragedy," "Elizabethan Tragedy," "Neo-Classical Tragedy," and "Modern Tragedy." In developing MINSTREL, we have focused on classical tragedy as outlined by Aristotle. As the basis and precursor of all tragedy, classical tragedy has a rich usage and history that makes it an excellent vehicle for demonstrating MINSTREL's use of dramatic writing techniques to improve a story's literary quality.

5.3.1 Tragedy in *The Vengeful Princess*

One of the stories MINSTREL creates which has a tragic element is "The Vengeful Princess." In this story, a knight accidently kills the princess he loves:

The Vengeful Princess

Once upon a time there was a lady of the court named Jennifer. Jennifer loved a knight named Grunfeld. Grunfeld loved Jennifer. Jennifer wanted revenge on a lady of the court named Darlene because she had the berries which she picked in the woods and Jennifer wanted to have the berries. Jennifer wanted to scare Darlene. Jennifer wanted a dragon to move towards Darlene so that Darlene believed it would eat her. Jennifer wanted to appear to be a dragon so that a dragon would move towards Darlene. Jennifer drank a magic potion. Jennifer transformed into a dragon. A dragon moved towards Darlene. A dragon was near Darlene.

Grunfeld wanted to impress the king. Grunfeld wanted to move towards the woods so that he could fight a dragon. Grunfeld moved towards the woods. Grunfeld was near the woods. Grunfeld fought a dragon. The dragon died. The dragon was Jennifer. Jennifer wanted to live. Jennifer tried to drink a magic potion but failed. Grunfeld was filled with grief.

Moral: Deception is a weapon difficult to aim.

The tragedy in this story arises from Jennifer's character flaw: temper. She seeks revenge on another princess for a trivial reason. This leads inevitably to her downfall, an accidental death at the hands of Grunfeld. MINSTREL, recognizing the element of tragedy in this story, increases the impact of the tragedy by making Jennifer and Grunfeld lovers. The fact that Jennifer's tragic flaw leads to her death at the hands of someone who loves her intensifies the tragic aspect of this story.

One interesting aspect of this story is that the initial tragedy arises independent of the theme of the story. The theme of this story is to avoid using deception plans, and this theme can be illustrated without any element of tragedy, as for instance:

> Jennifer decided to scare her little brother by playing dead. She poured ketchup on herself and laid on the floor. But it was her mother who came into the room and was scared. Later, Jennifer was punished for her prank.

But in "The Vengeful Princess," MINSTREL's instantiation of the theme leads inadvertently to a tragic situation. MINSTREL doesn't intentionally instantiate Jennifer's motivation for deception as a trivial affront. But once instantiated in this way, MINSTREL recognizes the elements of tragedy and take steps to further develop this aspect of the story. Thus MINSTREL is able to react to and capitalize on a fortuitous aspect of the story it is telling to create a story with unexpected layers of meaning.

5.3.2 When is Tragedy Appropriate?

A tragedy in the classical form involves a character with a tragic flaw who suffers a downfall as a direct, but unintended, result of the tragic flaw. To recognize this situation in a story, MINSTREL looks for three elements:

1. A character suffers a goal failure.
2. The goal failure is the result of unanticipated side-effects of the character's own plans.
3. The plans are motivated by a character flaw.

If all three of these elements are found, then MINSTREL recognizes the tragic element in the story and creates a goal to augment the tragedy. MINSTREL's author-level plan to recognize tragedy is shown in Figure 5.4.

There are two interesting features of this plan.

First, note that in tragedy as in suspense, MINSTREL limits itself to important goals, so as to avoid trying to create a tragedy concerning a small, meaningless goal. Not only would tragedy revolving around an unimportant goal be ineffective, it would likely distract from the theme of the story, rather than augment the theme as the author desires.

Second, this plan requires determining if a character has a "character flaw."

Name:	ALP:Check-Scene-For-Tragedy
Goal Type:	&Check-Scene-For-Tragedy
Object:	*AL-OBJ*
Test:	1. Is *AL-OBJ* a thwarted &P-HEALTH or &C-HEALTH goal?
	2. Is *AL-OBJ* thwarted by an unintended side-effect of an action by the actor of the goal?
	3. Does the actor of *AL-OBJ* have an explicitly marked character flaw? Or does he perform a socially unacceptable action motivated by a character trait?
Body:	1. Create an author-level goal to &Add-Tragedy-to-Scene to *AL-OBJ*.

Figure 5.4 ALP:Check-Scene-For-Tragedy

The idea and implementation of character flaws in MINSTREL is a topic with several interesting facets.

Character flaws are personality traits such as greed, pride, or envy, which cause a character to act outside the bounds of acceptable behavior. For instance, a greedy character uses normally unacceptable plans to achieve money, such as theft and cheating. Character flaws can be contrasted to other character traits, which cause characters to act in unusual but acceptable ways. For instance, a compassionate character might give a large sum of money to a beggar, an unusual but socially acceptable act.

There are two ways MINSTREL can determine if a character has a character flaw.

First, the flaw can be marked explicitly. In stories based on the theme PAT:Pride ("Pride goes before a fall"), the main character is explicitly marked as having a character flaw (pride).

Second, the character flaw can be implicit in the character's actions. If a character is motivated by a character trait to use socially unacceptable plans to achieve his goals, that character trait can be recognized as a flaw. For example, MINSTREL can recognize that a character who is motivated by "greed" to cheat and steal has a character flaw. Whether or not MINSTREL knows anything further about "greed," it can recognize that in this case "greed" is a character flaw.

Currently, MINSTREL recognizes socially unacceptable plans as those that cause goal failures for other characters. For example, cheating and stealing are both recognized as socially unacceptable because they cause goal failures (failure to protect one's money) in other characters when used. Compare this to selling, where both characters involved have goal successes. Although this definition of socially acceptability works well for the King Arthur domain, more complete models of the valuation of goals and plans have been defined (see for example [Reeves, 1991]).

In summary, MINSTREL recognizes a tragic situation when a character with a character flaw performs an action that has unintended bad results for the character.

5.3.3   Writing Techniques for Building Tragedy

There are a variety of common patterns in classical tragedy that build upon the basic element of the flawed character. One such is the "mythical hero," in which the flawed character is a hero who arises from humble or unknown origins to ascend to kingship, only to die because of a tragic flaw, a pattern that is present in stories from Oedipus Rex to Robin Hood. Another common pattern, also present in Oedipus Rex, is "destroying what one loves," in which the flawed character not only causes his own downfall, but unwittingly also destroys or hurts someone he loves. MINSTREL implements one plan for increasing the tragedy of a story based on the idea of "Destroying what one loves."

"Destroying what one loves" increases the tragic effect of a story by sharing the tragic character's downfall with a character he loves. The reader's sense of justice is offended when an innocent character suffers, and is even more outraged when a loved character suffers at the hands of the one he loves, for shouldn't love be a protection against tragedy and injustice? Thus "destroying what one loves" increases the tragic effect of a story by combining the downfall of the tragic character with what is seen by the reader as the unfair loss of an innocent character.

5.3.3.1   ALP:Add-Tragedy-Via-Loved-One

MINSTREL's author-level plan for involving a loved one in the downfall of a tragic character is limited. It applies only if the tragic character dies inadvertently at the hands of another character. If this is true, then ALP:Add-Tragedy-Via-Loved-One increases the tragedy of this event by making the flawed character and the character responsible for the downfall lovers. ALP:Add-Tragedy-Via-Loved-One is illustrated in Figure 5.5.

Two things should be noted about ALP:Add-Tragedy-Via-Loved-One.

First, ALP:Add-Tragedy-Via-Loved-One requires that the death of the tragic character at the hands of the loved one be inadvertent. This avoids the paradoxical situation where a character knowingly kills someone he loves. In the hands of a skilled writer, this paradox can be resolved, and, indeed, form the basis of an even more powerful tragedy, but that is beyond the scope of MINSTREL.

Second, the version of "destroying what one loves" that ALP:Add-Tragedy-Via-Loved-One creates has a layered complexity. The tragic character's death does indeed destroy someone he loves, because the loved character is destroyed by the knowledge that he has killed someone he loved. But on a second level, that destruction rebounds back to the tragic character, because he is literally destroyed by the loved character. And so ALP:Add-Tragedy-Via-Loved-One

Name: ALP:Add-Tragedy-Via-Loved-One
Goal Type: &Add-Tragedy-To-Scene
Object: *AL-OBJ*
Test: Use if the flawed character's downfall is his death, and the death was caused by another character.
Body:
1. Determine the character who caused the death of the flawed character.
2. Create a scene that establishes that these two characters loved each other:
   a. Create an uninstantiated state schema.
   b. Set the Type feature of the new state to &Affect.
   c. Set the To feature to the flawed character.
   d. Set the Object feature to the other character.
   e. Set the Value feature to &Pos (positive).
   f. Set the Scale feature to &Strong.
   g. Add the new state to the establishing scenes of the story.
3. Create a scene in which the character who causes the death of the flawed character, and who loved the flawed character, grieves over the loss:
   a. Create an uninstantiated state schema.
   b. Set the Type feature of the new state to &Affect.
   c. Set the Object feature to the other character.
   d. Set the Value feature to &Neg (positive).
   e. Set the Scale feature to &Strong.
   f. Connect the new state schema to the death of the flawed character by a &reaction link.

Figure 5.5 ALP:Add-Tragedy-Via-Loved-One

creates a complex situation in which the tragedy and destruction are intertwined on several levels.

5.4   Characterization

The art of creating and portrayal of convincing characters is called *characterization*. Poor characterization in a story causes critics to speak of "cardboard" or "one-dimensional" characters: characters whose personalities are very simple and shallow, and who act on the simplest and most obvious of motivations. To portray a convincing, deep character, the author must both create a character with the aspects of a real person and show how those aspects impact the character's life.

5.4.1 Characterization in *The Proud Knight*

Characterization is particularly important in stories that turn upon a character trait. For a story of this sort to be successful, the author must be able to portray and establish the character trait in sufficient detail to justify the story development involving the trait.

The previous section showed how a character flaw drove the development of tragedy in *The Vengeful Princess*. Another story MINSTREL tells which is driven by a character flaw is *The Proud Knight*. In this story, Lancelot is a proud man whose hot temper eventually leads him to a hasty killing. In the early part of this story, MINSTREL establishes Lancelot's hot temper:

The Proud Knight

It was the spring of 1089, and a knight named Lancelot returned to Camelot from elsewhere. Lancelot was hot-tempered. Once, Lancelot lost a joust. Lancelot wanted to destroy his sword. Lancelot struck his sword. His sword was destroyed...

MINSTREL establishes Lancelot's hot temper in two ways. First, MINSTREL simply states Lancelot's character trait: "Lancelot was hot-tempered." Secondly, MINSTREL invents a story episode that illustrates Lancelot's hot temper and shows how it leads him to make hasty and irrational decisions.

5.4.2 When Should Characterization be Used?

At first thought, it may seem like an author should always try to characterize his story characters as fully as possible. But that is not the case. There are several cases where characterization is not only unnecessary, but harmful.

For instance, it often harms a story if a minor character is given a full characterization. By spending time and detail on a character, the author creates in the reader an expectation that this character will be important. The reader, like the author, has a rough heuristic that the time and detail spent upon a portion of a story reflects its importance to the story. To go against this expectation creates "red herrings" which weaken the story. Skilled mystery writers sometimes take advantage of this bit of psychology to mislead the reader with false clues, but for less talented authors (like MINSTREL) it is best to avoid creating red herrings.

Characterization is also misplaced if it emphasizes the wrong aspect of the character. For example, if, in the beginning of *The Proud Knight*, MINSTREL had developed Lancelot as a very handsome character, Lancelot's later hot-tempered actions would have been inexplicable and unfounded. Thus characterization simply for the sake of characterization can have a detrimental effect on a story.

To avoid these types of problems, MINSTREL only tries to create characterization when a character has an explicitly marked character trait that is part of the story theme. In this way MINSTREL is assured that (1) the character is a major character, because he is part of the story theme, and (2) the character trait is important to the story development, because it is explicitly marked as necessary to the story theme. MINSTREL's author-level plan for determining when to apply characterization is shown in Figure 5.6.

5.4.3 Developing Characterization

Edgar Roberts, a professor of literature at City University of New York, writing about the role of characterization in literature, identifies four ways that an author can indicate character to the reader (Roberts, 1977, pp. 55-56):

1. *By what the character himself says (and thinks, from the author's third-person omniscient point of view).*
2. *By what the character does.*
3. *By what other characters say about him.*
4. *By what the author says about him, speaking as either the storyteller or an observer of the action.*

MINSTREL has implemented plans for characterization based on methods 2 and 4.

5.4.3.1 ALP:Add-Characterization-Statement

Of the characterization methods that Roberts identifies, author statement of a character trait is perhaps the simplest. In this method, the author simply states, third person, that a character possesses a particular trait, as MINSTREL does in *The Proud Knight*:

```
...Lancelot was hot-tempered...
```

Name:	ALP:Check-Story-For-Characterization
Goal Type:	&Check-Story-For-Characterization
Object:	*AL-OBJ*
Test:	Is the story based upon a theme?
Body:	1. Look at all the characters involved in the theme. If any of them have an explicitly marked character trait, create an author-level goal to &Add-Characterization for that character trait.

Figure 5.6 ALP:Check-Story-For-Characterization

ALP:Add-Characterization-Statement is the author-level plan that achieves this. ALP:Add-Characterization-Statement creates the character trait as an establishing scene in the story. Later, when the story is generated as English, this scene is generated as a third-person statement of the character trait. ALP:Add-Characterization-Statement is illustrated in Figure 5.7.

5.4.3.2   ALP:Add-Characterization-Example

A more subtle method of characterization is to have the character perform actions motivated by or predicated upon the character trait to be developed. Unlike author statement, this method of characterization does not baldly state the underlying character trait. Rather, it requires that the reader deduce from the character's actions the underlying character trait. Although this is more subtle, it can also be more effective, because it gives the reader a concrete example of the character's behavior.

In *The Proud Knight*, this method is used to illustrate Lancelot's hot temper:

```
...Once, Lancelot lost a joust. Lancelot
wanted to destroy his sword. Lancelot struck
his sword. His sword was destroyed...
```

By showing how Lancelot's hot temper affects his behavior, this method makes the characterization more immediate to the reader.

In MINSTREL, this method of characterization is implemented by the author-level plan ALP:Add-Characterization-Example. One might expect this plan to be much more complicated than the simple plan used to implement characterization through author statement, but ALP:Add-Characterization-Example is quite simple. MINSTREL already knows a lot about creating examples (recall that MINSTREL develops the theme of a story by creating an example of the theme), so all that is necessary to create a characterization example is to specify an abstract description of the example and then recursively use MINSTREL's existing author-level plans for creating examples (instantiation) to solve this new goal. ALP:Add-Characterization-Example is illustrated in Figure 5.8.

Name:	ALP:Add-Characterization-Statement
Goal Type:	&Add-Characterization
Object:	*AL-OBJ*
Test:	None.
Body:	1. Copy the character trait into the establishing scenes for the story being told.

Figure 5.7 ALP:Add-Characterization-Statement

Name:	ALP:Add-Characterization-Example
Goal Type:	&Add-Characterization
Object:	*AL-OBJ*
Test:	None.
Body:	1. Create a new, uninstantiated scene in which the character trait motivates a goal:

Body:

1. Create a new, uninstantiated scene in which the character trait motivates a goal:
    a. Make a new, uninstantiated goal schema.
    b. Set the Actor feature of the goal schema to the character being characterized.
    c. Connect the new goal schema to the character trait by a &motivates link.
2. Use author-level planning recursively to instantiate this goal.
3. If successful, add the instantiated goal to the story.

Figure 5.8 ALP:Add-Characterization-Example

5.5 Foreshadowing

Foreshadowing is a literary technique in which story incidents introduce, repeat, give casual allusion to, or hint at later story incidents. The purpose of foreshadowing is to build a sense of inevitability in the later story events (De Camp & De Camp, 1975). By foreshadowing important story elements, the author avoids having those elements appear contrived, and in addition, creates a sense of unity in the story.

5.5.1 Foreshadowing in *The Mistaken Knight*

MINSTREL uses foreshadowing in *The Mistaken Knight*. The climax of this story turns upon Lancelot unexpectedly seeing the woman he loves kissing another knight. MINSTREL accomplishes this by having Lancelot's horse act willful—pulling him into the woods where he sees Andrea with Frederick. To prevent this from appearing contrived, and to help unify the story, MINSTREL uses the same type of scene earlier in the story, when Lancelot meets Andrea:

The Mistaken Knight

It was the spring of 1089, and a knight
named Lancelot returned to Camelot from elsewhere. Lancelot was hot tempered. Once,
Lancelot lost a joust. Because he was hot tempered, Lancelot wanted to destroy his sword.
Lancelot struck his sword. His sword was
destroyed.
One day, a lady of the court named Andrea

wanted to have some berries. Andrea wanted to
be near the woods. Andrea moved to the woods.
Andrea was at the woods. Andrea had some
berries because Andrea picked some berries. *At
the same time, Lancelot's horse moved Lancelot
to the woods. This unexpectedly caused him to
be near Andrea.* Because Lancelot was near
Andrea, Lancelot loved Andrea.

*Some time later, Lancelot's horse moved
Lancelot to the woods unintentionally, again
causing him to be near Andrea.* Lancelot knew
that Andrea kissed with a knight named Frederick because Lancelot saw that Andrea kissed
with Frederick...

One interesting aspect of foreshadowing is that it requires the author to create early story events *after* he has created later events. In this case, MINSTREL
must create the scene in which Lancelot meets Andrea after the scene in which
Lancelot kills Frederick, i.e., out of story order.

Like a human author, MINSTREL does not necessarily write a story "from
beginning to end". Indeed, MINSTREL's representation of a story does not
even possess a linear structure; one of the tasks of presenting the story to the
reader is to determine the order in which to tell the story events. Instead, MIN-
STREL creates the events of the story in an order roughly determined by the
importance of the events to the story. MINSTREL may create important story
events near the end of the story (such as the resolution of the story theme) before
it even considers lower priority events near the beginning of the story (such as
scenes that introduce characters).

So there is no particular difficulty involved in creating earlier story events
after later story events, as must happen in foreshadowing. If necessary, MIN-
STREL can "jump back" to an earlier part of the story and create a new story
event, or if necessary, modify an existing story event.

5.5.2 Detecting Opportunities for Foreshadowing

As with other dramatic writing goals, the first step in using foreshadowing is to
determine when it is appropriate. MINSTREL uses two criteria to determine
when to apply foreshadowing.

First, MINSTREL applies foreshadowing only to story events that illustrate
the story theme. As with other dramatic writing techniques, MINSTREL
restricts foreshadowing to the story theme in order to focus the reader's attention
on the story theme and to avoid creating "red herrings."

Second, MINSTREL applies foreshadowing only to unique story events.

When deciding whether to foreshadow a story scene, MINSTREL compares that story scene to others in its memory. Only if the story scene has a unique feature or combination of features will MINSTREL choose to foreshadow the scene.

Because the purpose of foreshadowing is to create a sense of inevitability, foreshadowing is best applied to events which *might* seem contrived. Story events that are commonplace (i.e., similar to those MINSTREL has read about in the past) are unlikely to be seen as contrived or unexpected, and consequently there is no need to foreshadow these types of events. Story events that are unusual (i.e., unlike anything MINSTREL has previously encountered) might well be seen as contrived, and so it is to these types of events that MINSTREL applies foreshadowing.

MINSTREL's model of contrivance is admittedly weak. Not everything uncommon is contrived. Furthermore, if MINSTREL uses a contrived scene in several stories, it will begin to see the scene as common and hence uncontrived. Despite these flaws, choosing to foreshadow uncommon scenes remains a useful heuristic for several reasons. First, it is a domain-independent heuristic. It does not rely on any specific knowledge of the King Arthur domain to determine what might seem contrived. Rather, it uses the author's own experience in the story domain. Second, a simple form of learning can improve this heuristic. As the author reads other stories in the story domain, his or her knowledge of what is common and acceptable will increase. Finally, foreshadowing is not strictly limited to eliminating contrivance. It also serves to create a feeling of inevitability and to create a unifying story element. Both of these functions can be served even if the story event chosen for foreshadowing is not contrived. For these reasons, this model of how scenes for foreshadowing are selected has proven adequate for the kinds of stories MINSTREL currently tells.

MINSTREL's author-level plan to determine when foreshadowing is appropriate is shown in Figure 5.9.

ALP:Check-Story-For-Foreshadowing differs in two ways from the criteria just described.

First, ALP:Check-Story-For-Foreshadowing looks only for unique combinations of act and state schemas, rather than unique combinations of any schemas.

Name:	ALP:Check-Story-For-Foreshadowing
Goal Type:	&Check-Story-For-Foreshadowing
Object:	*AL-OBJ*
Test:	None.
Body:	1. Look at all the act/state combinations in the story. Use each combination as an index for recall. Save each combination that does not recall anything as a candidate.
	2. Select one candidate at random from the available candidates. Create an author-level goal to foreshadow the candidate event.

Figure 5.9 ALP:Check-Story-For-Foreshadowing

In the King Arthur domain, stories are "action driven," meaning that the most important story events are typically direct character actions. Rather than examine all the combinations of schemas present in a story, ALP:Check-Story-For-Foreshadowing concentrates instead on character actions (act schemas) and their results (state schemas). This allows MINSTREL to find foreshadowing opportunities much more efficiently, at the cost of possibly overlooking a foreshadowing opportunity that does not involve a character action.

A second addition that ALP:Check-Story-For-Foreshadowing makes to the criteria listed before is that ALP:Check-Story-For-Foreshadowing selects only one of the suitable candidates for foreshadowing. The purpose of this is to limit the amount of foreshadowing used in a story. This is purely an aesthetic judgment, the kind of "rule of thumb" a beginning author might learn to avoid overusing literary techniques such as foreshadowing.[7]

5.5.3 Creating Foreshadowing

Once the story scene to be foreshadowed has been selected, the next task is to create the foreshadowing scene. This is accomplished in two steps.

In the first step, the story is searched for points where a foreshadowing scene can be inserted. Because the scene to be foreshadowed consists of an act and a related state, MINSTREL looks through the remainder of the story for other act and state schemas similar to the foreshadowed schemas. If a match is found, it is saved as a possible candidate, and when all candidates are found, one is selected randomly as the point for foreshadowing.

For example, in *The Mistaken Knight*, the foreshadowed scene consists of Lancelot's horse taking an action which inadvertently caused Lancelot to be in a location. To find a point in the story where this can be foreshadowed, MINSTREL looks through the story for schemas representing (1) Lancelot being in a location, or (2) Lancelot's horse taking an action. A story event that matches the former is found: Lancelot must be in the same location as the Princess Andrea in order to meet her and fall in love with her. This is the only story event that matches the foreshadowed scene, so it becomes the candidate location for foreshadowing.

The second step is to copy the foreshadowed scene into the foreshadowing location. Human authors foreshadow subtly, by repeating only one or two key elements of the foreshadowed scene. MINSTREL's technique is more unrefined: It copies as much of the foreshadowed scene as is usable into the foreshadowing scene.

In the *The Mistaken Knight*, this results in a scene in which Lancelot meets

---

[7] In fact, opportunities for foreshadowing are rare in the stories that MINSTREL tells, and it is only in *The Mistaken Knight* that a suitable candidate is found and foreshadowing achieved, so this test could be dropped with no change in MINSTREL's behavior.

Name:	ALP:Add-Foreshadowing
Goal Type:	&Add-Foreshadowing
Object:	*AL-OBJ*
Test:	None.
Body:	1. Look at all the act and state schemas in the story. Save each schema that matches the schemas that represent the scene to be foreshadowed. When all candidates have been gathered, select one randomly.
2. If a candidate foreshadowing location was found, copy the foreshadowed scene into the foreshadowing location.

Figure 5.10 ALP:Add-Foreshadowing

Andrea inadvertently when his horse moves him unexpectedly into the woods. The entire act schema (representing Lancelot's horse moving unexpectedly into the woods) is copied from the foreshadowed scene. Consequently, Lancelot not only meets Andrea in the same unusual manner that he later discovers her with another man, but it also occurs in the same location.

MINSTREL's author-level plan that implements foreshadowing is shown in Figure 5.10.

5.6 Conclusions

MINSTREL implements four writing techniques as a way to explore the role of secondary author-level goals in storytelling. Although MINSTREL's implementation of these writing techniques is currently rudimentary, the effects they have on the stories MINSTREL tells demonstrate their value in creating complexity and depth in storytelling.

6 | Consistency Goals

6.1 Introduction

Here's an inexplicable little story:

The Story of John

One day, John passed a stranger on the street. John pulled a gun and shot him. The neighborhood priest saw John kill the man. The priest stopped his car and gave John a hug. John went home and gave his dog to his neighbor.

Although individually the events of this story are fine—even interesting—the story as a whole is confusing. The characters act almost randomly, pedestrians carry guns and no one seems to react properly to anything that happens. The story and the world it describes lack rhyme and reason. But the most curious thing about this story is that a little explanation changes its complexion entirely:

The Story of John, Redux

One day, John was walking home from his night job as a security guard. John passed a stranger on the street. John saw a tattoo on the man's hand which he remembered from the night his parents died. This man had to die. John drew his gun and shot the man. The neighborhood priest was driving by and saw John kill the man. The priest stopped his car and looked at the man. Then he turned to his brother and hugged him. They both cried. Then John went home, gave his dog to his neighbor, and waited for the police to arrive.

The Story of John—or rather, the two stories of John—illustrate the importance of story consistency. Readers expect a story to be understandable. The characters should act in ways that are familiar and easily understood; the world should operate as the reader expects. When they don't, the author must explain why not. The Story of John is unacceptable not because of what happens, but because of what is left unexplained.

In MINSTREL, story consistency is maintained by a collection of opportunistic goals that watch the developing story for inconsistencies and correct them. For example, MINSTREL has a story consistency goal that watches for situations where a character uses a plan without first fulfilling all the preconditions of the plan. When this occurs, MINSTREL adds scenes that fulfill the preconditions. In The Story of John, this goal would notice that John uses a plan (shooting someone with a gun) without fulfilling one of the preconditions of that plan (possessing a gun). MINSTREL would then add scenes explaining how John came to have a gun (perhaps by revealing that John was a security guard). In this way, MINSTREL assures that the stories it tells have internal consistency and plausibility.

6.2   How Story Inconsistencies Arise

One of the difficulties of storytelling is that it requires the author to solve a "problem" (writing a story) with many constraints. The author must create a story which fulfills a story theme, has literary value, is internally consistent, and so on. One method for problem solving under many constraints is to subdivide the problem and attack each set of constraints separately and serially.

For example, the writer can decide to work first on the parts of the story that illustrate the theme, without worrying about literary value or story consistency. Then he might move on to increasing the dramatic tension of the story while ignoring the other elements, or the characterization of the main actors. By moving back and forth between his various goals and constraints, the author reduces a very difficult monolithic problem to a series of more reasonable smaller problems.

But one consequence of this technique is that the author must be careful to review the story in light of all constraints. A scene created to fulfill one author-level goal might unwittingly violate another. If so, the problem must be corrected. This is how story inconsistencies arise, and this is why author-level goals and plans to detect and correct story inconsistencies are required.

As an example of how fulfilling one author-level goal can violate another, consider this scene, created by MINSTREL when telling *The Hermit and the Knight*:

```
Once upon a time, a knight named Cedric was
wounded.  A hermit named Bebe healed Cedric.
Cedric was grateful and vowed to return the
favor.
```

This scene is created to illustrate the first part of the story theme for *The Hermit and the Knight*: "A favor earned is soon returned." Bebe's kindness in healing Cedric will be returned when Bebe is in need. But although this scene illustrates the story theme, it violates several author-level goals of telling a consistent story. It lacks both an explanation of how Cedric came to be injured, and an explanation of how Bebe found the injured knight in order to heal him.

MINSTREL's author-level consistency goals detect and correct these and other types of story inconsistencies.

6.3 Organization of Consistency Goals

MINSTREL's consistency goals fall into three categories:

1. Planning Inconsistencies
2. Story World Inconsistencies
3. Emotional Inconsistencies

The first category deals with inconsistencies in the way characters plan. These goals assure that characters use appropriate plans to achieve their goals, create new goals in response to changes in the story world, and so on. The second category deals with the description of the story world. These goals make sure that things don't happen in the world without proper reason. The final category deals with how characters react emotionally to the events in their world. These goals provide characters with appropriate emotional reactions to goal failures and successes.

Every time MINSTREL creates or modifies a story scene, it also creates goals to check the consistency in each of the foregoing categories. So every part of the stories MINSTREL tells is checked for consistency. Altogether, MINSTREL has nine plans for maintaining story consistency. Most capture common sense knowledge about how people plan and how the world works; a few are more complex.

6.4　Planning Inconsistencies

As mentioned before, the scenes that MINSTREL creates to fulfill thematic and literary goals often contain incomplete planning sequences. Consider, for example, this scene from *Lancelot and Frederick*:

> One day, Lancelot wanted to kill Frederick. Lancelot fought with Frederick. Frederick was dead.

In this scene, Lancelot's goals are unclear. Why should Lancelot want to kill Frederick? A character who decides "out of the blue" to kill another character violates the reader's expectations of how people behave, and results in an inconsistent story. The reader expects characters in the story world to have understandable goals and pursue those goals in expected ways. If they do not, explanation is required.

MINSTREL has author-level goals and plans to detect and correct several types of planning inconsistencies.

6.4.1　Unmotivated Goals

The difficulty with the foregoing story fragment is that Lancelot's goal to kill Frederick is unmotivated. An unmotivated goal disrupts the story by causing the reader to ruminate over the unspoken reasons why the character would have this goal. A good author provides motivations for the goals that the characters in his story pursue.

In MINSTREL, there are three possible motivations for a goal:

1. it can be a role goal,
2. it can be a subgoal of another goal, or
3. it can be motivated by a state of the world.

Role goals are the "life goals" associated with character types such as knight and princess. These are goals that both the author and the reader assume that the character has based on his position and role in society. Role goals for knights, for example, include achieving status with their king and killing monsters. (To a certain extent, role goals define the character type: A character is a knight *because* he kills monsters, and tries to impress his king.) Role goals need no further motivation because the reader accepts them as typical and understandable goals for the character. The role goals used by MINSTREL are shown in Figure 6.1.

Role	Goals
King	none[8]
Knight	Achieve Status (&A-Status)
	Destroy Monsters (&Destroy)
	Achieve Love (&A-Love)
Princess	Pick Berries (&Atrans)
	Achieve Love (&A-Love)
Hermit	Pick Berries (&Atrans)
Monster	Satisfy Hunger (&S-Hunger)

Figure 6.1 Role Goals in MINSTREL

Role goals are an artifact of the shared culture between the author and the reader. They work because the author and the reader share a common understanding about roles in the story genre. Of course, if the author and reader don't share a common culture, the goals of characters in the story may be incomprehensible. Lack of a shared culture is one reason modern readers often struggle over stories from earlier times. MINSTREL assumes that the reader has enough familiarity with stories in the King Arthur genre that he or she won't be puzzled to read of a knight killing a monster. But if the reader lacks that background, he or she may well be confused.

Role goals are an example of a reader model. Who will read a story is an important consideration in how a story is told (Smith, 1982). The difference between children's stories and stories for adults—in content, subject matter, style, and explanation—is an excellent example of how a reader model affects the writing process.

MINSTREL assumes that the reader has the same knowledge that MINSTREL itself has, that is, MINSTREL writes for itself as a reader. This is the simplest and easiest reader model. It requires no special reasoning about what the reader knows or understands. Future work in computer models of storytelling may examine in more detail the role of the reader model in storytelling, but for MINSTREL, this simple reader model has proven effective and convenient.

A second possible motivation for a goal is for it to be a subgoal of another goal. The subgoals of a goal form a plan for achieving the goal. For instance, if Lancelot has a goal to become rich, his subgoals might include to be where Frederick is, to kill Frederick, and then to take Frederick's money. Together, the subgoals form a plan for achieving the goal of being rich. Subgoals are explained by their purpose in achieving the supergoal.

The third possible motivation for a goal is a change in the state of the world. Characters react to changes in their world by creating new goals for themselves.

---

[8] MINSTREL uses creativity to invent role goals for Kings when necessary (see Chapter 8).

For example, if Frederick drew his sword and charged at Lancelot, Lancelot might well react to this by creating the goal to kill Frederick. Lancelot's goal to kill Frederick is explained by the fact that Frederick is charging Lancelot with a drawn sword.

MINSTREL has one author-level plan for detecting unmotivated character goals, and two plans for correcting unmotivated character goals.

6.4.1.1 ALP:Check-Consistency-Goal

ALP:Check-Consistency-Goal determines if a goal is unmotivated by checking to see that it is not (1) a role goal, (2) a subgoal or (3) motivated by a story event. If none of these conditions are true, ALP:Check-Consistency-Goal creates an author-level goal to create a motivation for this goal. ALP:Check-Consistency-Goal is illustrated in Figure 6.2.

6.4.1.2 ALP:Make-Consistent-Supergoal

ALP:Make-Consistent-Supergoal tries to make an unmotivated goal consistent by creating a super-goal, that is, by making the unmotivated goal a step in a plan to achieve another goal. To do this, MINSTREL uses author-level planning recursively to try to recall or invent a plan that involves the unmotivated goal. ALP:Make-Consistent-Supergoal is illustrated in Figure 6.3.

One place ALP:Make-Consistent-Supergoal is used is in *The Hermit and the Knight*. This story is based on the theme "Good deeds do not go unrewarded." In the first part of this story, a hermit named Cedric does a favor for a knight

Name:	ALP:Check-Consistency-Goal
Goal Type:	&Check-Consistency
Object:	*AL-OBJ*
Test:	1. Is *AL-OBJ* of type &Goal?
	2. Is *AL-OBJ* a role goal for the actor of the goal?
	3. Is *AL-OBJ* the sub-goal of another goal?
	4. 4. Is *AL-OBJ* motivated by a state of the world?
Body:	1. If none of the tests are true, create an author-level goal to make *AL-OBJ* consistent (&Make-Consistent).
	2. Otherwise, the goal is consistent and no further work needs to be done.

Figure 6.2 ALP:Check-Consistency-Goal

Name:	ALP:Make-Consistent-Supergoal
Goal Type:	&Make-Consistent
Object:	*AL-OBJ*

Test:
1. Make *AL-OBJ* the sub-goal of a new, uninstantiated goal:
   a. Make a new, uninstantiated goal schema.
   b. Connect the new goal schema to *AL-OBJ* by a &sub-goal link.
2. Use author-level planning recursively to try to instantiate the super-goal:
   a. Make a new author-level goal to &Instantiate the new goal schema.
   b. Call author-level planning to achieve the new author-level goal.

Body:
1. If instantiation succeeds, add the instantiated super-goal to the story.

Figure 6.3 ALP:Make-Consistent-Supergoal

named Bebe when Bebe is injured fighting a dragon. Here is an initial version of the story:

> Once upon a time, there was a hermit named Bebe and a knight named Cedric. One day, Cedric was in the woods when he was attacked by a dragon and wounded. Bebe wanted to be in the woods. Bebe went to the woods. Bebe healed Cedric. Cedric was grateful and vowed to return the favor.

The difficulty with this initial version of the story lies in Bebe's trip to the woods. The theme of this story requires that Bebe heal Cedric, and that in turn requires that Bebe be in the same location as Cedric. Consequently, Bebe goes to the woods. But why? Although Bebe's goal to be in the woods serves an author purpose, it is unmotivated at the character level, resulting in an inconsistent story.

ALP:Make-Consistent-Supergoal corrects this by inventing a reason for Bebe to be in the woods. MINSTREL uses author-level planning recursively to find a goal for Bebe, which has a subgoal of being in the woods. In this case, MINSTREL uses ALP:General-Instantiate and recalls a previous story scene in which a Hermit went to the woods as a subgoal of picking berries. This is then used to instantiate the supergoal in the current scene as "Bebe wanted to pick some berries."

If the recursive instantiation succeeds, the instantiated scene is added to the story as an explanation of the originally inconsistent scene:

> Once upon a time, there was a hermit named Bebe and a knight named Cedric. One day, Cedric was in the woods when he was attacked by a dragon and wounded. Bebe, *who was in the woods picking berries*, healed Cedric. Cedric was grateful and vowed to return the favor.

Unlike Bebe's goal to be in the woods, Bebe's goal to pick berries is consistent. Picking berries is a role goal for hermits. It is something readers expect hermits to be doing, and no further explanation is needed.

6.4.1.3 ALP:Make-Consistent-Motivating-State

An alternate explanation for an unmotivated goal is a motivating state. Goals can arise as characters react to the state of the world. Consider this fragment from *Lancelot and Frederick*:

> Lancelot believed that Andrea loved Frederick. Lancelot wanted Andrea to love him. But Andrea loved Frederick. Lancelot hated Frederick... Lancelot wanted to kill Frederick.

This fragment contains an unmotivated goal: Lancelot wants Andrea to love him. Most readers of this fragment "fix" this problem by assuming that Lancelot loves Andrea. This state of the world explains why Lancelot would want Andrea to love him and be upset if she did not. The reader is following the same strategy as ALP:Make-Consistent-Motivating-State.

ALP:Make-Consistent-Motivating-State makes an unmotivated goal consistent by trying to invent or recall a state of the world that would motivate the goal. In the case of this example, ALP:Make-Consistent-Motivating-State finds the same solution most readers find—"Lancelot loves Andrea":

> Lancelot believed that Andrea loved Frederick. Lancelot loved Andrea. Because Lancelot loved Andrea, Lancelot wanted to be the love of Andrea. But he could not because Andrea loved Frederick. Lancelot hated Frederick... Lancelot wanted to kill Frederick.

ALP:Make-Consistent-Motivating-State tries to repair an unmotivated goal by creating a new state of the world that would motivate the goal, that is, it tries to make the character's goal a reaction to something that happened in the story world.   Like   ALP:Make-Consistent-Supergoal,   ALP:Make-Consistent-Motivating-State achieves this by using author-level planning recursively to recall or invent a state that can motivate the unmotivated goal. ALP:Make-Consistent-Motivating-State is illustrated in Figure 6.4.

ALP:Make-Consistent-Motivating-State   creates   an   uninstantiated   state schema which it uses as a "placeholder" motivation for the unmotivated goal. Author-level planning is then used recursively to try to fill in the placeholder. At the recursive level, author-level plans for instantiation are used to fill in the state schema. If instantiation succeeds, the instantiated state can be used to motivate the inconsistent goal.

6.4.2 Motivating States

Just as a state of the world *can* be used to motivate a goal, so some states *should* motivate goals. Changes in the world—especially ones that affect important character goals—should motivate new goals in the characters they affect. A world in which characters did not react to their environment would be strange indeed:

> John was walking to work. He saw a thousand dollar bill on the side-walk. John kept walking to work. John walked by the bank just as some robbers came out. John was hit by a stray bullet. John kept walking to work...

These kinds of inconsistencies are corrected by ALP:General-Motivating-

Name:	ALP:Make-Consistent-Motivating-State
Goal Type:	&Make-Consistent
Object:	*AL-OBJ*
Test:	1. Create an uninstantiated motivating state:
	a. Make a new, uninstantiated state schema.
	b. Connect the new state to the unmotivated goal by a &motivates link. (The new state represents an unknown motivation for the goal.)
	2. Use author-level planning recursively to try to instantiate the new state:
	a. Make a new author-level goal to &Instantiate the new state schema.
	b. Call author-level planning to achieve the new author-level goal.
Body:	1. If instantiation succeeds, add the instantiated state to the story.

Figure 6.4 ALP:Make-Consistent-Motivating-State

State. MINSTREL's initial solution to these problems was to use an author-level plan very specific to the King Arthur story world. In the King Arthur story world, the primary story events that characters must react to are dangers to their health. This knowledge was captured in an author-level plan called ALP:Make-Consistent-P-Health. Later, a more general author-level plan which used episodic memory to reason about how states motivate goals was created.

6.4.2.1   ALP:General-Motivating-State

Initially, MINSTREL's solution to the problem of motivating states was an author-level plan call ALP:Make-Consistent-P-Health, which was very specific to the King Arthur domain. Because almost all inconsistencies of this sort in the King Arthur domain are events that endanger the lives of characters, ALP:Make-Consistent-P-Health simply looked for these situations and corrected them.

Although ALP:Make-Consistent-P-Health is very effective, it is also quite inflexible. ALP:Make-Consistent-P-Health can make a character react correctly to having his life threatened, but not make him react correctly to finding a pot of gold. To generalize ALP:Make-Consistent-P-Health and add the ability to learn new motivating states, a new author-level plan was created which uses episodic memory to recognize motivating states.

The idea behind ALP:General-Motivating-State is to use episodic memory to determine if a state can motivate a goal. If so, ALP:General-Motivating-State can use the knowledge it finds in episodic to correct the inconsistencies in the current story.

For example, suppose that MINSTREL is telling a story in which a knight finds a pot of gold. ALP:General-Motivating-State uses that state as an index for recall, and remembers this story fragment from a story that MINSTREL had previously read:

Joshua was wandering through the desert when he found a hoard of silver and jewels. Joshua wanted to be rich, so he took the hoard.

In this story fragment, finding something valuable motivates a character to have a goal of being rich and accomplishing that by taking the valuable item. This knowledge can then be applied to the current story by making the pot of gold motivate the knight to want to be rich.

Because ALP:General-Motivating-State is driven by episodic memory, it can adapt to different story genres and change as the author learns more about a story genre. Thus ALP:General-Motivating-State is flexible in ways that ALP:Make-Consistent-P-Health was not.

However, ALP:General-Motivating-State has one problem that ALP:Make-Consistent-P-Health did not. Just because a state *could* motivate a goal does not necessarily mean that it *should*. For example, seeing a beautiful princess can cause a knight to fall in love, but not every knight should fall in love with every princess he sees. The purpose of ALP:General-Motivating-State is to maintain story consistency. Rather than add every possible motivated goal, it should add only those without which the story would be inconsistent.

Determining this, however, is difficult. Ultimately, the author must rely on his acquired knowledge of the story genre to know what goals are important to each type of character. This can be modeled by semantic knowledge of important character goals, much in the same way that role goals were modeled. For the King Arthur domain, MINSTREL assumes that only protection goals (i.e., protect one's health, protect one's possessions, protect one's status, etc.) are important enough to warrant inclusion in the story purely for consistency reasons. ALP:General-Motivating-State is illustrated in Figure 6.5.

Like ALP:Make-Consistent-Supergoal and ALP:Consistent-Motivating-State, ALP:General-Motivating-State uses author-level planning recursively to find knowledge it needs to make the story consistent. The power of this technique is that it permits MINSTREL to apply all of the knowledge it has about instantiation towards achieving a different type of author-level goal: building consistency.

Name: ALP:General-Motivating-State
Goal Type: &Make-Consistent
Object: *AL-OBJ*
Test: 1. *AL-OBJ* is a state which does not motivate a goal.
Body: 1. Create an uninstantiated goal motivated by *AL-OBJ*:
       a. Make a new, uninstantiated goal schema.
       b. Connect the original state (*AL-OBJ*) to the new goal schema by a &motivates link (i.e., the original state motivates the new, uninstantiated goal).
    2. Use author-level planning recursively to instantiate the uninstantiated goal:
       a. Make a new author-level goal to &Instantiate the new goal schema.
       b. Call author-level planning to achieve the new author-level goal.
    3. If instantiation succeeds and the instantiated goal is a protection goal, then add the new goal to the current story.

Figure 6.5 ALP:General-Motivating-State

6.4.3 Missing Preconditions

A precondition for an action is a state of the world that must be true before the action can be performed. For example, a precondition for fighting someone is to be colocated with that person. Similarly, possessing something is a precondition for giving it away.

Inconsistency arises if an action is performed without first achieving all of its preconditions. To prevent this type of inconsistency from appearing in its stories, MINSTREL has an author-level plan to detect and correct missing preconditions.

6.4.3.1 ALP:Check-Act-Preconds

ALP:Check-Act-Preconds is an author-level plan that examines each act schema in a story for missing preconditions, and creates the missing preconditions. ALP:Check-Act-Preconds is shown in Figure 6.6.

ALP:Check-Consistent-Precond relies upon semantic knowledge of what the necessary preconditions are for a given action. Although this knowledge could be deduced from episodic memory by recalling past uses of an action, the assumption is that knowledge about preconditions is used frequently enough and changes infrequently enough that it is compiled into a more convenient form (i.e., semantic memory). MINSTREL's knowledge of preconditions is shown in Figure 6.7.

ALP:Check-Consistent-Precond operates by looking up the preconditions needed for an action in the table shown in Figure 6.6. If a precondition for an action is missing from the story, ALP::Check-Consistent-Precond creates a state of the world that fulfills the precondition and adds it to the story.

Name:	ALP:Check-Act-Preconds Goal	
Type:	&Make-Consistent	
Object:	*AL-OBJ*	
Test:	1.	Is *AL-OBJ* an act schema?
Body:	1.	Determine what the preconditions for this type of action are. (The preconditions of an action is a list of states that must be true before the action can occur.)
	2.	For each precondition, search the story to see if the precondition is already true.
	3.	For each precondition that is not true:
		a. Make a new, uninstantiated state schema.
		b. Copy the current precondition into the new state schema.
		c. Connect the new state schema to the action by a &precond link.

Figure 6.6 ALP:Check-Consistent-Precond

An example of the use of ALP:Check-Consistent-Precond occurs in the story *The Proud Knight*. In this story, a knight is warned that fighting a dragon will result in doom. Being proud, he fights the dragon nonetheless, and is hurt in the process. The fight scene as MINSTREL initially creates it is:

```
Grunfeld fought with the dragon in the woods.
The dragon was destroyed but Grunfeld was hurt.
```

After this scene is created, ALP:Check-Act-Preconds notices that the precondition for fighting the dragon has not been met: Grunfeld is not in the same location as the dragon. ALP:Check-Act-Preconds creates a state that achieves this precondition and adds it to the story:

```
Grunfeld was near the dragon.  Grunfeld fought
with the dragon in the woods.  The dragon was
destroyed but Grunfeld was hurt.
```

The preconditions for fighting the dragon have now been satisfied. Grunfeld and the dragon are now colocated.

Of course, this new addition to the story itself seems inconsistent. There is no explanation of how Grunfeld came to be near the dragon, or why he wanted to be there. This type of inconsistency—an inconsistent state of the world—and how to correct it, is discussed in the following section.

6.5 Story World Inconsistencies

Just as the reader expects characters to act in familiar ways, he or she also expects the world to act in familiar ways. Unusual events should not happen at random or without explanation, and the ways in which the characters interact with the world should not violate the reader's common-sense understanding of the world.

In MINSTREL's stories, the world is represented by state schemas. Each

Identifier	Meaning	Preconditions
&M-Heal	Healing a character	Healer in same location as patient.
&M-Fight	Fighting someone	Combatants in same location.
&Mtrans	Witnessing something	Witness in same location as witnessed event.
&Ptrans	Physical movement	Physical control of object.
&Atrans	Change of ownership	Object to be transferred must be possessed.

Figure 6.7 Table of Preconditions

state schema represents a fact or "state" of the world. Like goals, most states require an explanation – a reason why they exist. In MINSTREL, there are two possible explanations for a state:

1. it can be a default state of the world, or
2. it can be the result of a character action.

Default states are analogous to role goals. They are states of the world that both the author and the reader accept as reasonable without further explanation. Default states represent any typical state of the world, such as the existence of an object or place. If the author assumes that a forest exists in the story world, the reader will not object, because the existence of forests is a commonplace state of the real world.

The second explanation for a state is that it results from a character's actions. The purpose of action is to change the state of the world. That a character's actions should change the world is both expected and consistent.

(A third possible explanation for a state is that it can be caused by an inanimate actor, such as "Nature" or gravity. Although this is a commonly used explanation in human storytelling, MINSTREL does not currently use inanimate actors to explain story events. Adding inanimate actors to MINSTREL would not, however, pose any difficulties.)

MINSTREL has three author-level plans for maintaining story world consistency. The first plan, ALP:Check-Consistency-State, determines whether or not a state is consistent. If it is not, the state is made consistent by one of the other two author-level plans: ALP:Make-Consistent-State or ALP:Make-Consistent-Colocation.

6.5.1 ALP:Check-Consistency-State

ALP:Check-Consistency-State determines if a state is unexplained by checking to see if it is (1) a default state, or (2) explained by a character action. If neither of these conditions are true, ALP:Check-Consistency-State creates an author-level goal to create an explanation for this state. ALP:Check-Consistency-State is illustrated in Figure 6.8.

6.5.2 ALP:Make-Consistent-State

ALP:Make-Consistent-State tries to make an unexplained state consistent by creating a character action which results in the state. To do this, MINSTREL uses author-level planning recursively to try to recall or invent an action that causes the state. ALP:Make-Consistent-State is illustrated in Figure 6.9.

To see how ALP:Make-Consistent-State works, let's return to the example

Name:	ALP:Check-Consistency-State
Goal Type:	&Check-Consistency
Object:	*AL-OBJ*
Test:	1. Is *AL-OBJ* a state schema?
	2. Does *AL-OBJ* represent the existence of an object or location? (I.e., is *AL-OBJ* a common state?)
	3. Is *AL-OBJ* the result of a character action?
Body:	1. If neither 2 nor 3 is true, then create an author-level goal to &Make-Consistent-State *AL-OBJ*.
	2. Otherwise, *AL-OBJ* is consistent.

Figure 6.8 ALP:Check-Consistency-State

Name:	ALP:Make-Consistent-State
Goal Type:	&Make-Consistent
Object:	*AL-OBJ*
Test:	1. Make *AL-OBJ* the result of a new, uninstantiated character action:
	a. Make a new, uninstantiated act schema.
	b. Connect the new act schema to the inconsistent state by an &intends link (i.e., the state is an intentional result of the action).
	2. Use author-level planning recursively to try to instantiate the character action:
	a. Make a new author-level goal to &Instantiate the new act schema.
	b. Call author-level planning to achieve the new author-level goal.
Body:	1. If instantiation succeeds, add the instantiated action to the story.

Figure 6.9 ALP:Make-Consistent-State

used in describing ALP:Check-Consistent-Preconds. In that example, MIN-STREL had started with a scene in which a knight fights a dragon:

```
Grunfeld fought with the dragon in the woods.
The dragon was destroyed but Grunfeld was hurt.
```

At this point, ALP:Check-Act-Preconds noticed that a precondition for fighting the dragon had not been met: Grunfeld is not in the same location as the dragon. ALP:Check-Act-Preconds then created a state that achieves this precondition and added it to the story:

```
Grunfeld was near the dragon.  Grunfeld fought
with the dragon in the woods.  The dragon was
destroyed but Grunfeld was hurt.
```

Now ALP:Make-Consistent-State comes into play. Because the state created to fulfill the precondition is not a default state (the existence of an object or location), and not the result of a character action, ALP:Make-Consistent-State recognizes it as inconsistent. ALP:Make-Consistent-State is then used to make the state consistent.

ALP:Make-Consistent-State uses author-level planning to find an action that a knight can do which would result in the knight being in the woods. When it finds a suitable action it adds it to the story:

```
Grunfeld wanted to be near the dragon.  Grun-
feld moved to the dragon.  Grunfeld was near
the dragon.  Grunfeld fought with the dragon in
the woods.  The dragon was destroyed but Grun-
feld was hurt.
```

The inconsistent state has now been explained by making it the result of a character action. Grunfeld being near the dragon is no longer puzzling. It is the direct result of Grunfeld's desire to be near the dragon, and his subsequent move in that direction.

But interestingly enough, the new explanation is itself inconsistent. Although Grunfeld's goal of being near the dragon explains his move towards the dragon, it lacks motivation. This inconsistency is detected by ALP:Check-Consistent-Goal. ALP:Make-Consistent-Supergoal corrects the problem by making the inconsistent goal a step in a larger plan:

```
Grunfeld wanted to kill the dragon.  Grunfeld
wanted to be near the dragon.  Grunfeld moved
to the dragon.  Grunfeld was near the dragon.
Grunfeld fought with the dragon in the woods.
The dragon was destroyed but Grunfeld was hurt.
```

However, the new goal is still inconsistent! Grunfeld's goal to kill the dragon is neither a role goal for a knight nor motivated by a change in the world. So ALP:Make-Consistent-Supergoal is used again, making the inconsistent goal a subgoal of a larger plan:

```
Grunfeld wanted to impress the King.  Grunfeld
wanted to kill the dragon.  Grunfeld wanted to
be near the dragon.  Grunfeld moved to the
dragon.  Grunfeld was near the dragon.  Grun-
feld fought with the dragon in the woods.  The
dragon was destroyed but Grunfeld was hurt.
```

Now (finally) the scene is consistent. Impressing the king is a role goal for knights and so needs no further explanation. As this example has illustrated, correcting the inconsistencies in a story scene may require several steps, and each correction may introduce inconsistencies of its own, which must also be corrected.

6.5.3 ALP:Make-Consistent-Colocation

MINSTREL's second author-level plan for making a state consistent is used when ALP:Make-Consistent-State fails, that is, when MINSTREL cannot recall or invent an act that intends the inconsistent state. ALP:Make-Consistent-Colocation guesses that a state may occur because all the elements of the state come together in a location. In other words, ALP:Make-Consistent-Colocation explains states of the world as simply "happy coincidences."

For example, in telling *Richard and Lancelot*, MINSTREL creates the following story scene (see ALP:Make-Consistent-Motivating-State):

Lancelot loved Andrea. Because Lancelot loved Andrea, Lancelot wanted to be the love of Andrea. But he could not because Andrea loved Frederick. Lancelot hated Frederick... Lancelot wanted to kill Frederick.

This scene is inconsistent because it lacks an explanation of why Lancelot loves Andrea. What's more, ALP:Make-Consistent-State fails to make the scene consistent, because MINSTREL knows of no action that results in one person loving another. So ALP:Make-Consistent-Colocation is applied. ALP:Make-Consistent-Colocation suggests that Lancelot may love Andrea simply because the two came together at some point:

One day, a lady of the court named Andrea wanted to have some berries. Andrea wanted to be near the woods. Andrea moved to the woods. Andrea was at the woods. Andrea had some berries because Andrea picked some berries. *Lancelot's horse moved Lancelot to the woods. This unexpectedly caused him to be near Andrea. Because Lancelot was near Andrea, Lancelot loved Andrea.*

ALP:Make-Consistent-Colocation works for two reasons. First, humans understand that people and the world are sometimes mysterious. The thought process of people and the causal processes of the world are complicated and often unfathomable. It *does* sometimes seem that people fall in love with each other simply because they happen to meet. Second, readers strive to make sense of what they read. A reader encountering a scene such as:

```
Lancelot met Andrea.  They fell in love.
```

will use his considerable knowledge of people and the world to construct explanations for these happenings. So in some cases, the author need not provide an explanation; the reader will invent one of his or her own.

There are, however, two difficulties with ALP:Make-Consistent-Colocation. The first is that a story filled with such happy coincidences would strain the reader's credulity. The second is that there are many states that *aren't* explainable by colocation, for example:

```
Lancelot   met   Andrea.    They   both   turned   into
spiders.
```

Consequently, it is best to use ALP:Make-Consistent-Colocation only when other, better explanations cannot be found. For this reason, ALP:Make-Consistent-Colocation is a low-priority plan that is attempted only when ALP:Make-Consistent-State fails.

6.6   Emotional Inconsistencies

The final class of story inconsistencies that MINSTREL detects and corrects are emotional inconsistencies. Just as readers expect story characters to be rational, goal-seeking actors, they also expect story characters to have appropriate emotional reactions to events in their lives. Characters should be happy when they succeed and unhappy when they fail.

6.6.1   The Tone Plus Goal Situation Model of Emotions

MINSTREL uses a "tone plus goal situation" model of emotions based upon models developed in Dyer (1983, 1987) and Oatley and Johnson-Laird (1987). There are two fundamental theoretical claims made by tone plus goal situation models of emotion.

The first claim is that emotions are caused by goal resolutions, that is, the failure or success of a goal. The term "resolution" is used rather broadly here, because emotions are often caused by the *anticipated* resolution of a goal. We feel happy not only when we succeed at some goal, but also when something happens that suggests we will succeed.

In the case of self-goals, the relationship between goal resolutions and the resulting emotions is specific: goal successes cause euphoric emotions and goal failures cause dysphoric emotions. That is to say, we feel happy when we succeed and sad when we fail. Further, the strength of emotion is related to the importance and difficulty of the goal resolved. Although both are goal successes, the birth of a first child is cause for more celebration than finding a lost comb. Emotional reactions to the goal resolutions of other people are more problematic. We may feel happy, sad, or indifferent, depending upon our relationship to that other person.

The second theoretical claim of the tone plus goal situation model is that all emotions can be represented as a basic tone (happiness, sadness, anxiety, anger and disgust in Oatley and Johnson-Laird (1987); positive and negative in Dyer (1987) and MINSTREL) coupled with an abstract goal situation. Consider, for example, the emotion "feeling grateful." When we say we are feeling grateful, we mean that we are happy towards someone because they have helped us in some way. In the tone plus goal situation model, this is represented as a positive (happy) basic tone caused by having a goal achieved by a third party. The claim of the tone plus goal situation model is that *all* emotions can be represented this way. Figure 6.10 shows a lexicon of emotions and their tone plus goal situation representations based on a similar lexicon in Dyer (1987).

MINSTREL's tone and goal situation model is based primarily on Dyer (1987). Each emotion as represented as a state schema with the following slots:

TYPE: The type slot of state schemas which represent emotions is set to &AFFECT. &AFFECT is a symbol which acts only to identify the representation of emotions; it has no other meanings.

VALUE: The value slot contains &POS or &NEG to identify the basic tone of the emotion.

OBJECT: The character who is feeling the emotion.

Emotion	Character	Tone	Toward	Goal Situation
happy	x	pos		G(x) achieved
sad	x	neg		G(x) thwarted
grateful	x	pos	y	G(x) achieved by y
angry-at	x	pos	y	G(x) thwarted by y
scared	x	neg	y	G(x) thwarted by y, G(x) a health goal
proud	x	pos	y	G(y) achieved by x
guilty	x	neg	y	G(x) thwarted by y
gloating	x	pos		G(y) thwarted
envious	x	neg		G(y) achieved
felicitating	x	pos		G(y) achieved
condoling	x	neg		G(y) thwarted.

Figure 6.10 Sample Lexicon of Emotions

TO: The character the emotion is directed at, if any.

SCALE: The strength of the emotion, either &STRONG, &NOR-MAL, or &WEAK.

State schemas which represent emotions may also have named links to other schemas:

&G-SITU: This link is a pointer to the goal situation which caused this emotion.

&MOTIVATES: Like any state, an emotion can be motivation for a goal, that is, being angry at a character might be motivation for having the goal to harm them. The &MOTIVATES link of an emotion points to any goals the emotion has motivated.

&SUPERSEDES: An emotion can supersede another emotion.

Figure 6.11 shows how MINSTREL represents the situation "Andrea was grateful when Lancelot killed the dragon." Andrea's grateful emotion is captured as a state schema with a &G-SITU pointer to the representation of "Lancelot killed the dragon." Note that the representation includes Andrea's unmentioned goal of wanting the dragon to be killed.

The following sections show how MINSTREL uses the two fundamental features of the tone plus goal situation model to detect and correct emotional inconsistencies in the stories it tells.

6.6.2 Maintaining Emotional Consistency

MINSTREL's primary concern with emotions is to maintain the emotional consistency of the story characters, that is, assure that they have the proper emotional reactions to events. To do this requires (1) detecting when a character should feel an emotion, and (2) building the proper schema-based representation for the emotion.[9] The tone plus goal situation model of emotions has several features which make these tasks easy to achieve.

First, the relationship between goal resolutions and emotions provides a method to detect when characters should feel emotions. Whenever a goal is resolved, MINSTREL knows that the character who held the goal should feel either euphoric (if the goal was successful) or dysphoric (if the goal was unsuccessful). For example, if Richard thwarts Lancelot's goal of possessing the

---

[9] In addition, MINSTREL must (1) make judgments about which emotions should be included in the story, that is, the author may choose to express only strong emotions, and (2) decide how to express emotions in language.

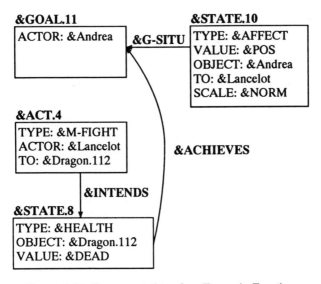

Figure 6.11   Representation of an Example Emotion

sword Excalibur by stealing it, then Richard should feel happy (because his goal to thwart Lancelot succeeded) and Lancelot should feel unhappy (because his goal failed).

Second, once the goal resolution has been found, creating the appropriate emotion is simple because the emotion is already implicitly represented in the goal resolution:

1. The resolution of the goal (success or failure) defines the basic tone (positive or negative).
2. The goal, it's resolution, and related schemas are the "goal situation" part of the representation of the emotion.
3. The character feeling the emotion is the actor of the resolved goal.
4. The character toward whom the emotion should be directed is the actor who caused the goal resolution.

These four elements can be combined to create the schema-based representation of the proper emotion. In the foregoing case of Richard and Lancelot, the emotion for Lancelot consists of a basic tone, negative, which is determined by the goal resolution (a failure), the causative goal situation (Lancelot's goal thwarted by Richard), and the character the emotion is directed towards (Richard, because he was the actor who caused the goal failure). Combined into a state schema, this is the representation for "Lancelot was angry at Richard."

Maintaining emotional story consistency is thus a matter of (1) detecting goal resolutions, and (2) building representations for the emotions caused by the goal resolutions using the information already present in the goal situation. The author-level plan which implements these tasks is called ALP:Check-Affects. (The problem of third-person reactions to goal resolutions is more difficult and is discussed later.)

6.6.3 ALP:Check-Affects

The purpose of ALP:Check-Affects is to look at every goal resolution in a story (including goal resolutions of secondary characters and monsters) and determine whether the actor of the goal has an emotional reaction to the goal resolution. If he does not, then a state schema representing his reaction is created and added to the story. ALP:Check-Affects is shown in Figure 6.12.

ALP:Check-Affects proceeds in three steps. First it creates the state schema that represents the emotional reaction to the goal resolution, filling in the

Name: ALP:Check-Affects
Goal Type: &Check-Consistency
Object: *AL-OBJ*
Test: Is *AL-OBJ* a resolved goal schema that lacks an emotional reaction?
Body:
1. Create the state schema:
   a. Make a new, uninstantiated state schema.
   b. Set the Type feature to &Affect.
   c. Set the Object feature to the actor of the resolved goal.
   d. Connect the new state schema to the resolved goal by a &g-situ link. (The &g-situ link points from an affect to the goal situation that caused the emotion.)
2. Determine the strength of the emotion:
   a. If *AL-OBJ* is an important goal (&P-HEALTH, &C-HEALTH, or &A-LOVE), then the strength of the emotion is &STRONG.
   b. Otherwise, the strength is &NORMAL.
   c. Set the Scale feature of the new state schema to the selected strength.
3. Determine the character the emotion is directed towards:
   a. If *AL-OBJ* was achieved or thwarted by an intentional action, then the emotion is directed towards the actor of the action.
   b. If *AL-OBJ* was achieved or thwarted by an unintentional action, then the emotion is directed towards the actor of the action, but the strength of the emotion is &WEAK.
   c. Set the To feature of the state schema to the selected character.

Figure 6.12 ALP:Check-Affects

character who is feeling the emotion, and the link to the goal resolution. Then it determines the strength of the emotion, and finally, the character towards whom the emotion is directed (if any).

ALP:Check-Affects uses knowledge about the relative importance of character goals to determine how strong the emotional reaction should be. Currently, MINSTREL uses a fixed scale of goal importance in which three goals, &P-HEALTH, &C-HEALTH and &A-LOVE are important enough to warrant a strong emotional reaction. These are the goals to, respectively, protect one's health, save one's life and achieve love. A more sophisticated approach would be to model goal priorities for each character (by using, for instance, goal trees [Carbonell, 1981]) and use this information to determine the strength of emotional reactions. Currently, however, MINSTREL uses the fixed scale of goal importance outlined above.

The strength of emotion is also affected by how the goal was resolved. The third step of ALP:Check-Affects determines which character the emotion should be directed at by looking at how the goal was achieved or thwarted. If the goal is achieved or thwarted unintentionally, the strength of the goal is reduced to &WEAK. If Richard accidently breaks Lancelot's magic sword, Lancelot may still be angry at Richard, but that anger will be less than if Richard had broken the sword intentionally.

An interesting aspect of ALP:Check-Affects is that it also maintains emotional consistency for *anticipated* goal resolutions. To understand how this happens, it is necessary to describe how MINSTREL represents an anticipated goal resolution.

In MINSTREL, anticipated events are represented as predictive beliefs. For example, when Princess Andrea sees a dragon moving toward her, she has the predictive belief that the dragon will eat her, thwarting her goal of protecting her health (Figure 6.13). Andrea's belief (&Belief.13) has two parts: the evidence, which is the dragon moving towards her, and the event that she predicts, the dragon eating her.

What happens when the scene represented in Figure 6.13 appears in a story? The mental-event portion of Andrea's belief contains a goal resolution (Andrea's thwarted &P-HEALTH goal). This triggers ALP:Check-Affects, which builds an emotion based on this goal resolution. Because there is nothing in ALP:Check-Affects to detect goal resolutions which are part of beliefs, it treats Andrea's anticipated goal resolution just as if it had actually occurred. The emotion ALP:Check-Affects creates is shown in Figure 6.14.

The emotion ALP:Check-Affects creates is "Andrea was very scared of the dragon." ALP:Check-Affects acts as if the anticipated goal resolution had actu-

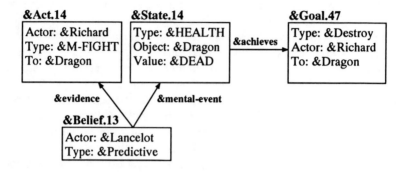

Lancelot sees Richard fighting a dragon and
believe that Richard will kill the dragon.

Figure 6.13 Representation of Anticipated Goal Resolution

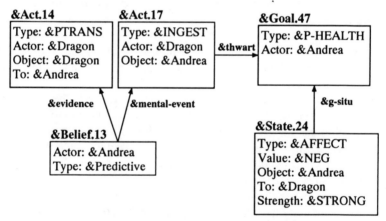

Andrea saw a dragon moving towards her and
believed that she would be eaten. Andrea was
very scared of the dragon.

Figure 6.14 Anticipated Goal Resolution and Emotion

ally occurred, creating the emotion that Andrea would feel[10] if she were eaten.
This behavior captures our intuitive understanding of how people react to anticipated outcomes: they react as if the event anticipated had occurred. This phe-

---

[10] At least momentarily.

nomenon is an important part of daydreaming (Mueller, 1989), and probably serves to reduce the effect of strong emotions by habituation.

Thus ALP:Check-Affects not only maintains the proper reactions to resolved goals, it also maintains the proper reactions to anticipated goal resolutions.

6.6.4 Third Person Emotions

To this point, our discussion of emotional consistency in MINSTREL has focused on the reactions of characters to the resolution of their personal goals. This task is relatively straightforward because the basic tone of the emotion is determined by whether the goal was achieved or thwarted. The same cannot be said, however, about third person reactions to goal resolutions. When Lancelot achieves a goal, the emotional reaction of Andrea depends upon her emotional relationship to Lancelot. To illustrate this point, consider the following story fragments:

> Andrea {loved, admired, was grateful to} Lancelot. When Andrea heard that Lancelot lost an important joust with Richard, she felt sad.

> Andrea {hated, was angry at, was envious of} Lancelot. When Andrea heard that Lancelot lost an important joust with Richard, she felt happy.

> Although Andrea had heard of Lancelot, she didn't know him. When Andrea heard that Lancelot lost an important joust with Richard, she was neither upset nor happy.

Andrea's reaction to Lancelot's goal failure is determined by her emotional relationship with Lancelot. If she has a positive relationship with Lancelot, then she shares empathically in his emotions. If she has a negative relationship with Lancelot, then she feels the opposite of his emotions. And if Andrea and Lancelot have no relationship, or a neutral one, then Andrea feels nothing in response to Lancelot's goal resolutions.

What is most interesting about this theory is that the emotional reaction of a third person to a goal resolution depends on the emotions he is feeling toward the actor of the goal. This is all the more apparent when we realize that character relationships like "love" can be viewed as long-lasting emotions. Thus emotions beget emotions in kind. If someone we view positively succeeds at something, we feel happy for him. If someone causes him to fail, we are angry at that person ("The enemy of my friend is my enemy"). This cycle of emotions begetting emotions serves to reinforce emotional relationships by making positive relationships more positive and negative relationships more negative.

Name:	ALP:Check-Affects-Others
Type:	&Check-Consistency
Object:	*AL-OBJ*
Test:	1. Is *AL-OBJ* a resolved goal schema? Does the actor of *AL-OBJ* have a &STRONG emotional reaction to *AL-OBJ*?
Body:	1. For each third-person character in the story, look through the story to see if there exists any emotional relations between the character and the actor of the goal *AL-OBJ*.
	2. If a positive relationship exists, then create a normal strength emotional reaction to this goal resolution equivalent to the reaction of the actor of *AL-OBJ*.
	3. If a negative relationship exists, then create a normal strength emotional reaction to this goal resolution opposite to the reaction of the actor of *AL-OBJ*.

Figure 6.15 ALP:Check-Affects-Others

MINSTREL's author-level plan which captures this knowledge is called ALP:Check-Affects-Others.[11]

6.6.5   ALP:Check-Affects-Others

The purpose of ALP:Check-Affects-Others is to look at each goal resolution in a story and determine whether any third party characters in the story should have a reaction to the goal resolution. As with ALP:Check-Affects, if an emotion is missing it is created. ALP:Check-Affects-Others is shown in Figure 6.15.

ALP:Check-Affects-Others adds one feature to the model of third-person emotional reactions. In ALP:Check-Affects-Others, third persons have empathic emotional reactions only to strong emotions. The idea here is that emotions felt empathically should be weakened in proportion to the strength of the empathy. Since MINSTREL has only one level of empathy, it arbitrarily reduces the strength of empathic emotions one level. A more detailed and robust model might have several levels of empathy (acquaintance, friend, comrade, love) and corresponding effects on empathic emotions.

---

[11] Although described here in some detail, ALP:Check-Affects-Others was never implemented.

7 | Annotated Trace

7.1 Introduction

This chapter contains an annotated trace of MINSTREL as it tells the story *The Mistaken Knight*:

The Mistaken Knight

It was the spring of 1089, and a knight named Lancelot returned to Camelot from else-where. Lancelot was hot tempered. Once, Lancelot lost a joust. Because he was hot tem-pered, Lancelot wanted to destroy his sword. Lancelot struck his sword. His sword was destroyed.

One day, a lady of the court named Andrea wanted to have some berries. Andrea wanted to be near the woods. Andrea moved to the woods. Andrea was at the woods. Andrea had some berries because Andrea picked some berries. At the same time, Lancelot's horse moved Lancelot to the woods. This unexpectedly caused him to be near Andrea. Because Lancelot was near Andrea, Lancelot loved Andrea. Some time later, Lancelot's horse moved Lancelot to the woods unintentionally, again causing him to be near Andrea. Lancelot knew that Andrea kissed with a knight named Frederick because Lancelot saw that Andrea kissed with Frederick. Lancelot believed that Andrea loved Frederick. Lancelot loved Andrea. Because Lancelot loved Andrea, Lancelot wanted to be the love of Andrea. But he could not because Andrea loved Frederick. Lancelot hated Frederick. Andrea loved Frederick. Because Lancelot was hot tempered, Lancelot wanted to kill Frederick. Lancelot wanted to be near Frederick. Lancelot moved to Frederick. Lancelot was near Frederick. Lancelot fought with Frederick. Frederick was dead.

Andrea wanted to be near Frederick. Andrea moved to Frederick. Andrea was near Frederick. Andrea told Lancelot that Andrea was siblings with Frederick. Lancelot believed that Andrea was siblings with Frederick. Lancelot wanted to take back that he wanted to kill Frederick. But he could not because Frederick was dead. Lancelot hated himself. Lancelot became a hermit. Frederick was buried in the woods. Andrea became a nun.

MORAL: Done in haste is done forever.

The purpose of this trace is to show how MINSTREL's various author-level goals come together to create a finished story. This trace will also identify places in the storytelling process where MINSTREL's mechanisms fail. This is important not only in order to present this research honestly, but also to identify areas of future research.

In telling *The Mistaken Knight*, MINSTREL attempts 654 author-level goals and achieves 182. The trace of this processing is nearly 200 single-spaced pages; far too long to include here in its entirety. In order to reduce the length of this trace and highlight the interesting sections, the trace has been edited. This has consisted primarily of removing failed author-level goals, failed attempts at creativity, and repetitive portions of the trace.

7.2   The Mistaken Knight

```
USER>  (goal nil
           :actor (human nil
                      :type &knight)
           :new-state (state nil)
           &thwarted-by (state nil))

&GOAL.216

USER>  (goal nil
           :actor &MINSTREL
           :type &tell-story
           :object &goal.216
           :priority 100)

&GOAL.217
```

The trace begins with the human user of the program suggesting a topic. The user specifies (using list notation for a goal schema) a character goal (&GOAL.216). The actor of the goal is a knight, and the goal is thwarted. What the goal is, how it is achieved, and how it is thwarted are left unspecified. The user then creates an author-level goal for MINSTREL to tell a story about the suggested character-level goal (&GOAL.217).

The purpose of this is to simulate "exterior input" to MINSTREL. Since MINSTREL does not have the life experience that human authors have, it has no source of inputs to suggest stories or jog its memory. To simulate this, the user provides a scene or fragment of a scene to act as an initial "seed" for the story-telling process. This scene won't necessarily be incorporated as part of the final story. Rather, as we see shortly, it serves as an index for recall. The shape and content of the final story will depend not so much upon this scene fragment as upon what the fragment recalls.

The next step is to begin MINSTREL's storytelling process on the initial storytelling goal:

User	USER>(alp:run &goal.217)
	+++
Goal	Author goal &TELL-STORY applied to &GOAL.216.
Plan	TRAM Cycle: &GOAL.217.
Recall	Executing TRAM-AL-STD-PROBLEM-SOLVING. Recalling: NIL. ...TRAM failed. Executing TRAM-GENERALIZED-AL-PLANS. Recalling: (&GOAL.171 &GOAL.170). ...TRAM succeeds: (&GOAL.223 &GOAL.222). TRAM Cycle succeeds: (&GOAL.223 &GOAL.222).
Plans	Found plans: ALP:TELL-STORY ALP:FIND-STORY-THEME.
Plan	Trying author plan ALP:TELL-STORY.
Execution	Trying author plan ALP:FIND-STORY-THEME. Recalling using &GOAL.216 as an index: (&GOAL.143). Created theme &PAT.8 from &PAT-HASTY. Creating author goal &TELL-STORY applied to &PAT.8. Author-level planning succeeded. +++

alp:run is the top-level function used to begin the author-level problem solving process. alp:run repeatedly takes the highest priority goal off the author-level goal agenda and applies author-level problem solving. In this case, the only goal on the author-level goal agenda is the initial goal to tell a story about the user suggestion, so that is popped off the goal agenda and solved. This process repeats until the goal agenda is empty.

The trace of each cycle of the problem solving process is bordered by two lines of pluses. The first line inside the borders (labeled *Goal*) identifies the highest priority goal on the goal agenda. This is the goal MINSTREL is trying to achieve during the current problem solving cycle:

Author goal &TELL-STORY applied to &GOAL.216.

This line identifies the type of the goal (&TELL-STORY) and the part of the story it is applied to (&GOAL.216). In this case, the goal is the one just created by the user—to tell a story about the user suggestion.

The next portion of the trace (labeled *Plan Recall*) shows MINSTREL using the current goal to recall possible plans. As discussed in Chapter 3, this involves creativity at the author level. The trace of the creative recall process begins with the line "TRAM Cycle..." and ends with the line "TRAM Cycle succeeds...":

```
TRAM Cycle: &GOAL.217.
    Executing TRAM-AL-STANDARD-PROBLEM-SOLVING.
        Recalling:    NIL.
    ...TRAM failed.
    Executing TRAM-GENERALIZED-AL-PLANS.
        Recalling:    (&GOAL.171 &GOAL.170).
    ...TRAM succeeds: (&GOAL.223 &GOAL.222).
TRAM Cycle succeeds: (&GOAL.223 &GOAL.222).
Found plans: ALP:TELL-STORY ALP:FIND-STORY-THEME.
```

At the author-level, MINSTREL has available two creativity heuristics, TRAM-AL-STANDARD-PROBLEM-SOLVING, and TRAM-GENERALIZED-AL-PLANS. These are used to recall similar past problem solving situations and the plans that were used on those occasions. TRAM-AL-STANDARD-PROBLEM-SOLVING recalls very similar past problem solving situations while TRAM-GENERALIZED-AL-PLANS recalls more generalized past situations. (See Chapter 3 for a detailed explanation of these TRAMS.) If either heuristic succeeds, the plans associated with the past goals are applied to the current goal.

In this case, TRAM-GENERALIZED-AL-PLANS succeeds in recalling two past problem solving situations (&GOAL.223 and &GOAL.222). The plans from these past situations (ALP:TELL-STORY and ALP:FIND-STORY-THEME) will now be applied to the current goal.

The creative recall process at the author level is similar for all of MINSTREL's author-level goals. TRAM-AL-STANDARD-PROBLEM-SOLVING is applied first, and if that heuristic fails to recall any similar past goals, then TRAM-GENERALIZED-AL-PLANS is applied. Although the past problem solving situations recalled vary depending upon the author-level goal being solved, the process and the trace of this process remains largely the same. For this reason, the trace of author-level creative recall has been suppressed for the remainder of this chapter, leaving only the line that indicates which plans were found.

The final step in the author-level problem solving process (labeled *Plan Exe-*

cution) is to apply the plans found until one is found that achieves the current goal:

```
Trying author plan ALP:TELL-STORY.
Trying author plan ALP:FIND-STORY-THEME.
  Recalling using &GOAL.216 as an index:
    (&GOAL.143).
  Created theme &PAT.8 from &PAT-HASTY.
  Creating author goal #{TELL-STORY} applied
    to &PAT.8.
Author-level planning succeeded.
```

Lines beginning "Trying..." indicate that MINSTREL is applying the named plan to the current goal situation. Plans are tried in the order they are recalled[12] until one succeeds.

In this case, ALP:TELL-STORY is applied without success. Generally, MINSTREL's author-level plans do not produce any trace when they fail. However, plan failure should be apparent to the reader because another plan is immediately applied. Had the original plan succeeded, author-level planning would have succeeded and there would be no need to try another plan.

Next, ALP:FIND-STORY-THEME is tried. This author-level plan uses the story fragment suggested by the user as an index for recall. If the story fragment recalls a past story, MINSTREL uses the theme from the past story as the theme for a new story.

In this case, the story fragment suggested by the user ("A knight has a thwarted goal"—represented as &GOAL.216) recalls a similar scene from memory (&GOAL.143), as shown by the line:

```
  Recalling using &GOAL.216 as an index: (&GOAL.143).
```

&GOAL.143 represents a small part of a story based on the theme "Done in haste is done forever":

Thwarted Love[13]

Once upon a time, Arthur loved Jennifer and wished that she loved him also. Jennifer said that she didn't love Arthur. Arthur was upset. Arthur wanted to kill himself. Arthur hit himself with his sword. When Jennifer saw that Arthur was dying, she told Arthur that she did love him. Arthur regretted that he had killed himself. Arthur died.

---

[12] Plans can also be executed in random order.

[13] This story has a conceptual representation in MINSTREL's episodic memory. The English version shown here was prepared by the author.

The original user suggestion ("A knight has a thwarted goal") recalls the first event in this story, in which Arthur has his goal of being Jennifer's love thwarted. In turn, this story recalls the theme PAT:Hasty-Impulse-Regretted. ALP:FIND-STORY-THEME makes a copy of this abstract theme (&PAT.8) to use as the theme for a new story, and merges the original user suggestion with the recalled story to create the beginnings of a new story:

The Mistaken Knight 1

Once upon a time, a knight named Lancelot loved a princess named Andrea but his love was thwarted. This caused him to make a hasty decision.

Later, he discovered that his hasty decision was incorrect. He wished he could take back what he did. But he couldn't.

MINSTREL's internal representation of the story theme is shown in Figure 7.1. For the reader's convenience, the actors are shown as &Lancelot and &Andrea; in fact they are represented by schemas named &HUMAN.138 and &HUMAN.137. As this figure shows, the initial story skeleton consists of a largely uninstantiated theme.

After creating this new story skeleton based on the user's suggestion and the recalled theme, MINSTREL creates an author-level goal to tell a story based on this skeleton:

```
Creating author goal &TELL-STORY applied
    to &PAT.8.
Author-level planning succeeded.
+++++++++++++++++++++++++++++++++++++++++++++++++++++++++
```

This concludes this cycle of the author-level problem solving process. However, ALP:FIND-STORY-THEME created another author-level goal (to tell a story about &PAT.8), so the author-level goal queue is no longer empty. The top priority goal in the queue is popped and problem solving repeats on this new goal:

```
+++++++++++++++++++++++++++++++++++++++++++++++++++++++++
Author-level goal &TELL-STORY applied to &PAT.8.
Found plans: ALP:TELL-STORY ALP:FIND-STORY-THEME.
Trying author plan ALP:TELL-STORY.
    Creating goal &INSTANTIATE (&BELIEF.28).
    Creating goal &CONNECT (&PAT.8).
    Creating goal &INSTANTIATE (&BELIEF.29).
```

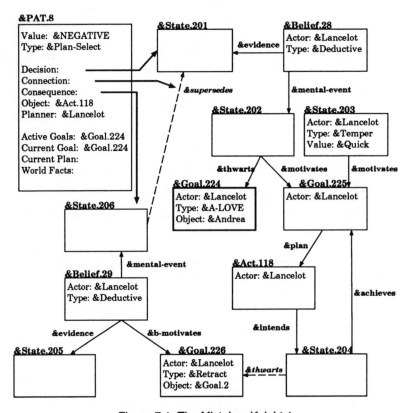

Figure 7.1 The Mistaken Knight 1

```
Creating goal &CHECK-STORY-SUSPENSE (&STORY.1).
Creating goal &CHECK-STORY-TRAGEDY (&STORY.1).
Creating goal &CHECK-STORY-FORESHADOWING...
Creating goal &CHECK-STORY-CHARACTERIZATION...
Creating goal &ADD-STORY-INTROS (&STORY.1).
Creating goal &ADD-DENOUEMENTS (&STORY.1).
Creating goal &GENERATE-ENGLISH (&STORY.1).
Author-level planning succeeded.
+++++++++++++++++++++++++++++++++++++++++++++++++++++++++++
```

This goal is the same type as the previous goal (&TELL-STORY) but applied to a new type of object: a story theme (&PAT.8). The same author-level plans are applied, but this time the first plan (ALP:TELL-STORY) succeeds. ALP:TELL-STORY tells a story about a particular story theme by creating goals to:

1. Instantiate the parts of the theme (&BELIEF.28, &BELIEF.29).
2. Achieve dramatic writing goals (suspense, tragedy, etc.).
3. Achieve presentation goals (add story introductions, denouements, etc.).

These goals are prioritized in the order listed and are added to the author-level goal queue.

7.3 Instantiating the Theme

ALP:TELL-STORY creates three goals to instantiate the story theme. Two of these goals are to instantiate the Decision (&BELIEF.28) and Consequence (&BELIEF.29) of the theme, and the third is to create the Connection between the Decision and the Consequence.

As shown in Figure 7.1, the Decision portion of the theme "Done in haste is done forever" involves an actor who makes a hasty decision based on a mistaken belief. MINSTREL's first goal in instantiating the theme is to instantiate this belief. The first plan tried to achieve this goal is ALP:GENERAL-INSTANTIATE:

```
++++++++++++++++++++++++++++++++++++++++++++++++++++
Author-level goal &INSTANTIATE (&BELIEF.28).
Found plans: ALP:DONT-INSTANTIATE...
Trying author plan ALP:DONT-INSTANTIATE.
Trying author plan ALP:GENERAL-INSTANTIATE.
TRAM Cycle: &BELIEF.28.
    Executing TRAM-STANDARD-PROBLEM-SOLVING.
        Recalling:    NIL.
    ...TRAM failed.
    Executing TRAM-GENERALIZE-ACTOR.
        Recalling:    (&FIGHT2 &KNIGHT-FIGHT).
        Recalling:    NIL.
    [TRAM Recursion: &BELIEF.59.]
        [...]
    ...TRAM failed.
    Executing TRAM-LIMITED-RECALL.
        Recalling:    NIL.
    [TRAM Recursion: &BELIEF.73.]
        Executing TRAM-STANDARD-PROBLEM-SOLVING.
            Recalling: NIL.
        ...TRAM failed.
    ...TRAM failed.
TRAM Cycle fails.
```

```
ALP:GENERAL-INSTANTIATE failed.
```

ALP:GENERAL-INSTANTIATE uses the object being instantiated as an index for creative recall. If something similar can be recalled or invented, the recalled object can be used to fill in (instantiate) the object from the current story. In this case, despite applying a number of TRAMs, MINSTREL can neither recall nor invent a suitable belief. So ALP:GENERAL-INSTANTIATE fails. (For the remainder of this chapter, when creativity fails the detailed trace of the creative cycle is deleted to save space.)

```
Trying author plan ALP:INSTANTIATE-AFFECT.
Trying author plan ALP:INSTANTIATE-DECEPTION.
Trying author plan ALP:INSTANTIATE-REVENGE.
Trying author plan ALP:INSTANTIATE-BELIEF.
  Creating goal &INSTANTIATE applied to
    &STATE.202, &STATE.201.
  Creating goal &CHECK-NEW-SCENE applied to
    &BELIEF.28, &STATE.202, &GOAL.225, &ACT.118,
    &STATE.204, &HUMAN.138, &GOAL.224, &STATE.207,
    &HUMAN.137, &STATE.203, &STATE.201.
Author-level planning succeeded.
++++++++++++++++++++++++++++++++++++++++++++++++++++
```

A number of other plans are recalled but do not apply to the current goal. These plans are ALP:INSTANTIATE-AFFECT, etc. Each of these plans is a specialized author-level plan for instantiating a particular kind of story situation (i.e., a deception, revenge, or affect). In this case, none of these plans apply because the particular story scene being instantiated (&BELIEF.28) is not a deception, revenge, or affect.

Eventually, ALP:INSTANTIATE-BELIEF is applied and succeeds. ALP:INSTANTIATE-BELIEF is an author-level plan specifically for instantiating beliefs. Like ALP:TELL-STORY, ALP:INSTANTIATE-BELIEF instantiates a belief by creating author-level goals to instantiate the parts of the belief. The parts of a belief are the mental-event (the thing believed) and the evidence for the belief. In this case, the mental-event is represented by &STATE.202 and the evidence by &STATE.201, so ALP:INSTANTIATE-BELIEF creates author-level goals to instantiate these two schemas. The remainder of the goals created by ALP:INSTANTIATE-BELIEF are author-level goals to check the consistency of all of the schemas which make up &BELIEF.28. This ensures that after the belief is instantiated it will be checked for consistency.

The new author-level goal to instantiate the mental-event of the belief is now the top goal in the author-level goal queue:

```
+++++++++++++++++++++++++++++++++++++++++++++++++++++++++
Author-level goal &INSTANTIATE (&STATE.202).
Found plans: ALP:DONT-INSTANTIATE...
Trying author plan ALP:DONT-INSTANTIATE.
[...]
Trying author plan
   ALP:INSTANTIATE-THWARTING-STATE.
   Copying achieving state into thwarting state.
   Replacing &HUMAN.138 with &HUMAN.274.
   Instantiated object is &STATE.202.

   (STATE &STATE.202
      :TYPE        &AFFECT
      :VALUE       &LOVE
      :OBJECT      &HUMAN.137
      :TO          &HUMAN.274
      &MOTIVATES <==>   (&GOAL.225)
      &EVENT-IN  <==>   (&BELIEF.28)
      &THWARTS   <==>   (&GOAL.224))

Author-level planning succeeded.
+++++++++++++++++++++++++++++++++++++++++++++++++++++++++
```

&STATE.202 is the mental-event portion of &BELIEF.28 (see Figure 7.1). &STATE.202 represents the state of the world that thwarts Lancelot's initial goal to have Andrea love him. After a number of plans fail to instantiate this schema, a plan called ALP:INSTANTIATE-THWARTING-STATE succeeds.

ALP:INSTANTIATE-THWARTING-STATE is an author-level plan that instantiates a state which thwarts a goal by "reversing" the goal. That is, MINSTREL knows that many goals can be thwarted by states that are the reverse of the state which would achieve the goal. For example, possession of an object is thwarted if someone else possesses the object, the goal to be somewhere is thwarted by being somewhere else, and so on. ALP:INSTANTIATE-THWARTING-STATE instantiates a thwarting state by making a copy of the state that would achieve the goal and then "reversing" the copy.

The first step of ALP:INSTANTIATE-THWARTING-STATE is to determine what state would achieve the thwarted goal. In this case the thwarted goal is "Lancelot wants to achieve love with Andrea" and MINSTREL determines that the state "Andrea loves Lancelot" would achieve this goal. Once this is determined, the achieving state is copied into the thwarting state (i.e., &STATE.202, the state being instantiated).

The next step is to turn the achieving state into a thwarting state by "reversing" the state. ALP:INSTANTIATE-THWARTING-STATE knows that if a state is directed toward something, then the state can be reversed by directing it toward a different but similar object. In this case, the achieving state represents Andrea's love directed toward Lancelot, so the achieving state can be turned into a thwarting state by replacing Lancelot with another character. MINSTREL invents a new, uninstantiated character (&HUMAN.274) and replaces Lancelot with this new character, creating the new thwarting state "Andrea loves some other person."

The end result of this plan is that the state that thwarts Lancelot's goal to achieve love with Andrea has been instantiated as "Andrea loves some other person." This is shown in Figure 7.2.

The thwarting state was the mental-event portion of the belief which makes up the Decision portion of PAT:Hasty-Impulse-Regretted. The next author-level goal is to instantiate the evidence for this belief:

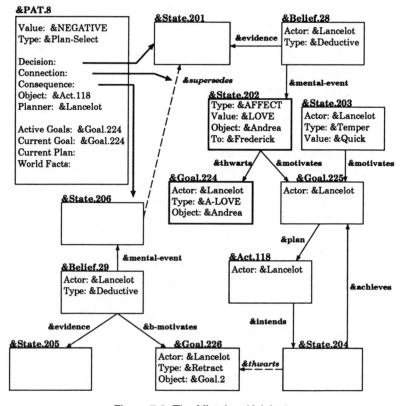

Figure 7.2 The Mistaken Knight 2

```
+++++++++++++++++++++++++++++++++++++++++++++++++++++++++++++
Author-level goal &INSTANTIATE (&STATE.201).
Found plans: ALP:DONT-INSTANTIATE
             ALP:GENERAL-INSTANTIATE...
Trying author plan ALP:DONT-INSTANTIATE.
[...]
Trying author plan ALP:INSTANTIATE-EVIDENCE.
Initial motivation chain is &GOAL.483.

(GOAL &GOAL.483
   :ACTOR          &HUMAN.137
   &MOTIVATED-BY <==> (STATE &STATE.694
                      :TYPE    &AFFECT
                      :VALUE   &LOVE
                      :OBJECT  &HUMAN.137
                      :TO      &HUMAN.274))
```

To instantiate the evidence for the belief, MINSTREL applies
ALP:INSTANTIATE-EVIDENCE. ALP:INSTANTIATE-EVIDENCE is an
author-level plan that invents evidence for a belief by generating a motivational
chain from the belief to some action that can be observed. For example, to generate evidence for the belief "The dragon is going to eat Andrea"
ALP:INSTANTIATE-EVIDENCE might reason that "The dragon is going to eat
Andrea" could motivate the goal "Andrea wants to be away from the dragon,"
which in turn could be achieved by the action "Andrea runs away." From this it
can be deduced that seeing Andrea running away from the dragon is reasonable
evidence to support the belief "The dragon is going to eat Andrea":

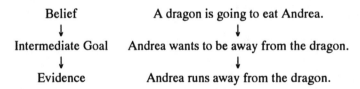

	Belief	A dragon is going to eat Andrea.
	↓	↓
	Intermediate Goal	Andrea wants to be away from the dragon.
	↓	↓
	Evidence	Andrea runs away from the dragon.

Thus ALP:INSTANTIATE-EVIDENCE invents reasonable evidence by
starting at the belief and building a motivational chain until it reaches an action
or result that can be observed.
    In this case, ALP:INSTANTIATE-EVIDENCE is trying to create a moti-
vation chain beginning with "Andrea loves a person." To do this,
ALP:INSTANTIATE-EVIDENCE tries to find a goal this state could motivate,
and then an act that would achieve that goal. If this is possible the act (not the
intermediate goal) can serve as evidence for the belief.
    The first step is to find an intermediate goal that could be motivated by the

belief. To find a goal that "Andrea loves a person" could motivate, ALP:INSTANTIATE-EVIDENCE begins by building an uninstantiated goal motivated by this state. In the trace, this is shown as &GOAL.483:

```
Initial motivation chain is &GOAL.483.

(GOAL &GOAL.483
    :ACTOR           &HUMAN.137
    &MOTIVATED-BY <==> (STATE &STATE.694
                        :TYPE    &AFFECT
                        :VALUE   &LOVE
                        :OBJECT  &HUMAN.137
                        :TO      &HUMAN.274))
```

&GOAL.483 is a goal belonging to &HUMAN.137 (Andrea). The goal is motivated by Andrea's love for &HUMAN.274, but is otherwise uninstantiated. To instantiate this goal, ALP:INSTANTIATE-EVIDENCE uses this goal as an index to imaginative memory. If a similar past goal (i.e., a goal motivated by love) can be recalled or invented, then the past goal can be used to instantiate this intermediate goal in the motivation chain. The next portion of the trace shows the recall process:

```
Imaginative recall using index &GOAL.483:
 TRAM Cycle: &GOAL.483.
    Executing TRAM-STANDARD-PROBLEM-SOLVING.
      Recalling:    (&AR-AFFECTION).
    ...TRAM succeeds: (&AR-AFFECTION).
 TRAM Cycle succeeds: (&AR-AFFECTION).
Reminding is &AR-AFFECTION.

(GOAL &AR-AFFECTION
    :TYPE            &A-LOVE
    :ACTOR           &HUMAN.361
    :OBJECT          &HUMAN.362
    :NEW-STATE       &STATE.698
    &MOTIVATED-BY <==>    (&STATE.699)
    &PLAN <==>           (&ACT.212)
    &ACHIEVED-BY <==>    (&STATE.698))
```

&GOAL.483 recalls &AR-AFFECTION from MINSTREL's episodic memory. &AR-AFFECTION represents the following scene:

Motivated by her love of a knight, a princess wanted to achieve the love of a knight, so she kissed him.

Recall succeeded in finding a past goal motivated by love. This reminding can now be used to instantiate the goal motivated by "Andrea loves a person" as "Andrea wants the person to love her," that is, loving someone motivates you to want them to love you back.

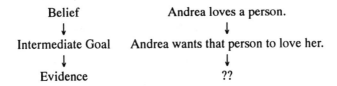

The next step in building the motivational chain is to find an action that can achieve the intermediate goal. Fortuitously, the reminding found for the previous step already contains a plan. In the reminding, the plan for achieving the goal of having someone love you is to kiss that person. This same action can be used in the current motivation chain:

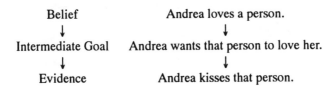

The trace shows the representation of evidence after this instantiation:

```
Evidence after instantiation:

(STATE 'STATE.201
   :OBJECT   '&HUMAN.137
   :TO   '&HUMAN.274
   :TYPE   &KISS
   &EVIDENCE-FOR   '&BELIEF.28 )
```

Author-level planning succeeded.
++

This yields the scene:

```
Lancelot knew that Andrea kissed a knight named Fred-
erick because Lancelot saw that Andrea kissed Freder-
ick.  Lancelot believed that Andrea loved Frederick.
```

Figure 7.3 shows the state of theme after this instantiation.

There are two interesting things about this instantiation. The first is that the intermediate goal does not appear as part of the story. It exists only temporarily during the execution of ALP:INSTANTIATE-EVIDENCE. In the final story there is no mention of Andrea's goal to have Frederick love her, or how that goal connects the evidence and the belief. Instead, the reader is presented with the belief and the evidence and reconstructs the motivation chain himself.

The second item of note is that instantiating the evidence has the side-effect of instantiating the character that Andrea loves. In the reminding, the princess

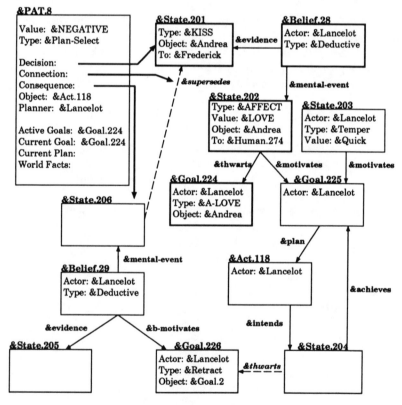

Figure 7.3 The Mistaken Knight 3

loves a knight, and this information is copied over into the person Andrea loves in the story, resulting in &HUMAN.274 being instantiated as a knight:

```
(HUMAN 'HUMAN.274
 :SEX    'MALE
 :NAME   'FREDERICK
 :TYPE   &KNIGHT)
```

(The name "Frederick" is chosen randomly from a list of male character names.)

MINSTREL has now instantiated the belief that makes up the first part of the plot of *The Mistaken Knight*. The story so far is:

The Mistaken Knight 3

Once upon a time, a knight named Lancelot loved a princess named Andrea. Lancelot saw Andrea kiss a knight named Frederick. Lancelot believed that Andrea loved Frederick. Lancelot wanted to be the love of Andrea. But he could not because Andrea loved Frederick. This caused him to make a hasty decision.

Later, he discovered that his hasty decision was incorrect. He wished he could take back what he did. But he couldn't.

With the completion of the goals to instantiate the belief that makes up the first half of the theme, the lower priority goals to check the consistency of the instantiated belief now rise to the top of the author-level goal queue. These goals are achieved by ALP:CHECK-NEW-SCENE:

```
+++++++++++++++++++++++++++++++++++++++++++++++++++++++++++++++
Author-level goal &CHECK-NEW-SCENE (&BELIEF.28).
Found plans: ALP:CHECK-NEW-SCENE
Trying author plan ALP:CHECK-NEW-SCENE.
  Creating goal &CHECK-CONSISTENCY.
  Creating goal &CHECK-AFFECTS.
  Creating goal &CHECK-SCENE-FOR-SUSPENSE.
  Creating goal &CHECK-SCENE-FOR-TRAGEDY.
  Creating goal &CHECK-SCENE-FOR-FORESHADOWING.
Author-level planning succeeded.
+++++++++++++++++++++++++++++++++++++++++++++++++++++++++++++++
```

In each case, ALP:CHECK-NEW-SCENE checks the consistency of a story scene by creating a number of subgoals. These goals include a goal to instantiate the scene (if it has not already been instantiated), to check the (causal) consistency of the scene, to check the affect consistency of the scene, and to check various author-level dramatic writing goals.

This plan is applied to &BELIEF.28 and all its parts. These include the mental-event and the evidence as well all other schemas attached to the evidence and mental-event via causal links (see Figure 7.3: &GOAL.225, &STATE.203, &GOAL.224, &ACT.118, and &STATE.204).

One of these attached schemas is &GOAL.225. &GOAL.225 is Lancelot's goal that is motivated by the state "Andrea loves Frederick" (which in turn thwarts Lancelot's goal of achieving love with Andrea). The top priority goal created by ALP:CHECK-NEW-SCENE (above) is to instantiate &GOAL.225, so this goal is popped off the priority queue and solved:

```
+++++++++++++++++++++++++++++++++++++++++++++++++++++++++++++++
Author-level goal &INSTANTIATE (&GOAL.225).
Found plans: ALP:DONT-INSTANTIATE...
Trying author plan ALP:DONT-INSTANTIATE.
[...]
Trying author plan ALP:INSTANTIATE-UNTHWARTS.

To unthwart a goal, kill the actor
who is thwarting the goal: &HUMAN.274.

(GOAL &GOAL.225
    :TYPE           &DESTROY
    :ACTOR          &HUMAN.138
    :OBJECT         &HUMAN.274
    :NEW-STATE      &STATE.204
    &PLAN <==>          (&ACT.118)
    &ACHIEVED-BY <==>   (&STATE.204)
    &SUBGOAL-OF <==>    (&GOAL.224)
    &MOTIVATED-BY <==>  (&STATE.202 &STATE.203))

Author-level planning succeeded.
+++++++++++++++++++++++++++++++++++++++++++++++++++++++++++++++
```

ALP:INSTANTIATE-UNTHWARTS is applied. This is an author-level plan that knows how to unthwart a goal. It applies in this case because the goal being instantiated (&GOAL.225) is motivated by a state (&STATE.202) that thwarts a goal (&GOAL.224). If something occurs that thwarts an actor's goal, then that can motivate the actor to unthwart his goal. ALP:INSTANTIATE-

UNTHWARTS will try to instantiate &GOAL.225 as something that will unthwart &GOAL.224.

One way to unthwart a goal is to kill the person who is thwarting the goal, that is, to unthwart Lancelot's goal to have Andrea love him, kill the actor who is thwarting the goal: Frederick. So ALP:INSTANTIATE-UNTHWARTS instantiates &GOAL.225 as a goal to &DESTROY Frederick, which (by means of some as yet uninstantiated action) results in Frederick being dead. The state of the theme after this instantiation is shown in Figure 7.4.

MINSTREL's attention now turns to the act that achieves Lancelot's newly instantiated goal to destroy Frederick. The top goal on the author goal queue is to check this scene. Achieving this puts the goal to instantiate this scene next on the queue:

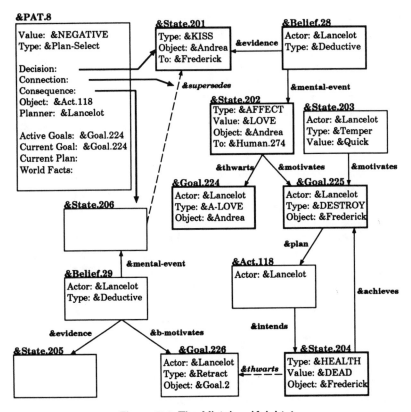

Figure 7.4 The Mistaken Knight 4

```
++++++++++++++++++++++++++++++++++++++++++++++++++++++++++++
Author-level goal &INSTANTIATE (&ACT.118).
Found plans: ALP:DONT-INSTANTIATE...
Trying author plan ALP:DONT-INSTANTIATE.
Trying author plan ALP:GENERAL-INSTANTIATE.
Imaginative recall using index: &ACT.118.
 TRAM Cycle: &ACT.118.
   [...]
   Executing TRAM-GENERALIZE-ACTOR.
      Recalling: NIL.
      [TRAM Recursion: &ACT.280.]
        [...]
        Executing TRAM-SIMILAR-OUTCOMES.
        ...TRAM succeeds: (&ACT.375).
TRAM Cycle succeeds: (&ACT.376).

Found a reminding for instantiation: &ACT.376.

(ACT &ACT.376
    :AT        &SETTING.42
    :TO        &HUMAN.706
    :ACTOR     &HUMAN.705
    :TYPE      &M-FIGHT
    &PLAN-OF  <==>   (&GOAL.756)
    &INTENDS  <==>   (&STATE.1083))
```

&ACT.118 is instantiated by the author-level plan ALP:GENERAL-INSTANTIATE. This plan tries to instantiate a schema by using it as an index to creative recall. If a similar schema can be recalled or invented, the recalled schema can be used to fill out the current schema.

In this case, MINSTREL is not initially able to recall any schemas similar to &ACT.118, because MINSTREL does not know anything about knights killing knights. But by using two creativity heuristics (TRAM-GENERALIZE-ACTOR and TRAM-SIMILAR-OUTCOMES), MINSTREL is able to invent a similar schema, and use this to fill in &ACT.118.

TRAM-GENERALIZE-ACTOR is a creativity heuristic which generalizes the actor of the recall index. If recall succeeds with the new, modified index, then TRAM-GENERALIZE-ACTOR adapts any recalled episodes back to the original problem by replacing the generalized actor with the original actor.

In this example, TRAM-GENERALIZE-ACTOR replaces Lancelot (the actor of &ACT.118) with a monster. (By noticing that both knights and monsters engage in violent acts, TRAM-GENERALIZE-ACTOR reasons that they are similar enough to interchange in many situations.) This replacement is also done on all the schemas connected to &ACT.118, and the new recall index is: "A monster wanted to destroy Frederick and did something to achieve that goal." However, this also fails to recall anything, because MINSTREL does not have any episodes in memory in which a monster kills a knight.

Creativity is again applied. A new TRAM is used, TRAM-SIMILAR-OUTCOMES. TRAM-SIMILAR-OUTCOMES is a creativity heuristic that modifies the intended result of an action. TRAM-SIMILAR-OUTCOMES replaces the intended result of an action with a similar but different outcome.

In this example, TRAM-SIMILAR-OUTCOMES reasons that being wounded is similar to being killed, and replaces the death of Frederick with the wounding of Frederick. The twice-modified index is "A monster wanted to kill a knight and did something which wounded the knight." This index succeeds in recalling a scene from MINSTREL's episodic memory:

> One day, a dragon wanted to kill a knight so it attacked the knight. The dragon wounded the knight but was killed by the knight.

In this scene, a dragon tries to kill a knight and only wounds him, matching the modified index. The next step is for TRAM-SIMILAR-OUTCOMES and TRAM-GENERALIZE-ACTOR to adapt this recalled episode to the original problem.

TRAM-SIMILAR-OUTCOMES begins the adaptation by changing the wounding in the recalled episode back to death:

> One day, a dragon wanted to kill a knight so it attacked the knight in the woods. The dragon killed the knight but was killed by the knight.

Next TRAM-GENERALIZE-ACTOR replaces the generalized actor (a monster) with the actor from the original index for recall:

> One day, Lancelot wanted to kill a knight so he attacked the knight in the woods. Lancelot killed the knight but was killed by the knight.

Now the adapted recalled episode can be used to fill in &ACT.118 as an attack on Frederick by Lancelot. The extraneous events in the recalled episode (namely Lancelot also dying in the attack) can be ignored because they do not match events already existing in the story. The instantiated result of &ACT.118 is:

After instantiation: &ACT.118.

```
(ACT &ACT.118
   :AT        &SETTING.43
   :TO        &HUMAN.274
   :TYPE      &M-FIGHT
   :ACTOR     &HUMAN.138
   &PLAN-OF  <==>  (&GOAL.225)
   &INTENDS  <==>  (&STATE.204))
```

This represents "Lancelot fought Frederick in the woods." By using creative recall, ALP:GENERAL-INSTANTIATE is able to invent an act by which Lancelot can kill Frederick, even though prior to telling this story MINSTREL knew nothing about knights fighting knights. Figure 7.5 shows the state of the theme after this instantiation.

The next theme-related goal MINSTREL achieves is the goal to connect the two halves of the theme. This is achieved by a simple author-level plan that creates the causal links connecting the two halves of the theme. In this theme, there are two connections: a supersedes link between the mental-events of the two beliefs and a thwarts link between &STATE.204 and &GOAL.226 (see Figure 7.5).

```
+++++++++++++++++++++++++++++++++++++++++++++++++++++++++++++++
Author-level goal &CONNECT (&PAT.8).
Found plans: ALP:CONNECT
Trying author plan ALP:CONNECT.
  Creating &SUPERSEDES link between &STATE.206
     and &STATE.201.
  Creating &THWARTS link between &STATE.204
     and &GOAL.226.
Author-level planning succeeded.
+++++++++++++++++++++++++++++++++++++++++++++++++++++++++++++++
```

Next, MINSTREL begins instantiating the Consequence portion of the story theme. As it happens, the Consequence portion of this theme is also a belief. The Consequence is a new belief that will supersede the Decision belief ("Andrea loves Frederick") while remaining consistent with the evidence for the earlier belief ("Andrea kisses Frederick").

The new belief (&STATE.206) is instantiated by ALP:INSTANTIATE-

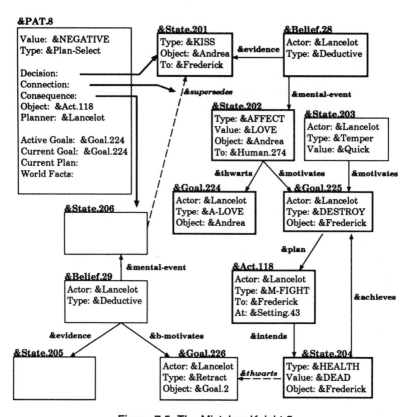

Figure 7.5 The Mistaken Knight 5

SUPERSEDING-BELIEF, This author-level plan instantiates a state that supersedes a belief by finding an alternate explanation for the evidence of the belief:

```
++++++++++++++++++++++++++++++++++++++++++++++++++++++++++++
Author-level goal &INSTANTIATE (&STATE.206).
Found plans: ALP:DONT-INSTANTIATE...
[...]
Trying author plan ALP:INSTANTIATE-
          SUPERSEDING-BELIEF.

Try to recall an alternate explanation for the
   following state:

(STATE &STATE.4403
   :TYPE      &KISS
```

```
:TO        &HUMAN.274
:OBJECT    &HUMAN.137
&ACHIEVES <==>  (&GOAL.2787))
```

In this case, Lancelot's belief that Andrea loves Frederick is based on the evidence that Andrea kissed Frederick, so ALP:INSTANTIATE-SUPERSEDING-BELIEF tries to find an alternate explanation for this evidence, that is, it tries to find another reason why Andrea might have kissed Frederick.

To do this, ALP:INSTANTIATE-SUPERSEDING-BELIEF creates a copy of the evidence of the first belief ("Andrea kisses Frederick") and uses this as an index for creative recall, in the hopes of finding an alternate goal that the evidence might achieve:

```
Imaginative recall using index: &STATE.4403.
 TRAM Cycle: &STATE.4403.
   [...]
   Executing TRAM-GENERALIZE-OBJECT.
     Recalling:    (&SHOW-AFFECTION).
   ...TRAM succeeds: (&STATE.4423).
 TRAM Cycle succeeds: (&STATE.4423).
```

Reminding is:

```
(STATE &STATE.4423
  :TYPE   &RELATION
  :VALUE  &SIBLINGS
  :OBJECT &HUMAN.1878
  :TO     &HUMAN.1876
  &ACHIEVES (&GOAL.2807))
```

Alternate explanation is:

```
(GOAL &GOAL.2807
   :TYPE        &A-AFFECTION
   :OBJECT      &HUMAN.1878
   :TO          &HUMAN.1876
   &ACHIEVED-BY <==>   (&STATE.4423))
```

Using a creativity heuristic called TRAM-GENERALIZE-OBJECT, imaginative memory invents an episode in which two people kiss to show their affection for one another because they are siblings. The recalled episode is then used to instantiate the mental-event of Lancelot's new belief as Andrea and Frederick being siblings:

```
Instantiated state:

(STATE &STATE.206
  :TYPE    &RELATION
  :VALUE   &SIBLINGS
  :OBJECT  &HUMAN.137
  :TO  &HUMAN.274)
```

Thus the alternate belief is "Andrea and Frederick are brother and sister" and this motivates them to show affection for one another, which they achieve by kissing one another. Note that as with the previous belief, the intermediate steps in this reasoning chain (in particular the goal to express affection) are not expressed in the story. The instantiated theme to this point is shown in Figure 7.6.

The next author-level goal is to instantiate additional evidence for the new belief. The first plan tried to achieve this goal is ALP:INSTANTIATE-EVIDENCE, the author-level plan used to create the evidence for Lancelot's original belief that Andrea and Frederick were lovers:

```
++++++++++++++++++++++++++++++++++++++++++++++++++++++++++++++
Author-level goal &INSTANTIATE (&STATE.205).
Found plans: ALP:DONT-INSTANTIATE...
[...]
Trying author plan ALP:INSTANTIATE-EVIDENCE.

Initial motivation chain is &GOAL.2999.

(GOAL &GOAL.2999
   :NEW-STATE      &STATE.4826
   :ACTOR          &HUMAN.137
   &PLAN <==>          (&ACT.2166)
   &ACHIEVED-BY <==>   (&STATE.4826)
   &MOTIVATED-BY <==>  (&STATE.4825))
```

As with the instantiation of the evidence for Lancelot's first belief, ALP:INSTANTIATE-EVIDENCE is applied to find a motivation chain from the belief ("Andrea and Frederick are siblings") to some evidence to support that belief. This time, however, ALP:INSTANTIATE-EVIDENCE fails, because

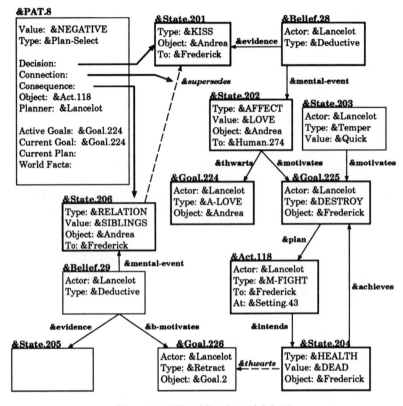

Figure 7.6 The Mistaken Knight 6

MINSTREL cannot invent any goals that might be motivated by Andrea and Frederick being siblings:

```
Imaginative recall with index: &GOAL.2999
  TRAM Cycle: &GOAL.2999.
    Executing TRAM-STANDARD-PROBLEM-SOLVING.
      Recalling:    NIL.
    ...TRAM failed.
    [...]
  TRAM Cycle fails.

Reminding is NIL.
Instantiation fails: cannot invent motivation chain.
```

Problem solving falls through to a second plan, ALP:INSTANTIATE-

EVIDENCE-2. This plan says that another form of evidence for a belief is being told that the belief is true by an authority. ALP:INSTANTIATE-EVIDENCE-2 creates evidence for a belief by having the believer be told the belief is true by an authority figure. The authority can be a character involved in the belief or an authority figure such as a king.

In this case, ALP:INSTANTIATE-EVIDENCE-2 instantiates the evidence of the belief as Lancelot knowing that Andrea and Frederick are siblings after being told so by Andrea. Since Andrea is one of the characters involved in the belief, being told it is true by her carries weight.

```
Trying author plan ALP:INSTANTIATE-EVIDENCE-2.
Making the evidence a &know event: &STATE.205.

(STATE &STATE.205
    :TYPE           &KNOW
    :TO             &HUMAN.138
    :OBJECT         &STATE.4915
    &EVIDENCE-FOR <==>   (&BELIEF.29))


(STATE &STATE.4915
    :TYPE   &RELATION
    :VALUE  &SIBLINGS
    :OBJECT &HUMAN.137
    :TO   &HUMAN.274)


Making the evidence the intended result of
    an MTRANS: &ACT.2218.

(ACT &ACT.2218
    :TYPE       &MTRANS
    :ACTOR      &HUMAN.137
    :TO         &HUMAN.138
    :OBJECT     &STATE.4915
    &INTENDS <==>   (&STATE.205))
```

&ACT.2218 represents Andrea transferring information ("Andrea and Frederick are siblings") to Lancelot. The result of this instantiation on the theme is shown in Figure 7.7.

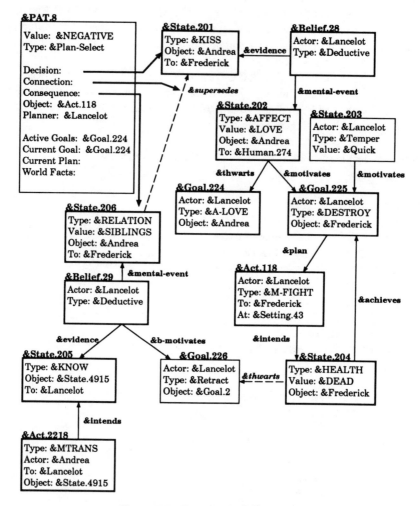

Figure 7.7 The Mistaken Knight 7

At this point, instantiation of the theme is complete. MINSTREL has created the elements of the story that illustrate the story theme:

The Mistaken Knight 7

Once upon a time, a knight named Lancelot loved a princess named Andrea. Lancelot saw Andrea kiss a knight named Frederick. Lancelot believed that Andrea loved Frederick. Lancelot

wanted to be the love of Andrea. But he could
not because Andrea loved Frederick. Lancelot
decided to kill Frederick. Lancelot fought
with Frederick. Frederick was dead.

   Later, Andrea told Lancelot that Andrea and
Frederick were siblings. Lancelot believed
that Andrea and Frederick were siblings.
Lancelot wanted to take back that he wanted to
kill Frederick. But he could not because Frederick was dead.

Now that the theme has been instantiated, MINSTREL's remaining tasks are to
(1) check the story for consistency, (2) apply dramatic writing techniques, and
(3) present the story to the reader.

7.4 Consistency Checking

As author-level goals are achieved and the story modified, MINSTREL must
continuously check the story for inconsistencies, and try to correct any that it
finds. Depending on the priorities of the pending author-level goals, this checking may occur immediately after a scene is created or later, after more important
intervening goals have been addressed. The previous section illustrated how
several consistency goals contributed to the development of the theme. In this
section we look at some additional consistency goals and how they are achieved.

   The first problem MINSTREL's consistency goals detect in the story so far
concerns &GOAL.224:

```
(GOAL &GOAL.224
  :TYPE   &A-LOVE
  :ACTOR  &HUMAN.138
  :OBJECT &HUMAN.137)
```

This represents Lancelot's goal to achieve love with Andrea. MINSTREL finds
this goal inconsistent because there is no explanation in the story so far of why
Lancelot has this goal. There is no state that motivates this goal, and this is not
one of the goals that MINSTREL expects knights to normally have (i.e., it is not
a "role goal"). So this goal is inconsistent, and MINSTREL creates an author-
level goal to make the goal consistent:

```
++++++++++++++++++++++++++++++++++++++++++++++++++++++++++++
Author-level goal &MAKE-GOAL-CONSISTENT (&GOAL.224).
Found plans: ALP:MAKE-CONSISTENT-SUPERGOAL
             ALP:MAKE-CONSISTENT-OBJECT
```

```
                 ALP:MAKE-CONSISTENT-MOTIVATING-STATE
[...]
Trying author plan ALP:MAKE-CONSISTENT-
MOTIVATING-STATE.

Recalling a motivating state:
  TRAM Cycle: &GOAL.1183.
    Executing TRAM-STANDARD-PROBLEM-SOLVING.
      Recalling:    (&AR-AFFECTION).
      ...TRAM succeeds: (&AR-AFFECTION).
  TRAM Cycle succeeds: (&AR-AFFECTION).

A motivating state for &GOAL.224 was created:

(STATE &STATE.1470
  :TYPE   &AFFECT
  :VALUE  &LOVE
  :OBJECT &HUMAN.138
  :TO   &HUMAN.137
  &MOTIVATES   &GOAL.224)

Creating author goal &CHECK-NEW-SCENE
  (&STATE.1470).
Author-level planning succeeded.
++++++++++++++++++++++++++++++++++++++++++++++++++++++++++++++++
```

MINSTREL knows three plans for making a goal consistent. The first two fail, but the third succeeds. The third plan is ALP:MAKE-CONSISTENT-MOTIVATING-STATE, which tries to make a goal consistent by inventing a state of the world that could motivate the goal. To do this, ALP:MAKE-CONSISTENT-MOTIVATING-STATE uses the goal as an index for creative recall. If a past scene can be recalled with a similar goal, the motivation for that past scene can be adapted to the current scene.

In this case, recall succeeds in finding a similar past scene: &AR-AFFECTION. In &AR-AFFECTION, a princess is motivated to achieve love with a knight because she loves the knight. This is adapted to the current scene by substituting Lancelot for the princess and Andrea for the knight, resulting in a motivating state for Lancelot's goal to achieve love with Andrea: "Lancelot loves Andrea."

(It is interesting to note at this point that &AR-AFFECTION was recalled and used earlier to instantiate a different part of the story, &STATE.201. &STATE.201 represents the kiss between Andrea and Frederick. MINSTREL's creative recall enables it to make maximum use of what it knows, adapting the same knowledge for a variety of tasks and situations.)

MINSTREL has now created a motivating state for Lancelot's goal of achieving love with Andrea. But his new motivating state is itself inconsistent, because there is no explanation for why Lancelot loves Andrea. The author-level goal created at the end of ALP:MAKE-CONSISTENT-MOTIVATING-STATE detects this inconsistency and creates an author-level goal to make the motivating state consistent:

```
++++++++++++++++++++++++++++++++++++++++++++++++++++++++++++
Author-level goal &CHECK-CONSISTENCY (&STATE.1470).
Found plans: ALP:MAKE-CONSISTENT-STATE
   ALP:MAKE-CONSISTENT-STATE-COLOCATION
   ALP:MAKE-CONSISTENT-P-HEALTH
Trying author plan ALP:CHECK-CONSISTENCY-
   STATE.
Trying author plan ALP:MAKE-CONSISTENT-
   STATE-COLOCATION.
```

MINSTREL knows several plans for making a state consistent. The primary plan, ALP:MAKE-CONSISTENT-STATE, uses creative recall to try to find an act that could have the inconsistent state as a result. In this case, ALP:MAKE-CONSISTENT-STATE tries to find an action that could result in Lancelot loving Andrea. This fails, because MINSTREL can neither recall nor invent an action which has the intended result of causing someone to be in love.

The next plan tried is ALP:MAKE-CONSISTENT-STATE-COLOCATION. ALP:MAKE-CONSISTENT-STATE-COLOCATION tries to explain a state by making it an unintended result of the principal elements of the state being colocated. For example, if ALP:MAKE-CONSISTENT-STATE-COLOCATION were used to explain the state "Lancelot possesses a magic sword," it would try to invent a scene where Lancelot and the magic sword became unexpectedly colocated. In this case, ALP:MAKE-CONSISTENT-STATE-COLOCATION tries to invent a scene in which Lancelot and Andrea become unexpectedly colocated.

To do this, ALP:MAKE-CONSISTENT-STATE-COLOCATION uses creative recall to try to recall or invent a scene in which a knight unexpectedly becomes colocated with a princess:

```
Attempting to recall an unintentional colocation:
  TRAM Cycle: &ACT.673.
       Executing TRAM-STANDARD-PROBLEM-SOLVING.
          Recalling:     NIL.
       ...TRAM failed.
       Executing TRAM-CROSS-DOMAIN-REMINDING.
```

```
Recalling:     (&SPOT-DART).
...TRAM succeeds: (&ACT.690).
TRAM Cycle succeeds: (&ACT.690).
```

Created unintended colocation to explain state:

```
(ACT &ACT.673
  :TYPE   &PTRANS
  :ACTOR  &ANIMAL.5
  :OBJECT &HUMAN.138
  :TO &SETTING.215
  &UNINTENDED   '&STATE.1470
  &UNINTENDED   '&STATE.1800)
```

MINSTREL's episodic memory does not contain any scenes where a knight and a princess unexpectedly meet, so noncreative recall (using TRAM-STANDARD-PROBLEM-SOLVING) fails. However, a creativity heuristic called TRAM-CROSS-DOMAIN-REMINDING succeeds in inventing a suitable episode. TRAM-CROSS-DOMAIN-REMINDING is a creativity heuristic that tries to recall a parallel scene from a different domain and adapt it to the current domain. In this case, TRAM-CROSS-DOMAIN-REMINDING succeeds in recalling the following scene from the "modern" domain:

A Willful Dog

One day, a businessman named Tim was out walking his dog Spot. Suddenly, Spot darted through a hole in a hedge, dragging Tim with him. At first Tim was angry with Spot, but on the other side of the hedge he saw his long-lost friend Tom. What luck that Spot had darted through the hedge!

TRAM-CROSS-DOMAIN-REMINDING and ALP:MAKE-CONSISTENT-STATE-COLOCATION adapt this reminding to the King Arthur domain, creating a scene in which Lancelot's horse (represented by &ANIMAL.5) carries Lancelot to a location where he unexpectedly meets and falls in love with Andrea:

At the same time, Lancelot's horse moved Lancelot to the woods. This unexpectedly caused him to be near Andrea. Because Lancelot was near Andrea, Lancelot loved Andrea.

Note that MINSTREL has already determined that Lancelot loves Andrea, and is explaining here how they came to love one another. MINSTREL doesn't make every character that comes near another character fall in love. Indeed, MINSTREL doesn't have any knowledge at all about what makes characters fall in love. It is only by using ALP:MAKE-CONSISTENT-STATE-COLOCATION and creativity that MINSTREL is able to invent a reason for Lancelot and Andrea to fall in love.

After creating this scene, MINSTREL detects another inconsistency: What is Andrea doing in the woods where Lancelot unexpectedly meets her? This inconsistency is corrected by inventing a reason for Andrea to be in the woods. Several other inconsistencies are also corrected, and eventually, the explanation for why Lancelot wants Andrea to love him results in the following story scenes:

> One day, a lady of the court named Andrea wanted to have some berries. Andrea wanted to be near the woods. Andrea moved to the woods. Andrea was at the woods. Andrea had some berries because Andrea picked some berries. At the same time, Lancelot's horse moved Lancelot to the woods. This unexpectedly caused him to be near Andrea. Because Lancelot was near Andrea, Lancelot loved Andrea. Because Lancelot loved Andrea, Lancelot wanted to be the love of Andrea.

The schema representation for these scenes is shown in Figure 7.8.

This example illustrates two interesting features of MINSTREL. First, this example shows how storytelling is achieved by a large number of interacting author-level goals. Achieving one author-level goal can give rise to a number of new author-level goals, and adding one element to the story can require the addition of many more elements. This example started with the single author-level goal to make Lancelot's goal to achieve love with Andrea consistent, and ended only after the invention of a number of new story events. As this example illustrates, storytelling cannot be understood as a single, straightforward process, but rather as a complicated interaction between large numbers of competing goals.

Second, it is interesting to note that not all of what MINSTREL invents during storytelling will necessarily be expressed in the final story. The dotted box in Figure 7.8 encloses an explanation of where Lancelot was before he came to the woods and met Andrea. MINSTREL creates the events in the dotted box to improve the consistency of the story, but later decides not to express them when presenting the story to the reader in natural language. This illustrates another facet of a system involving competing goals. In a system with many goals, the goals must necessarily be semi-independent. Each goal cannot take into account

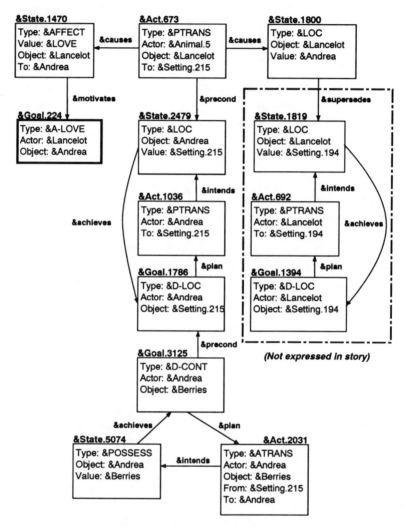

Figure 7.8 Illustration of Consistency Scenes

all the other goals. Therefore, goal conflicts will arise. One goal may make a decision only to be overruled later by another goal.

Before we look at author-level dramatic writing goals, we examine one other type of consistency goal. The previous example dealt with causal inconsistencies: problems in the way characters planned or in the way the world behaved. Another type of inconsistency is emotional inconsistency. Not only should characters plan properly, they should also have the proper emotional reactions to events in the story world.

During the processing of *The Mistaken Knight*, MINSTREL discovers an emotional inconsistency in &GOAL.224. &GOAL.224 is Lancelot's thwarted goal to achieve love with Andrea. Important thwarted goals should cause an emotional reaction in the actor of the goal. This inconsistency is detected by the author-level goal &CHECK-AFFECTS:

```
++++++++++++++++++++++++++++++++++++++++++++++++++++++++++++
Author-level goal &CHECK-AFFECTS (&GOAL.224).
Found plans: ALP:CHECK-AFFECT-THWARTED-GOAL
Trying author plan ALP:CHECK-AFFECT-THWARTED-GOAL.

Creating emotional reaction:

(STATE &STATE.1478
   :VALUE    &HATE
   :TO       &HUMAN.274
   :OBJECT   &HUMAN.138
   :TYPE     &AFFECT
   &TRIGGER &GOAL.224)

Author-level planning succeeded.
++++++++++++++++++++++++++++++++++++++++++++++++++++++++++++
```

ALP:CHECK-AFFECT-THWARTED-GOAL is an author-level plan which checks a thwarted goal to see if the actor of the goal had an emotional reaction. If he did not, ALP:CHECK-AFFECT-THWARTED-GOAL adds a negative emotional reaction directed toward the character who thwarted the goal. In this case, ALP:CHECK-AFFECT-THWARTED-GOAL creates the reaction "Lancelot hates Frederick."

Maintaining causal and emotional consistency during storytelling is important to creating a believable story. For a more detailed discussion of MINSTREL's goals and plans for maintaining story consistency, see Chapter 6.

7.5 Dramatic Writing Goals

After the story events which illustrate the theme have been created and checked for consistency, MINSTREL's next priority is to apply dramatic writing techniques to improve the literary quality of the story. In this story, MINSTREL is able to create foreshadowing and characterization; we'll examine how MINSTREL creates foreshadowing.

Foreshadowing is a literary technique in which story incidents introduce, repeat, give casual allusion to, or hint at later story incidents. The purpose of foreshadowing is to build a sense of inevitability in the later story events (De

Camp & De Camp, 1975). By foreshadowing important story elements, the author avoids having those elements appear contrived, and in addition, creates a sense of unity in the story.

MINSTREL's author-level plan for creating foreshadowing looks through the story theme for unique events and then checks to see if those events can be repeated elsewhere in the story. By repeating events, MINSTREL hopes to improve the unity of the story; by repeating *unique* events, MINSTREL hopes to make this repetition noticeable to the reader.

MINSTREL's author-level plan for foreshadowing begins with any element of theme and looks through *all* the theme-related story events for foreshadowing possibilities:

```
++++++++++++++++++++++++++++++++++++++++++++++++++++++++++++
Author-level goal &CHECK-STORY-FOR-FORESHADOWING
   applied to &BELIEF.28.
Found plans: ALP:CHECK-STORY-FOR-FORESHADOWING
Trying author plan ALP:CHECK-STORY-FOR-
   FORESHADOWING.


Checking possible candidates:
   Recalling &STATE.1800: NIL.
   Recalling &STATE.1470: NIL.
Candidates = (&STATE.1800 &STATE.1470).
```

The first step in ALP:CHECK-STORY-FOR-FORESHADOWING is to find possible candidates for foreshadowing. To do this ALP:CHECK-STORY-FOR-FORESHADOWING looks through the story events which illustrate the theme for unique combinations of states and acts. To determine whether or not a particular combination is unique, MINSTREL uses the combination as an index for recall.

If a particular combination of states and acts recalls something from episodic memory, then it is clearly not unique, because MINSTREL has encountered similar combinations before. On the other hand, if it recalls nothing, then it is unique in MINSTREL's experience. This is the same type of test that MINSTREL uses to determine whether a problem solution is creative (see Chapter 2), and indicates again how a properly organized episodic memory can be useful for determining the originality of an episode.

In this case, MINSTREL finds two combinations that do not recall similar past episodes: &STATE.1800 and &STATE.1470. Both states have to do with Lancelot's willful horse. &STATE.1470 represents Lancelot's willful horse unintentionally causing Lancelot to fall in love with Andrea; &STATE.1800 represents the related unintentional meeting of Lancelot and Andrea. MINSTREL's episodic memory does not contain any states similar to these two scenes (recall that this scene was invented using the TRAM-CROSS-DOMAIN-REMINDING creativity heuristic), so they are judged suitable for foreshadowing.

Once acceptable candidates for foreshadowing have been found, the next step is to see if these candidates can be inserted elsewhere in the story. This is achieved by looking through the story for states similar to the candidate states. In this case, that means looking for states representing two people being unexpectedly in the same location, or one person unexpectedly loving another person.

```
Insertions for &STATE.1800 are: (&STATE.6950).
New foreshadowing state is &STATE.17630.
New foreshadowing act is &ACT.9768.

Insertions for &STATE.1470 are NIL.
No foreshadowing created.

Author-level planning succeeded.
+++++++++++++++++++++++++++++++++++++++++++++++++++++++++++++++++
```

One match is found: &STATE.6950. This state represents Lancelot and Andrea being in the same location so that Lancelot can see Andrea kissing Frederick. &STATE.6950 was created by a combination of consistency goals which noticed that (1) Lancelot must see the evidence for his belief, that is, he must witness the kiss, and (2) Lancelot must be in the same location as the event in order to witness it. These consistency goals also created an explanation for how Lancelot comes to unexpectedly witness the kiss:

```
Some time later, Lancelot wanted to kill a
dragon.  Lancelot rode to the woods, causing
him to be near Andrea.  Lancelot knew that
Andrea kissed with a knight named Frederick
because Lancelot saw that Andrea kissed with
Frederick.
```

This explanation is created by finding a typical goal for a knight that would take him to the location where he should unexpectedly be. This is accomplished by the same consistency goals that invented the scenes in which Andrea goes to the woods to pick berries (so that she can unexpectedly be where Lancelot sees her and falls in love).

However, this explanation is about to be replaced by a new explanation. ALP:CHECK-STORY-FOR-FORESHADOWING has noticed that &STATE.6950 (which represents Lancelot unexpectedly meeting Andrea when he sees her kissing Frederick) matches &STATE.1800 (which represents Lancelot unexpectedly meeting Andrea when he falls in love with her). In order to create foreshadowing, ALP:CHECK-STORY-FOR-FORESHADOWING deletes the existing explanation for &STATE.6950 ("Lancelot was in the woods to kill a dragon") and replaces it with the same explanation used for the early scene ("Lancelot's willful horse took him to where Andrea was"). The result is that the early scene in which Andrea and Lancelot meet foreshadows the later scene in which Lancelot sees Andrea and Frederick kiss:

> One day, a lady of the court named Andrea wanted to have some berries. Andrea wanted to be near the woods. Andrea moved to the woods. Andrea was at the woods. Andrea had some berries because Andrea picked some berries. At the same time, Lancelot's horse moved Lancelot to the woods. This unexpectedly caused him to be near Andrea. Because Lancelot was near Andrea, Lancelot loved Andrea...
>
> Some time later, Lancelot's horse moved Lancelot to the woods unintentionally, again causing him to be near Andrea. Lancelot knew that Andrea kissed with a knight named Frederick because Lancelot saw that Andrea kissed with Frederick.

It is interesting to note that just as MINSTREL earlier created story scenes that were not expressed in the final version of the story, here MINSTREL creates story scenes only to discard them later in favor of different scenes. As these examples illustrate, the final story is not an accurate record of the storytelling process. Just as human authors revise and discard, so MINSTREL sometimes creates story scenes only to later discard, revise, or choose not to express them.

7.6 Presentation Goals

The final step in the storytelling process is presenting the story to the reader. This involves (1) creating any new scenes needed to improve the presentation of the story, such as character introductions and denouements, and (2) generating the story in language.

MINSTREL creates two types of story introductions. The first introduction scene establishes the location and time of the story. The second scene identifies the main character of the story. (For the type of theme-based stories MINSTREL tells, the main character is the character who makes the planning decision identified by the Decision portion of the theme.) In this story, the main character is Lancelot. Both introductory scenes are created by ALP:CREATE-STORY-INTROS:

```
+++++++++++++++++++++++++++++++++++++++++++++++++++++++++++++++
Author-level goal &ADD-STORY-INTROS (&STORY.1).
Found plans: ALP:CREATE-STORY-INTROS
Trying author plan ALP:CREATE-STORY-INTROS.

Creating establishing scene.
Year is 1089.

(STATE &STATE.24407
  :VALUE  &SPRING
  :OBJECT  '1089
  :TYPE  &DATE)

Creating introduction scene.
Location is &CAMELOT.
Main character is: &HUMAN.138.

(STATE &STATE.24406
  :VALUE  &CAMELOT
  :OBJECT  &HUMAN.138
  :TYPE  &LOC
  &SUPERSEDES &STATE.24405 )

Author-level planning succeeded.
+++++++++++++++++++++++++++++++++++++++++++++++++++++++++++++++
```

The first introductory scene is a state schema representing the current date, Spring of 1089. (The year is generated randomly in range of credible years for the King Arthur genre.) The second introductory scene is a state schema representing the main character's return to the current location from elsewhere. This serves both to establish the current location and introduce the main character. These scenes are later generated as the first sentence of the story:

```
              The Mistaken Knight

        It  was  the  spring  of  1089,  and  a  knight
    named  Lancelot  returned  to  Camelot  from  else-
    where...
```

Note that MINSTREL's language generation goals have combined the two state schemas into a single sentence to produce a more fluent introduction.

As well as creating introduction scenes, MINSTREL's presentation goals also create denouement scenes. Denouement scenes are used by MINSTREL to resolve character fates. By telling the reader briefly how the events of the story affected the characters in the story, MINSTREL provides the reader with a feeling of closure. MINSTREL creates denouement scenes only for characters that have unhappy fates. In *The Mistaken Knight*, that includes Lancelot, Andrea, and Frederick.

The first denouement created is for Andrea. Andrea is a tragic character because she suffers some important goal failures during the course of the story. For a tragic character of this sort, MINSTREL creates a denouement scene in which the tragedy motivates the character to change roles:

```
+++++++++++++++++++++++++++++++++++++++++++++++++++++++++++++++
Author-level goal &MAKE-DENOUEMENT (&HUMAN.137).
Found plans: ALP:BURIAL-DENOUEMENT...
Trying author plan ALP:BURIAL-DENOUEMENT.
Trying author plan ALP:TRAGIC-DENOUEMENT.

&HUMAN.137 is tragic because of &GOAL.2808.
&HUMAN.137 is currently a &PRINCESS.
Most different role from &PRINCESS is &HERMIT.
Created denouement scene:

(STATE &STATE.24494
  :VALUE   &HERMIT
  :TYPE    &ROLE-CHANGE
  :OBJECT  '&HUMAN.138 )

Author-level planning succeeded.
+++++++++++++++++++++++++++++++++++++++++++++++++++++++++++++++
```

ALP:TRAGIC-DENOUEMENT begins by checking to make sure that the character it is being applied to is in fact a tragic character. For Andrea, ALP:TRAGIC-DENOUEMENT finds a thwarted goal to express affection toward her brother (thwarted because Lancelot has killed her brother). This establishes Andrea as a tragic character.

The next step is to determine a suitable role change for Andrea. Currently Andrea is a princess, which has the features of being &SOCIABLE and &NON-VIOLENT. By comparing these features to the features of other roles, MINSTREL is able to determine that the most different role is &HERMIT, which has the features .&UNSOCIABLE and &NON-VIOLENT. ALP:TRAGIC-

DENOUEMENT then creates a state schema representing a role change for Andrea to a hermit and adds this to the story. This will later be generated as:

```
Andrea became a nun.
```

MINSTREL's natural language component generates female hermits as "nuns."
A similar process occurs for Lancelot and for Frederick, resulting in the scenes:

```
Lancelot became a hermit.
Frederick was buried in the woods.
```

After the story introductions and character denouements have been created, all that remains is to generate the story in English. This is accomplished by author-level goals that control the order in which the story scenes will be generated, and a phrasal generator, which does the actual translation of schemas to English. Rather than trace all of the author-level goals and phrasal generator calls involved in expressing *The Mistaken Knight* in English, we look here at a few representative examples.

ALP:GENERATE-BELIEF is an example of an author-level plan for generation. ALP:GENERATE-BELIEF generates the parts of a character belief in an order that emphasizes the argument structure of the belief:

```
+++++++++++++++++++++++++++++++++++++++++++++++++++++++++++++++
Author-level goal &GENERATE-ENGLISH (&BELIEF.28).
Found plans: ALP:GENERATE-BELIEF.
Trying author plan ALP:GENERATE-BELIEF.

Generating establishing scene from belief:

(ONE DAY *COMMA* A LADY OF THE COURT NAMED
ANDREA WANTED TO HAVE SOME BERRIES
*PERIOD* ANDREA WANTED TO BE NEAR THE
WOODS *PERIOD* ANDREA MOVED TO THE WOODS
*PERIOD* ANDREA WAS AT THE WOODS *PERIOD*
ANDREA HAD SOME BERRIES BECAUSE ANDREA
PICKED SOME BERRIES *PERIOD* AT THE SAME
TIME LANCELOT *POSSESSIVE* HORSE MOVED
LANCELOT TO THE WOODS *PERIOD* THIS
UNEXPECTEDLY CAUSED HIM TO BE NEAR ANDREA
*PERIOD* BECAUSE LANCELOT WAS NEAR ANDREA
*COMMA* LANCELOT LOVED ANDREA *PERIOD*)
```

ALP:GENERATE-BELIEF begins by generating the scenes need to establish the belief. These scenes represent the preconditions of the belief, and were created by consistency goals to explain why Lancelot wanted Andrea to love him (the goal that is thwarted by Lancelot's belief that Andrea loves Frederick). The trace shows the actual output from the RAP phrasal generator. Note that punctuation is represented with keywords such as "*COMMA*." These are later filtered into their proper form by a separate program.

```
Generating b-precond:

(SOME TIME LATER *COMMA* LANCELOT
 *POSSESSIVE* HORSE MOVED LANCELOT TO THE
 WOODS UNINTENTIONALLY *COMMA* AGAIN
 CAUSING HIM TO BE NEAR ANDREA *PERIOD*)
```

Next ALP:GENERATE-BELIEF generates the belief preconditions. These represent the preconditions for attaining the evidence of the belief. In this case, the evidence is "Andrea kisses Frederick," and the preconditions are that Lancelot must be in the same location as Andrea to witness the kiss.

```
Generating evidence:

(LANCELOT KNEW THAT ANDREA KISSED WITH
 A KNIGHT NAMED FREDERICK BECAUSE LANCELOT
 SAW THAT ANDREA KISSED WITH FREDERICK
 *PERIOD*)
```

Now ALP:GENERATE-BELIEF generates the evidence for the belief. This consists of Lancelot viewing the kiss.

```
Generating mental-event:

(LANCELOT BELIEVED THAT ANDREA LOVED
 FREDERICK *PERIOD* LANCELOT LOVED ANDREA
 *PERIOD* BECAUSE LANCELOT LOVED ANDREA
 *COMMA* LANCELOT WANTED TO BE THE LOVE OF
 ANDREA *PERIOD* BUT HE COULD NOT BECAUSE
 ANDREA LOVED FREDERICK *PERIOD* LANCELOT
 HATED FREDERICK *PERIOD* ANDREA LOVED
 FREDERICK *PERIOD* BECAUSE LANCELOT WAS
 HOT TEMPERED *COMMA* LANCELOT WANTED TO
 KILL FREDERICK *PERIOD* LANCELOT WANTED TO
 BE NEAR FREDERICK *PERIOD* LANCELOT MOVED
```

```
TO FREDERICK *PERIOD* LANCELOT WAS NEAR
FREDERICK *PERIOD* LANCELOT FOUGHT WITH
FREDERICK *PERIOD* FREDERICK WAS DEAD
*PERIOD*)
```

Author-level planning succeeded.
+++

Finally, ALP:GENERATE-BELIEF generates the mental-event of the belief (i.e., what Lancelot believes) and the story events that are causally dependent upon this belief.

The actual generation of each part of the belief is handled by MINSTREL's natural language component, RAP. RAP is a phrasal parser (Arens, 1986; Reeves, 1991; Wilensky & Arens, 1980) which uses a lexicon of phrases that pair concepts and words. To generate a concept in English, it is matched against concepts in the lexicon, and when a match is found, the corresponding words are output.

To illustrate how RAP produces English language from conceptual representation, we trace the production of the evidence portion of &BELIEF.28:

```
(LANCELOT KNEW THAT ANDREA KISSED WITH
A KNIGHT NAMED FREDERICK BECAUSE LANCELOT
SAW THAT ANDREA KISSED WITH FREDERICK
*PERIOD*)
```

Figure 7.9 shows the conceptual representation of the evidence for Lancelot's belief that Andrea loves Frederick. &STATE.24508 represents Andrea kissing Frederick. &ACT.13689 represents Lancelot's viewing of the kiss, which intends his knowledge of the kiss, represented by &STATE.24509. For technical reasons,[14] the identifiers for the schemas shown in Figure 7.9 are different from the ones shown previously. Similarly, although we have labeled the characters "&Lancelot," "&Frederick," and "&Andrea" in Figure 7.9, these characters are actually represented by schemas &HUMAN.5369, &HUMAN.5370, and &HUMAN.5368.

To begin generation, the RAP generator is called with the keyword :sentence and the act representing Lancelot's seeing the kiss. The keyword :sentence indicates that RAP is to generate this concept as a full sentence, including any necessary clauses or secondary sentences to convey the full meaning of the concept:

---

[14] The RAP generator creates copies of the concepts it generates so that any changes made to the conceptual structures during the course of generation won't affect the actual conceptual structure of the story being told.

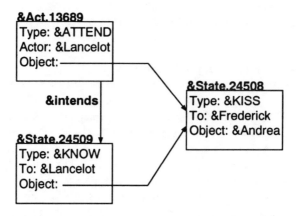

Figure 7.9 Conceptual Representation of Evidence of &BELIEF.28

```
RHAPSODY-USER>(rap:gen (list :sentence &act.13689))

Applying Phrase RAP:INTENTIONAL-RESULTS:

  (:SENTENCE
      &ACT.13689) ->
  (:CLAUSE &STATE.24509 BECAUSE :SENTENCE
      &ACT.13747).
```

Each step of the trace of RAP shows the phrase applied and the action that phrase took. The first phrase applied is RAP:INTENTIONAL-RESULTS, which rewrites the initial pattern into a new pattern in which the intentional result of Lancelot's action is generated as a clause followed by "because," and then the action that intended the result. RAP:INTENTIONAL-RESULTS appears this way in the phrasal lexicon:

```
(rap:phrase intentional-results
  (input :sentence
    (*and* ?act
      (act nil
           &intends (*and* ?ul (*value* ?ul))))))
  (output
    :clause ?ul because :sentence
    (:wo ?act &intends)))
```

The input portion of this phrase matches against acts that are being generated as sentences and which have intentional results. Matching acts are rewritten to a keyword ":clause" followed by the intended state, followed by "because" and then the original act generated as a sentence. (The ":wo" function removes the link between act and the intended result, so that RAP won't get trapped recursively applying this phrase.)

The next step is to generate the opening clause:

```
Applying Phrase RAP::CLAUSE-KNEW:
  (:CLAUSE &STATE.24509) ->
  (:SUBJECT &HUMAN.5369 KNEW THAT
   :OBJECT &STATE.24508).
```

This is accomplished by RAP:CLAUSE-KNEW, a phrase that knows how to generate states representing knowledge as a clause:

```
(rap:phrase clause-knew
  (input :clause (state nil
                  :type &know
                  :object ?what
                  :to ?who))
  (output :subject ?who knew that :object ?what))
```

RAP:CLAUSE-KNEW is applied when a state with &KNOW in the type slot is generated as a clause. RAP:CLAUSE-KNEW breaks out portions of the state (the object that is known and who is knowing it) and generates that as a simple declarative clause with the knower as the subject and the thing known as the object. The first step of generating this as a clause is to generate the subject:

```
Applying Phrase RAP:SIMPLE-CHAR-NAME:
  (:SUBJECT &HUMAN.5369) -> (LANCELOT).
```

```
Outputting: (LANCELOT KNEW THAT).
```

Except when first introducing a character, RAP generates a character by using the name of the character. After this has been done for the subject of the introductory clause, the name and the words "knew that" (which were produced by RAP:CLAUSE-KNEW) are output. The remaining portion of the input pattern is:

```
Remaining: (:OBJECT &STATE.24508 BECAUSE
            :SENTENCE &ACT.13747).
```

A similar process of recursive application of phrasal patterns is used to generate first the object of the initial clause and then the second independent clause. The final result is:

```
(LANCELOT KNEW THAT ANDREA KISSED WITH
 FREDERICK BECAUSE LANCELOT SAW THAT ANDREA
 KISSED WITH FREDERICK *PERIOD*)
```

A postprocessor later capitalizes the sentence and proper names and replaces keywords like "*PERIOD*" with the proper punctuation.

8

Evaluation of
MINSTREL's Computer Model

8.1 Introduction

The research in any area of science falls into two broad categories: the discovery and definition of problems, and the discovery and definition of solutions. Every field has a mix of these two types of research. New areas of science tend to concentrate on the exploration of problems; established fields tend to be more heavily weighted towards solutions.

As a relatively young discipline, cognitive science concentrates on the first type of research. The ultimate goals of cognitive science are (1) to understand human intelligence, and (2) to build intelligent computer programs. But those goals are currently so distant as to seem unattainable. The immediate goal of cognitive science is to discover, explore, and define the principles of intelligence. Not necessarily to solve those problems, but rather to form a good understanding of what the problems are.

MINSTREL is research into the problems and issues in creativity. MINSTREL is neither a solution to the problem of creativity, nor a performance model of creativity. It is instead an *exploration* of the creative process in humans and computers. It is hoped that by building a theory and computer model of creativity consistent with human creativity, MINSTREL will provide foundations and directions for further research, in both human and computer creativity.

How, then, should MINSTREL be evaluated? Were MINSTREL intended as a solution to the "creativity problem" evaluation would be straightforward. MINSTREL could be given a standardized creativity test, or matched against humans in creativity exercises. Or MINSTREL could be asked to publish a

213

story. However, none of these are appropriate evaluations because MINSTREL is not a human-level performance model.

As explorative research in creativity, MINSTREL should achieve two goals. First, it should increase our understanding of the creative process. MINSTREL should be consistent with, elucidate, and extend the current theories about the processes of creativity. Second, MINSTREL should test the theories and models it proposes to determine their strengths, limitations, and to discover new areas of research.

To determine how well MINSTREL has achieved these goals, this chapter evaluates MINSTREL in two ways. First, MINSTREL is compared to previous work in psychology, creativity, and storytelling. This reveals how MINSTREL fits in with established knowledge about the creative process, shows how MIN-STREL elucidates that knowledge, and indicates how MINSTREL extends the current understanding of human creativity. Second, MINSTREL's performance as a computer model is evaluated. Although MINSTREL is not a human-level performance model of creativity, it must still demonstrate a level of performance that supports the plausibility of its process model. MINSTREL is tested both in comparison to human storytellers and by performing extensive experimentation with MINSTREL as a computer model. Together, these evaluations should give the reader a better understanding of the scope and value of this research.

8.2 How MINSTREL Fits In With Previous Research

Because MINSTREL addresses a number of areas in cognitive science, there is a large amount of related work. In this section, MINSTREL is evaluated by comparing it to the most closely related research in psychology, artificial intelligence, and cognitive science.

8.2.1 Psychological Models of Creativity

The traditional psychological model of creativity descends from Wallas (1926). Wallas in turn was inspired by the theory and experiences of Henri Poincare (1913). Wallas proposed a four-step model of the creative process:

1. Preparation—problem investigation from all directions.
2. Incubation—subconscious consideration of problem.
3. Illumination—occurrence of a "happy idea."
4. Verification—consideration and debugging of solution.

This model was later elaborated in different ways by Reichenbach (1938), Koestler (1964), Boden (1991), and others. Reichenbach (1938) and others added steps to this process including elaboration (verification and debugging of the created solution) and communication (presentation of the solution to an audience). Koestler (1964) proposed that the basic process of illumination was *bisociation*, the bringing together of two previously related ideas, although he did not detail a mechanism to accomplish this. Boden (1991) suggests that the basic process of illumination is representational redescription (the changing of the underlying representation of conceptual structures).

This research recognized several important features of the creative process:

1. It was recognized that the creative process does not follow the steps outlined above in a linear fashion (Stein 1967). The creative process jumps from stage to stage in an erratic fashion. In particular, the elaboration stage leads back into preparation or incubation if problems are found in a solution.
2. There is much preparation involved in creative thinking. An extensive and deep knowledge of a field is crucial to productive creative thinking.
3. The creative process may involve changing the original problem. Following tangents is a well-known and important aspect of creative thinking.
4. There is emotional response to creativity. The well-known "Aha!" is indicative of the excited emotional response that results from discovering a solution to a particularly vexing or thorny problem.

Although the Wallas model is widely known and accepted, it has several major problems. First, the Wallas model is descriptive rather than explanatory. The crux of creativity—how a new idea comes to be—is left unilluminated. Second, the Wallas model fails to explain the links between problem solving and creativity. The Wallas model explains creativity as an unusual cognitive process quite different from ordinary problem solving, and fails to address how these processes might be interrelated.

Weisberg (1986) presents an alternative model of creativity that addresses the problems of the Wallas model. Weisberg proposes a model of creativity as an extension of problem solving. Weisberg rejects the notion of creativity as fundamentally different from ordinary problem solving. Instead, he views creativity as the interactions of a complex web of processes, many involving the recall and modification of previous problem solutions. Weisberg also believes that creativity is incremental. Weisberg sees creativity in nearly everything a person does because every situation in which a person finds himself is unique, and every response he makes novel. Thus great acts of creativity, like Picasso's *Guernica*, are only incrementally different from the acts of everyday life.

The MINSTREL model captures important features of both the Weisberg and Wallas models. Weisberg suggests three major features of creativity, all of which are modeled in MINSTREL:

1. Creativity is an extension of problem solving, driven by the failure of the problem solving process.
2. Creativity is strongly memory based, involving the recall and modification of previous knowledge.
3. Creativity is incremental, a process that is active in mundane problem solving as well as in great creative acts.

MINSTREL also captures the important observations of Wallas theory. MINSTREL's model supports nonlinear thinking, preparation, and problem restructuring.

More importantly, MINSTREL extends the current work in the psychology of creativity by proposing specific mechanisms for the processes of creativity. The major shortcoming of both the Wallas and Weisberg models of creativity is that they lack a process model of the creative process. Both are primarily behavioral models of the creative process. MINSTREL complements these models by providing a process model of creativity consistent with the accepted behavioral models.

8.2.2 Artificial Intelligence Models of Creativity

MINSTREL is not the first process model of creativity. Both AM (Lenat, 1976) and DAYDREAMER (Mueller, 1989) presented artificial intelligence models of creativity.

Lenat (1976) addressed the issue of creativity in the domain of mathematics. Lenat built a computer program called AM which looked at the problem of creative theory formation in mathematics: how to propose interesting new concepts and plausible hypotheses connecting them. Like MINSTREL, AM had a flexible, priority-based control structure and a large library of creativity heuristics used to explore a solution space for new solutions.

A major difference between AM and MINSTREL is in their styles of problem solving. AM was an exploratory system. It began with a small set of basic concepts and used creativity heuristics to explore a large problem space, relying on interestingness heuristics to identify worthwhile discoveries. AM doesn't have a specific goal to achieve, but can recognize an interesting result when it occurs.

MINSTREL, in contrast, is a goal-directed system. MINSTREL begins processing with a specific goal (normally to tell a story about a particular story theme) and creates and achieves new subgoals in an effort to satisfy that initial goal. MINSTREL has a specific goal to achieve and uses creativity to solve it.

MINSTREL is also a more integrated model of creativity than AM. By showing how creativity can be incorporated into the recall process, MINSTREL explains how creativity can be transparently available to all cognitive processes, rather than being specifically a function of problem solving.

DAYDREAMER (Mueller, 1989) also addressed the issue of creativity. DAYDREAMER was a computer program that produced daydreams in reaction to being rejected for a date by a famous movie star. Although DAYDREAMER was not primarily a model of creativity, it did address the role that creativity played in daydreaming. DAYDREAMER had two methods for creating new solutions to problems: serendipity ("the accidental juxtaposition of a recalled experience with a problem") and mutation ("a structural transformation of an unachieved action subgoal of [a] goal").

DAYDREAMER is similar to MINSTREL in that its creativity was driven by the failure of problem solving, and achieved by the use of transformation heuristics. It differs both in how it controls search (DAYDREAMER used spreading activation) and in that it applied creativity transformations to solutions, not to problems.

Perhaps the most interesting result of comparing MINSTREL, DAYDREAMER and AM is the role that problem constraints play in creativity. These three programs can be viewed as lying along a continuum of problem types from least constrained (daydreaming) to most constrained (mathematics). Fanciful inventions are commonplace in daydreaming, must be justified in storytelling, and have no place in mathematics. What reflection of this is there in these programs?

One apparent reflection is in the number of creativity heuristics. DAYDREAMER has two creativity heuristics, MINSTREL about twenty, and AM several hundred. It would appear that the more constrained the problem domain, the greater number and more specific the creativity heuristics required.

Perhaps more interesting is that the three programs share similar control structures. Although each program makes use of a different mechanism to control search (DAYDREAMER uses spreading activation, MINSTREL a limit to recursion, and AM interestingness heuristics), the underlying mechanism for all three programs is a priority-based agenda. This suggests both that creativity may be consistent across the continuum of problem constraints and that a flexible control mechanism may be an integral part of creative problem solving.

8.2.3   Artificial Intelligence Models of Storytelling

There have also been several previous works in artificial intelligence that looked at the problem of storytelling. Of these, the most important are TALESPIN (Meehan, 1976) and UNIVERSE (Lebowitz, 1985).

The seminal work in computer storytelling was James Meehan's TALESPIN program (Meehan, 1976). TALESPIN told stories about the lives of simple woodland creatures. The thrust of TALESPIN was planning; the process of telling a story involved giving some character a goal and then watching the development of a plan to solve that goal.

TALESPIN simulated a simple world populated by woodland creatures. To tell a story, TALESPIN assigned goals to each of the creatures (i.e., "Irving Bear wants to eat some honey") and then simulated the actions of each of the creatures as it tried to achieve its goals. The trace of these actions formed the story.

The most important result to come out of TALESPIN was that character-level planning was necessary but not sufficient for storytelling. TALESPIN's stories were plausible and consistent, but often uninteresting. The impact of this is seen in two ways in MINSTREL.

First, MINSTREL's consistency goals are a direct reflection of the need for consistent character-level planning in storytelling. MINSTREL's consistency goals make sure that character goals arise properly, are achieved, and that actions in the world effect the characters and the story world properly.

Second, MINSTREL's other author-level goals reflect the need for a level of storytelling purpose beyond character-level planning. By creating stories to fulfill the author-level goal of illustrating a theme, MINSTREL creates stories that have the purpose and interest that TALESPIN's stories lacked.

TALESPIN can be characterized as a "planful" storyteller, because it is most concerned with the plans and actions of its story characters, and MINSTREL can be characterized as a "thematic" storyteller, because its primary concern is to create a story that illustrates a particular theme. UNIVERSE (Lebowitz, 1985) is best characterized as a "character interaction" storyteller. UNIVERSE looks at the problem of developing stories which involve complex and continuing relationships between well-developed characters. This type of serial, character-based storytelling is best exemplified by soap operas.

There are two important elements to the UNIVERSE program: character descriptions and plot fragments. Character descriptions are detailed representations of story characters involving stereotypes, individual traits, individual goals, interpersonal relationships, and a history. Plot fragments are abstract descriptions of story events that will achieve particular author-level goals. To tell a story, UNIVERSE instantiates plot fragments from a library of character descriptions. Instantiating one plot fragment may generate opportunities for more plot fragments, resulting in a continuing, serial story.

While UNIVERSE can achieve author-level goals at a higher level than TALESPIN, it lacks MINSTREL's ability to reason about and manipulate a story as it is being created. For example, once UNIVERSE creates a story event, it can no longer reason about that event. This prevents UNIVERSE from using one story event to fulfill multiple goals, or to maintain consistency across multiple story events. UNIVERSE also has a limited representational vocabulary, which limits the types of goals it can achieve and the complexity of the stories it can create.

MINSTREL's primary advancement over both TALESPIN and UNIVERSE is its model of storytelling as a purposeful activity. By explicitly representing, reasoning about, and achieving author-level goals, MINSTREL is able to create stories that are more purposeful, interesting, and complex than either TALESPIN or UNIVERSE.

8.3 MINSTREL as a Computer Model

Having seen how MINSTREL fits in with previous work in creativity and storytelling, we now turn to evaluating MINSTREL as a computer model of the theory of creativity and storytelling presented in this book. We analyze MINSTREL's performance and present a number of experiments that have been made to determine the robustness and coverage of MINSTREL. But before we can present these results, we must first discuss the role of the computer model in this research.

In general, computer models play a number of roles in cognitive science research. First, a computer model provides an existence proof that a theory is rigorous enough to be implemented as a computer program that can perform useful and meaningful tasks. The computer acts as an idiot savant critic of the theory being implemented, constantly asking "How is this done?" When a computer model has been built for a cognitive theory, there is some assurance that the researcher has addressed details that might otherwise remain undiscovered or glossed over.

Second, the computer model gives the underlying cognitive theory *plausibility*. Theories in cognitive science explain the processes and knowledge needed to perform some particular reasoning task. The fact that the computer model can use the underlying theory to perform meaningful example tasks gives plausibility to the claim that the theory explains how that type of reasoning works. If the problem domain is well-defined stronger claims can be made about the computer model. But in general the reasoning tasks being studied in cognitive science are ill-defined and poorly understood, and consequently most computer models represent proofs of plausibility, not of correctness.

Third, the computer model is a testbed for the development and testing of a theory. The researcher can use the computer model to test the limits of his theory, to see where the theory succeeds and where it fails. Further, the researcher can use the computer model to extend and develop his theories, to test new hypotheses and possibilities: What if memory functioned differently? What happens when creativity is taken away? How do author-level goals interact with the creative process? The computer program is not only an embodiment of a theory, it is also a tool for the development of theory.

Finally, the computer model is useful for understanding the overall behavior of large systems. It is difficult to fully comprehend a cognitive model of a complicated task like storytelling. There are too many sources of knowledge and too many different processes using that knowledge. The computer program provides a tool for discovering and studying the behaviors that emerge when these many parts interact. And regardless of whether the emergent behaviors confirm or contradict the original theory, these behaviors contribute to the researcher's understanding of the problem domain and help refine and modify his theories.

The role of a computer model in cognitive research is thus four-fold:

1. to act as a painstaking critic of a theory,
2. to act as a plausibility proof of a theory's validity,
3. to act as a testbed for the development and testing of a theory, and
4. to act as a tool for discovering complicated, emergent behaviors.

MINSTREL's roles as (1) a critic and as (4) a tool for studying the behavior of a complicated system must be judged by the overall quality of this research. If the theories presented in this volume are detailed and comprehensive, that is partly due to MINSTREL's role as a critic of the theory. And if this volume presents interesting and unexpected ideas (such as imaginative memory) that is partly due to MINSTREL's value as a tool for studying the complicated behavior of a creative problem solver. In this chapter we address the roles of MINSTREL that can be evaluated more explicitly: (2) as a plausibility proof and (3) as a testbed for our theories about creativity and storytelling.

To evaluate MINSTREL as a plausibility proof, we examine MINSTREL's performance as a creator. We examine the *quality* and *quantity* of tasks that MINSTREL can perform and judge how well these support the theoretical claims of this research.

To evaluate MINSTREL as a testbed of our theories about creativity and storytelling, we present a number of experiments and studies we have performed to test the limits of MINSTREL's performance. These experiments have led to a number of interesting insights about creativity, which support MINSTREL's value as a theoretical testbed.

8.4 MINSTREL as a Plausibility Proof

The purpose of evaluating MINSTREL's performance is to show that it supports the plausibility of the underlying theory. Unfortunately, there are no objective standards for this judgment. There is no standard "storytelling problem" against which we can test MINSTREL's performance. And, as pointed out earlier, MINSTREL is not a human-level performance model of storytelling, so such a test is anyway irrelevant. Instead, we hope to show that MINSTREL's performance is *convincing*: that MINSTREL's performance on creative tasks is good enough to persuade the majority of the readers of this book that it is a plausible model of human creativity. To this end we evaluate MINSTREL's performance based on two criteria: quantity and quality.

First, to show the generality of the underlying theory of creativity,

MINSTREL should solve a number of different tasks. A program that solved only one example (whether simple or complex) would be unconvincing because there would be little reason to believe that the program (and consequently the underlying theory) was general enough to handle a wide range of problems. Instead, a computer model should handle a variety of problems, varying in content and difficulty. In the next section we present the range of problems that MINSTREL can handle and argue that they are sufficient to establish MINSTREL's generality.

Second, MINSTREL should solve difficult tasks at a high enough level of performance so that we can reasonably expect the underlying model to account for human creativity. A one-note program that solved only a very restricted, simple type of problem, no matter in what quantity, would be unconvincing as a model of human cognition because human cognitive abilities are very rarely so restricted. Instead, a computer model should handle difficult problems with an effectiveness that demonstrates: (1) the flexibility of the model, (2) the quality of the solutions, and (3) the interaction of the model with other cognitive processes. Following the next section we show how MINSTREL's performance achieves these goals.

8.4.1 Quantity

MINSTREL is primarily a storytelling program. It can tell complete stories based on four different themes. In addition, the creativity component of MINSTREL has been applied separately to the task of inventing methods of suicide, and to a simple mechanical invention task. Figure 8.1 lists the tasks MINSTREL performs and the output generated.

As this shows, MINSTREL can solve a variety of very difficult problems in creativity (telling stories) as well as a number of examples in simpler problem

Task	Output
PAT-GOOD-DEEDS-REWARDED	The Hermit and the Knight (two stories)
PAT-ROMEO	The Lady's Revenge
PAT-HASTY	Richard and Lancelot
PAT-PRIDE	The Proud Knight (five stories)[1]
Suicide Invention	Three methods for a knight to commit suicide.
Mechanical Invention	Three designs for staplers to use on a thick set of papers.[2]

[1] See 8.5, 8.6, and 8.7 for details.
[2] See Section 8.12 for details.

Figure 8.1 MINSTREL's Tasks

domains. This alone may convince the reader of MINSTREL's generality. But this summary of MINSTREL's performance is misleading. MINSTREL's basic problem unit is not the story, but rather the author-level goals that are satisfied during the invention of the story. The best measure of MINSTREL's performance is not how many complete stories it can tell, but how many author-level goals it solves.

To tell the stories listed above, MINSTREL solves 1025 author-level goals of 22 types using 44 plans. As these numbers show, MINSTREL solves a large number and variety of goals using a number of different plans. At the problem solving level, MINSTREL has an impressive range of performance.

Still, the fact remains that MINSTREL tells only a handful of stories. Why can't MINSTREL tell more stories? Why can't MINSTREL tell stories endlessly? There are several reasons.

First, the focus of this research has been on creativity: the creation of new solutions with *significant* differences from past solutions. The nine stories that MINSTREL tells are all very different from one another. It would be a simple matter to have MINSTREL tell additional stories not significantly different from the stories it already tells. We could, for example, add knowledge of three new types of berries to MINSTREL's episodic memory, and have MINSTREL generate three new variants of every story it tells which involves berries. And if we also added three new types of knights, MINSTREL could generate nine new variants of each story that involved berries and knights. Adding knowledge results in a combinatorial number of new stories. But such stories are neither interesting nor enlightening. MINSTREL is no more competent because it can tell ninety uninteresting stories in addition to ten interesting ones. The challenge of creativity research is to build a model that can explain interesting results, not uninteresting results.

Quantity alone is a poor measure of performance.

A more important explanation concerns MINSTREL's *in-depth* understanding of the stories it creates. MINSTREL tries to create stories that achieve a large number of specific constraints. The stories MINSTREL tells all illustrate a theme and are consistent in many different ways. Each constraint that MINSTREL must satisfy during storytelling acts as a "bottleneck" for the number of stories it can tell. If a theme involves deception, then MINSTREL can necessarily tell only as many stories about that theme as it can invent deceptions. If a theme involves a deception that later causes a goal failure for the deceiver, then MINSTREL can only tell as many stories as it can invent deceptions that *also* backfire. Similar bottlenecks occur with each of the hundreds of author-level goals MINSTREL achieves during the course of creating a story; each bottle-neck limits the number of complete stories MINSTREL can create (Figure 8.2).

In-depth understanding leads to a
combinatorial explosion of constraints.

This is in marked contrast to story grammars or more simply constrained systems like UNIVERSE (Lebowitz, 1985). These systems can generate many stories because they have only a limited understanding of the stories they generate. Propp's fairy tale grammar can be used to create many fairy tales, but none of them will illustrate a moral or be consistent except by random chance,

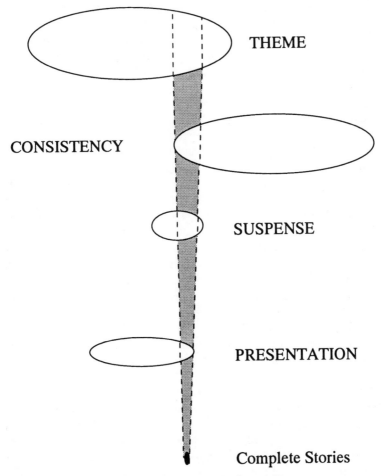

THEME

CONSISTENCY

SUSPENSE

PRESENTATION

Complete Stories

Figure 8.2 Bottlenecks in Storytelling

because Propp's grammar understands stories only at the level of what types of events follow other events.

The bottleneck problem is made even more difficult by MINSTREL's goal to be creative. Being creative is a constraint that eliminates most new solutions that would satisfy other constraints. Given knowledge about three new types of berries, MINSTREL would *not* tell three new variants of each berry story as suggested before. Rather, MINSTREL's goal to tell creative stories would reject these variants, correctly recognizing (by their similarity to stories already told) that the new stories were not creative. Thus the drive to be creative is an especially restrictive bottleneck, because it eliminates many solutions that would trivially satisfy other bottlenecks.

The drive to be creative eliminates trivial solutions.

In general, there is a tradeoff between quantity of performance and quality of performance. The complexity and depth of MINSTREL's understanding limits the number of complete, correct stories it can tell. In general, a system with deep understanding will require more knowledge and operate under more constraints, limiting the breadth of its performance.

In addition to the quantity of problems that MINSTREL solves, there is other evidence to support MINSTREL's generality.

First, MINSTREL was able to invent methods of suicide using the same author-level goals and plans used in telling stories. MINSTREL was able to solve a new problem with no modification. In fact, MINSTREL is capable of solving many new problems in the King Arthur and storytelling domains without changes of any sort (see, for example, Experiment #1 in this chapter, which describes how MINSTREL was able to solve all the problems involved in telling a story about a new theme with little additional knowledge). This indicates that MINSTREL is not restricted to the particular problems it currently handles, but rather has the generality to extend to other similar problems.

Second, with the addition of appropriate episodic memories and TRAMs, MINSTREL was able to invent mechanical devices (see Section 7 of this chapter for details). Although MINSTREL required new knowledge to perform the mechanical invention task (as would a human who knew nothing about mechanical devices), MINSTREL required no changes to the underlying model of creativity.

MINSTREL's number of solved examples and its simple extension to new problems and problem domains should be sufficient to establish the generality of the TRAM model of creativity. Of course, there is always the possibility that a new example will reveal a difficulty with the TRAM model, or that new research in psychology will establish that human creativity functions quite differently from the TRAM model. But the number and variety of examples MINSTREL solves clearly establish its plausibility.

8.4.2   Quality

Evaluating the quality of MINSTREL's output is even more difficult than evaluating the quantity. We can at least measure the quantity of MINSTREL's output, even if we have no accepted scale against which to judge it. In evaluating the quality of the output we have neither measure nor scale.

The standard measure of quality in creativity has been the marketplace. Getting published is the goal of the struggling writer; selling a patent the goal of the backyard inventor. Simply put, creative ideas are valuable. And so the marketplace has always been a good (albeit imperfect) judge of creativity.

If MINSTREL's stories were publishable, it would therefore be a strong argument for their quality. Alas, they are not. That's not an unexpected result. After all, MINSTREL is an ignorant infant competing against human experts with many thousands of years of human creative history on which to draw. In fact, if MINSTREL were able to produce publishable stories it would be more suspicious than auspicious. Asking MINSTREL to compete against human authors is too strict and demanding a criteria given MINSTREL's goals and the current state of research in creativity. How, then, to judge the quality of MINSTREL's stories?

The measure presented here is loosely based on the Turing Test. Suggested by the famous British mathematician Alan Turing, the Turing Test is intended as a measure of computer intelligence. A person acting as a tester (T) converses with a computer (C) and with another person (P) by some means that conceals their identities (such as a teletype). T converses with C and P separately. If, after some reasonable period of time, T cannot determine which is the computer, the computer is deemed intelligent. The intent of the Turing Test is to compare computer performance against human performance in an unbiased setting.

The variant of the Turing Test presented here is much less ambitious. Rather than asking a person to compare MINSTREL directly against a human in an interactive test, we asked subjects to judge MINSTREL against their knowledge of human performance. A survey which contained one of MINSTREL's stories and MINSTREL's invented suicides was given to a selection of subjects of varying backgrounds. The subjects (who were not aware that the story had been written by a computer) were asked to read the story and answer some simple questions about the author. The answers give some insight into how unbiased adults evaluate the quality of MINSTREL's output. The questionnaire used is shown in Figure 8.3 and Figure 8.4.

This survey was given to ten subjects solicited over the Internet. One subject did not respond. A summary of the other nine responses is shown in Figure 8.5. On average, the subjects judged MINSTREL to be about 16 years old with a high school education. They felt that MINSTREL had a good understanding of what a story is, and rated MINSTREL's story between mediocre and good. Of MINSTREL's suicide methods, they found taking a poison potion very effective

Personal Information
AGE:
SEX:
EDUCATIONAL LEVEL (High School, College, or Graduate School):

A subject was asked to write a short (a few paragraphs) story about King Arthur. The subject produced the following story:

In the Spring of 1089, a knight named Lancelot returned to Camelot from elsewhere. Lancelot was hot tempered. Once, when Lancelot lost a joust, he blamed his lance and wanted to destroy it. He struck his lance and broke it.

One day, a lady of the court named Andrea wanted to pick some berries. Andrea went to the woods. Andrea picked some berries. Lancelot's horse unexpectedly carried him into the woods. Lancelot was near Andrea and fell in love with her. Lancelot wanted Andrea to love him.

Some time later, Lancelot's horse again carried him into the woods. There he saw Andrea kissing a knight named Frederick. Because of this, Lancelot believed that Andrea loved Frederick. Because Lancelot loved Andrea, he wanted her to love him. Lancelot hated Frederick. Lancelot's hot temper made him mad. He wanted to kill Frederick. Lancelot moved to Frederick and fought him. Frederick was killed.

Andrea ran to Frederick. Andrea told Lancelot that Frederick was her brother. Lancelot wanted to take back that he wanted to kill Frederick, but he could not. Lancelot hated himself.

Lancelot became a hermit to hide his shame. Frederick was buried in the woods where he died, and Andrea became a nun.

Please answer the following questions about the author of this story:

1. How old do you think the author is?
2. How much education do you think the author has had?
3. Do you think the author is male or female?
4. Do you think the author understands what a story is?
5. Would you call this story "excellent", "good", "mediocre" or "poor"?
6. Do you feel you know or can guess anything else about the author?

Please rate the story from 1 to 5, where 5 indicates good or best on the following criteria:

Use of the English language:
Interesting or clever plot:
Attention to details:
Coherency:

Figure 8.3 Initial Survey, Part 1

A subject was asked to invent ways in which one of King Arthur's knights might commit suicide. Below are listed three answers:

1. The knight could hit himself with his sword until dead.
2. The knight could drink a potion that would kill him.
3. The knight could fight a dragon and lose on purpose.

Please rate these answers according to the listed criteria on a scale of 1-5, where 5 indicates good or best.

How effective do you rate each solution? I.e., will it work?

How clever or creative is each solution?

That's it! Thank you very much for participating. When you return this questionnaire, you will receive a short explanation of this research.

Figure 8.4 Initial Survey, Part 2

and fighting a dragon with intent to lose very creative.

Subject responses to the free-form response question were also interesting. A sampling of the free-form responses from the first survey indicate that even with MINSTREL's rough story expression, subjects still attributed human characteristics to the story's author:

Possibly poor. Possibly from a minority. Although there is an age implied by my guess of the amount of education I would not be surprised to learn that the author was much older and simply lacked the education... Probably reads romance novels.

The author likes violence and the idea of sex.

Since the "story" is rough and lacking in detail, the author either sees things in 'block-diagram' form, and is uninterested in detail, or finds detail difficult to supply.

An intelligent female with a knowledge of cause and effect and a sense of poetic justice.

I would guess that the author may have a problem with his temper.

The lack of detail in the story also makes me think the author is writing about something personal, and not describing something that might have happened many years ago. Perhaps the author has a hot temper and is in trouble for fighting someone by mistake. The problem might be recent, because Lancelot hasn't rejoined the round table, or the author might act withdrawn because he is embarrassed by his temper tantrums.

Question	Resp.	Max	Min
Respondents			
Number	9		
Average age	35.7	57	20
Average education	2.6^1	3	2
Responses			
Author age	15.8	25	12
Author education[1]	0.9	2	0
Author sex[2]	0.4		
Does the author understand what a story is?[3]	0.9		
On a scale of 1-5...			
Overall rating of story	1.5	3	1
Clever plot?	2.5	4	1
Attention to details?	2.8	5	1
Coherency?	3.6	5	2
Use of language?	2.1	3	1
Effectiveness of suicide solns (1-5)			
#1	2.6	5	1
#2	4.7	5	4
#3	3.9	5	1
Creativeness of suicide solns (1-5)			
#1	1.6	3	1
#2	3.6	5	2
#3	4.1	5	3

[1] 0 = Grade School, 1 = High School, 2 = College, 3 = Grad. School
[2] 0 = Female, 1 = Male
[3] 0 = No, 1 = Yes

Figure 8.5 Summary of Responses to Initial Survey

To determine how much the subjects' responses were affected by MIN-STREL's expression of the Lancelot story (i.e., the precise wording and English of the story), a second survey was conducted using a revised version of the Lancelot story. The revised story was produced by hand, and used language more fluently without changing the basic structure or events of the story (Figure 8.6).

The results of the second survey are summarized in Figure 8.7. As was expected, subjects in the second survey thought the use of language in the story better. Estimates of the author's age were also higher (possibly due to the association in Western culture of language expertise with maturity) and the author was thought to be more male. But in all other categories, responses were close to those in the first survey, indicating that the subjects' judgments of MIN-STREL's storytelling abilities and creativity were not overly affected by the particular expression of the sample story.

As a final test of the quality of MINSTREL's stories, the same survey was given to a third set of subjects using a story written by the 12-year-old daughter of a colleague. This story is shown in Figure 8.8.

Figure 8.9 shows the results of this survey and compares them with MIN-STREL's results. As Figure 8.9 shows, respondents rated the human author as older (17.9 years vs. 16.8 years), and the story as more clever (3.3 vs. 2.5 on a scale of 1-5), but also rated the story more poorly overall (1.1 vs. 1.4 on a scale of 1-5) and found it less coherent than the MINSTREL story (2.6 vs. 3.4 on a scale of 1-5).

In the Spring of 1089, a knight named Lancelot returned to Camelot from a quest. Lancelot was known as a hot tempered knight. Once, when Lancelot lost a joust, he blamed his lance and broke it in a fit of temper.

On the day Lancelot returned, a lady of the court named Andrea was in the woods picking berries. As Lancelot rode near the woods his horse suddenly darted into the woods, and he saw Andrea. He fell in love with her immediately, and wanted Andrea to love him.

A few days later, Lancelot was again riding near the woods, thinking about Andrea. Again, his horse carried him unexpectedly into the woods. There he saw Andrea kissing a knight named Frederick. Lancelot realized that Andrea loved Frederick. His hot temper boiled over, and he charged into the clearing and struck down Frederick. Frederick was killed by the first blow.

Andrea ran to Frederick and held his body. Crying, Andrea told Lancelot that Frederick was her brother. Lancelot was filled with remorse. He hated himself. He wanted to take back his hasty action but he could not.

Lancelot became a hermit to hide his shame. Frederick was buried in the woods where he died, and Andrea became a nun.

Figure 8.6 Revised Lancelot Story

Question	Resp.	Max	Min
Respondents			
Number	13		
Average age	32.9	22	53
Average education[1]	2	3	2.3
Responses			
Author age	17.5	10	37
Author education[1]	0.9	0	2
Author sex[2]	0.7		
Does the author understand what a story is?[3]	0.8		
On a scale of 1-5...			
Overall rating of story	1.4	3	1
Clever plot?	2.6	5	1
Attention to details?	2.8	5	2
Coherency?	3.2	5	2
Use of language?	3.3	4	1
Effectiveness of suicide solns (1-5)			
#1	1.9	4	1
#2	4.5	5	3
#3	3.4	5	1
Creativeness of suicide solns (1-5)			
#1	1.6	3	1
#2	2.5	5	1
#3	3.9	5	1

[1] 0 = Grade School, 1 = High School, 2 = College, 3 = Grad. School
[2] 0 = Female, 1 = Male
[3] 0 = No, 1 = Yes

Figure 8.7 Summary of Second Survey

More complete and careful study is needed to fully understand how people judge MINSTREL's stories, but these preliminary surveys indicate that MINSTREL's storytelling is equivalent to what people expect from a younger high-school age student.

8.4.3   Summary of Evaluation

The basic claim of this research is that MINSTREL is a plausible explanation of aspects of human creativity. As the foregoing sections show, MINSTREL is capable of solving a wide variety of creative tasks at an adult level. MINSTREL tells stories about four different themes, invents suicides and mechanical devices, and solves over 500 author-level goals using a variety of plans and mechanical heuristics. The stories MINSTREL tells are comparable to those of a younger high-school student, and at least one of MINSTREL's suicide solutions is viewed as very creative by older, college-educated subjects. Both the

Once upon a time, in a land over the sea and beyond the mountains, lay a kingdom and the royal family.

Well, it just so happens that the princess was a very unhappy child. All day long she would keep to herself and the animals. Princess Bunny was supplied abundantly with toys, dresses, three nannies, basically anything she asked for.

But every day, Bunny would play with her new toys for an hour or so, then go where the peasants were working with the animals.

Bunny's particular favorite animal was Henry the pig. She liked to visit Henry for hours each day. Then when it was feeding time, Bunny would go back into the castle and become dreary and lonely once more.

Bunny's daily visits to see Henry became rarer and rarer, until she stopped seeing him altogether, and the pig became very lonely. So did Bunny. The nannies tried their hardest to cheer Bunny up. Jesters came, dancers came, but nothing worked.

One morning Bunny woke up to the blast of the king's trumpets. "Someone has broken into the king's safe and stolen everything!" Upon hearing this, a smile cracked over Bunny's face.

Later that afternoon Bunny went to visit Henry. She passed a few pages and saw a peasant boy go into the barn next to Henry's pen.

Henry greeted Bunny with a pleasant oink and rubbed his head on her skirt, telling her in his way to scratch him.

"Henry," whispered Bunny. "Do you think Daddy and Mommy will love me and pay attention to me if they stop being King and Queen and loose all of their money?"

Henry oinked saying yes to this poor desperate child.

"Good, because I robbed my own father! I put the money under my bed."

Now the peasant boy who had gone in the barn heard all this and ran to the castle to confess what he'd just heard.

The king was very surprised at hearing this. He made promise to spend more time with Bunny, and the King, Queen, Bunny, the kingdom, and Henry lived happily ever after.

Figure 8.8 Third Survey Story

quality and quantity of MINSTREL's outputs indicate that MINSTREL can perform at the level of a creative problem solver, albeit on a limited set of problems.

8.5   Experiments With MINSTREL

The second purpose of this chapter is to evaluate MINSTREL as an experimental testbed. To this end, we have performed a number of experiments and studies to test the limits of MINSTREL's performance. These experiments have led to a number of interesting insights about the processes of creativity.

Question	Human Author	MINSTREL
Respondents		
Number	9	22
Average age	32.8	34.1
Average education	2.4	2.4
Responses		
Author age	**17.9**	**16.8**
Author education	1.0	0.9
Author sex[2]	0.2	0.6
Does the author understand what a story is?[3]	0.8	0.8
On a scale of 1-5...		
Overall rating of story	**1.1**	**1.4**
Clever plot?	**3.3**	**2.5**
Attention to details?	**2.4**	**2.8**
Coherency?	**2.6**	**3.4**
Use of language?	2.9	2.8

[1] 0 = Grade School, 1 = High School, 2 = College, 3 = Grad. School
[2] 0 = Female, 1 = Male
[3] 0 = No, 1 = Yes

Figure 8.9 Summary of Third Survey

8.6   Study #1: Abandoned TRAMs

During the development of MINSTREL, three particular TRAMs were implemented that were later abandoned. Examining these TRAMs and determining
why they were discarded provides insight into MINSTREL's creativity process
and will help evaluate the generality of the Transform-Recall-Adapt model of
creativity.

8.6.1   TRAM:Ignore-Neighbors

The first of the three TRAMs that were implemented and then later abandoned is
TRAM:Ignore-Neighbors. TRAM:Ignore-Neighbors suggests finding a problem
solution by ignoring all the knowledge structures immediately connected to the
problem description, finding a past problem that matches the modified problem
description, and then using the solution to that past problem (without adaptation)
to solve the current problem. Figure 8.10 shows the pseudo-code for this
TRAM.

In MINSTREL, problem descriptions are represented as goal, action and
state frames connected to one another by various kinds of links. For example,
the problem description "What action can a knight perform that will make him
famous and make a princess love him?" is represented as an unspecified action

TRAM:Ignore-Neighbors

Comment:	Find a reminding by ignoring connections.
Test:	Does problem description have any connections to other knowledge structures?
Transform:	Remove all connections to other knowledge structures.
Adapt:	No adaptation.

Figure 8.10 TRAM:Ignore-Neighbors

frame connected to other frames by causal links such as "&plan-of" and "&intends". MINSTREL's representation for this problem description is shown in Figure 8.11.

TRAM:Ignore-Neighbors transforms a problem by removing all connections to other knowledge structures. Given the problem description shown in Figure 8.11, TRAM:Ignore-Neighbors removes the "&plan-of" and "&intends" links from &Act.77. The transformed problem description is "What action can a knight perform?" If MINSTREL can recall any action that a knight can

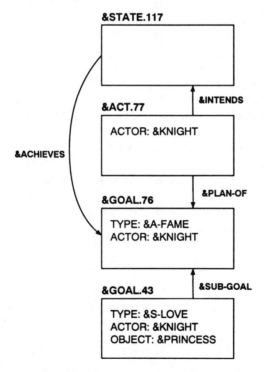

Figure 8.11 Graphical Representation of Problem Description

perform, that recalled action will be acceptable as a solution to the modified problem. Since TRAM:Ignore-Neighbors does no adaptation of any recalled solutions, the recalled episode will be used directly as a solution to the original problem. This can result in nonsensical solutions, such as a knight who becomes famous by sharpening his sword.

Interestingly enough, TRAM:Ignore-Neighbors is similar to the successful TRAM:Limited-Recall. TRAM:Limited-Recall transforms a problem description by removing all *distant* neighbors. That is, TRAM:Limited-Recall removes all of the knowledge structures connected to a problem description *except* the immediate connections. In the case of the problem shown in Figure 8.11, TRAM:Limited-Recall removes &Goal.43. The new problem description looks for actions that can make a knight famous, regardless of whether or not they were part of a plan to capture a princess's love. Consequently, the solutions discovered by TRAM:Limited-Recall will be much more usable than those discovered by TRAM:Ignore-Neighbors. TRAM:Limited-Recall is shown in Figure 8.12.

Why is TRAM:Limited-Recall useful and TRAM:Ignore-Neighbors not? The answer is that TRAM:Ignore-Neighbors uses a powerful problem transformation without a balancing solution adaptation. Removing all the connections to a problem description creates a new problem description that will match many more episodes in memory. But TRAM:Ignore-Neighbors cannot adapt those episodes to the original problem.

Of course, TRAM:Limited-Recall also has no adaptation process. But TRAM:Limited-Recall has a much weaker problem transformation, so that less adaptation of discovered solutions is necessary.

It is a tenet of this research that creative solutions to problems are found by small, precise heuristics that apply specific problem transformations and corresponding solution adaptations. TRAM:Ignore-Neighbors illustrates why powerful, broad creativity heuristics must fail: because the adaptation task created by a sweeping problem transformation is likely to be more difficult than the original problem. To be sure, a heuristic like TRAM:Ignore-Neighbors will sometimes discover a novel and useful solution. But most of the time it will simply create an adaptation task more difficult than the original problem (such as explaining why sharpening a sword would make a knight famous).

Does this mean that MINSTREL cannot discover the good solutions that

TRAM:Limited-Recall

Comment:	Find a reminding by removing distant connections.
Test:	Does problem description have any second-level connections to other knowledge structures?
Transform:	Remove all connections to second-level knowledge structures.
Adapt:	No adaptation.

Figure 8.12 TRAM:Limited-Recall

TRAM:Ignore-Neighbors would occasionally find? Not at all. MINSTREL must simply find those solutions using smaller and more specific steps. If a problem description has four immediate connections to other knowledge structures, MINSTREL must remove these connections singly, by using heuristics that know about these specific types of connections. (And if MINSTREL lacks a TRAM suited to removing a particular connection, it also lacks the knowledge necessary to adapt a solution that lacks that connection; and so no solution is lost.) By breaking the transformation problem into four smaller problems, MINSTREL has made the adaptation problem tractable.

8.6.2   TRAM:Switch-Focus

TRAM:Switch-Focus is the second of the abandoned TRAMs. This heuristic suggests that if MINSTREL is trying to find a state resulting from some action, it look instead for an action that intends that state. In this case, the problem description consists of two frames connected by an "&intended/&intended-by" link. This TRAM suggests considering the "other" frame to be the problem description. This transformation is shown graphically in Figure 8.13. The pseudo-code for TRAM:Switch-Focus is given in Figure 8.14.

TRAM:Switch-Focus was intended to allow MINSTREL to apply act-specific TRAMs to problems involving states. (Since MINSTREL has 11 TRAMs that apply to acts and only 6 that apply to states, this would seem to be

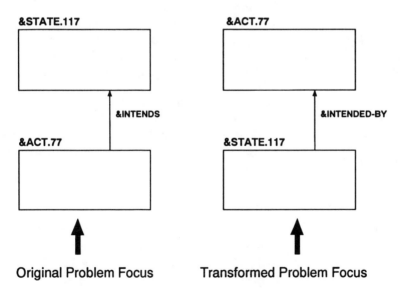

Figure 8.13 Graphical Explanation of TRAM:Switch-Focus

TRAM:Switch-Focus

Comment:	Look at this problem from the viewpoint of the act, instead of the state.
Test:	Is the problem description a state intended by an act?
Transform:	Use the intended act as the problem description.
Adapt:	The recalled episode is an act that intends a state. Return the state instead of the act.

Figure 8.14 TRAM:Switch-Focus

a worthwhile goal.) However, TRAM:Switch-Focus was never successfully applied.

The reason for this is twofold. First, TRAM:Switch-Focus will never by itself lead to a discovery, because it does not change the problem description. Any episode which involves both a state and an act will be indexed in episodic memory by both, so simply shifting the focus of recall in a problem description from an act to a state will not lead to any additional solutions. So as an individual creativity heuristic, TRAM:Switch-Focus is ineffective.

Second, TRAM:Switch-Focus often operated at odds with author-level goals. The author-level of MINSTREL specified problems by their most important features. If a problem specification focused on a state, that was usually because the state was the most critical component of the problem description. When TRAM:Switch-Focus moved the focus to an associated action, it reduced MINSTREL's chances of finding a solution.

There are two lessons to be learned from TRAM:Switch-Focus. First, the idea of "looking at something in a new way" is often touted as a creativity technique. What TRAM:Switch-Focus emphasizes is that the "different way" must be substantively different. A simple syntactic change is unlikely to lead to a creative realization.

Second, TRAM:Switch-Focus reveals an interaction between higher level cognitive processes (called the author-level in MINSTREL) and low-level creativity. Creativity should make use of high-level knowledge (such as domain-specific knowledge on where to focus creativity) to guide the search for a new solution to a problem.

8.6.3 TRAM:Remove-Slot-Constraint

TRAM:Remove-Slot-Constraint suggests transforming a problem description by removing a single slot of the problem description frame at random, recalling a solution based on the transformed description, and then adding the removed slot back to any discovered solution. The pseudo-code for this TRAM is given in Figure 8.15.

The purpose of TRAM:Remove-Slot-Constraints was to improve MINSTREL's chances of finding a solution when given a problem description that

TRAM:Remove-Slot-Constraint

Comment:	Randomly remove one slot of the description frame.
Test:	Does the frame have a slot other than :actor or :type?
Transform:	Randomly select and remove a slot other than :actor or :type.
Adapt:	Add the removed slot value to any solutions.

Figure 8.15 TRAM:Remove-Slot-Constraint

was overconstrained. When creating a large, interconnected structure like a story, filling in one part of the story will cause other parts of the story to be filled in. For instance, if the protaganist is a knight, he is a knight in every part of the story, not just in the scene where that decision is made. Consequently, when MINSTREL attempts to fill in a scene, there may be a number of possibly irrelevant constraints on that scene arising from other parts of the story. TRAM:Remove-Slot-Constraints was an attempt to write a TRAM that would remove some of these unnecessary constraints.

The difficulty with this TRAM lies in the random selection of slot constraints. There is nothing in TRAM:Remove-Slot-Constraints that attempts to decide whether a constraint is relevant or not. Consequently TRAM:Remove-Slot-Constraints removed important constraints as frequently as it removed irrelevant constraints. (In fact, more frequently, since there are generally more relevant constraints than irrelevant ones.) An early attempt to fix this problem is evident in the Test and Transform portions of the TRAM as shown in Figure 8.15. These portions of TRAM:Remove-Slot-Constraint prevent the removal of the :actor and :type slots, two slots that were discovered by experience to be almost always relevant. But this was patchwork fix that did not address the real problem.

The lesson to be learned from TRAM:Remove-Slot-Constraints is that care must be taken in removing or weakening problem constraints. Much shrift is given in popular creativity literature to removing problem constraints as a method for unlocking creativity. Yet the removal of important problem constraints will only lead to unworkable solutions or a very difficult adaptation problem. Better advice is to examine a problem carefully to discover what constraints are truly necessary and what constraints only appear to be necessary, and to remove those constraints that only appear necessary.

8.7   Experiment #1: Adding a New Theme to MINSTREL

To help evaluate MINSTREL as a computer model, a number of experiments with MINSTREL's knowledge, control structures, and task domains were performed. The first experiment was to have MINSTREL tell a story about a new theme. Assuming MINSTREL had the episodic memory, representation, author-level plans, and TRAMs needed to tell stories about three different themes, what additional knowledge would MINSTREL need to tell a story about a new theme? If MINSTREL required little or no additional knowledge, it would indicate that MINSTREL's author-level plans and creativity have some generality, at least for the task of storytelling within the King Arthur domain.

8.7.1 PAT:PRIDE

As the first step in this experiment, a new theme was represented and added to MINSTREL's episodic memory: PAT:PRIDE. PAT:PRIDE is based on the saying: "Pride goes before a fall." In particular, PAT:PRIDE represents the goal/plan situation in which an actor is warned that if he does something, it will result in a goal failure, but because he is overly proud, attempts the action anyway. &PAT:PRIDE is a knowledge structure which captures a piece of planning advice: "Don't let your pride get in the way of accepting useful advice." MINSTREL's representation of PAT:PRIDE is shown in Figure 8.16.

As with all themes in MINSTREL, this representation was hand coded by the author and added to MINSTREL's episodic memory. No examples of PAT:PRIDE were added to memory, only the abstract representation. It would be up to MINSTREL to invent story scenes to fit this new theme, using its existing episodic memories and creativity.

8.7.2 MINSTREL's Performance

After the representation for PAT:PRIDE was added to MINSTREL, MINSTREL was given the goal of telling a story about this theme. MINSTREL immediately ran into an interesting and typical problem.

Initially, the main character of PAT:PRIDE (?Planner in Figure 8.16) is uninstantiated. MINSTREL begins storytelling by determining a role for this actor from amongst the kinds of characters it knows about. As it happens, the actor is instantiated as a hermit. MINSTREL's next step is to instantiate the prideful act (&Act.2 in Figure 8.16). To do this, MINSTREL uses an episodic memory about a princess and some creativity heuristics to invent a scene in which a hermit picks berries in the woods.[15]

At this point, MINSTREL bogs down. MINSTREL cannot invent any bad consequences of picking berries. So MINSTREL is unable to fill in the "fall" portion of "Pride goes before a fall," and the story fizzles. Figure 8.17 shows an (author-supplied) English version of the failed story.

Being unable to continue a story because of a bad decision earlier is a common problem for MINSTREL. MINSTREL has a very limited planning model, and no effort was made to give MINSTREL plans for retracting bad solutions, or

---

[15] In fact, the instantiation of the actor occurs simultaneously with the instantiation of the prideful act. While this is indicative of the kinds of interactions that occur in the creation of a story, it is more easily understood if presented as two separate instantiations.

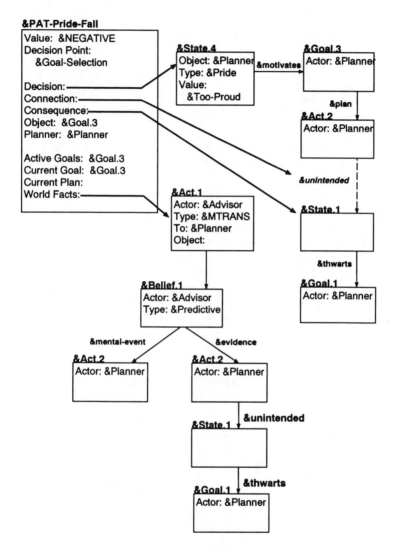

Figure 8.16 Representation of PAT:PRIDE

The Proud Hermit

Once upon a time there was a hermit. Someone warned him not to pick berries, but he went ahead and picked them anyway. Nothing bad happened.

Figure 8.17 Failed PAT:PRIDE Story

for recovery from decisions that resulted in a large number of failed goals. Consequently, when MINSTREL makes a decision that later causes difficulties, MINSTREL has no way to retract the earlier decision. MINSTREL's common errors and what they say about MINSTREL's model of creativity are discussed in more detail in Section 12 of this chapter.

There are several ways to address this problem without changing MINSTREL's planning model. One solution is to give MINSTREL a "hint" that will point it in a different direction. In this case, we suggest an alternative role for the main character. This is done by setting the role of the main character by hand to an appropriate value. Because MINSTREL knows the most about knights, we set the main character to be a knight.

The result after this hint is an almost-perfect story about a knight who fought a dragon despite a warning from a friendly hermit. The resulting story is shown in Figure 8.18.

"The Proud Knight" has two errors in it, as indicated by the italics in Figure 8.18. MINSTREL explains how Grunfeld got wounded twice, and (rather impishly) suggests that Grunfeld's injuries impress the king.

These errors occur during MINSTREL's creation of the scene in which Grunfeld is wounded. Because these errors give insight into MINSTREL's operation and the role of creativity heuristics, we provide a detailed analysis of the problem and its solution.

8.7.3 A Storytelling Error

In telling "The Proud Knight," MINSTREL invents a scene in which Grunfeld kills a dragon but is wounded in the process. After this scene is created, MINSTREL checks to see if it knows anything further about woundings that it should add to the scene. To do this, it tries to recall a previous scene in which a knight was wounded in a similar situation, and uses the recalled scene to further instantiate the story scene. Using two creativity heuristics (TRAM:Similar-Thwart-State and TRAM:Generalize-Actor), MINSTREL recalls the episode shown in Figure 8.19.

In fact, this is the same episode MINSTREL used to instantiate the main action of "The Proud Knight." In this case, however, "Knight Fight" is being

The Proud Knight

Once upon a time, a hermit named Bebe told a knight named Grunfeld that if Grunfeld fought a dragon then something bad would happen.

Grunfeld was very proud. Because he was very proud, he wanted to impress the king. Grunfeld moved to a dragon. Grunfeld fought a dragon. The dragon was destroyed, but Grunfeld was wounded. *Grunfeld was wounded because he fought a knight. Grunfeld being wounded impressed the king.*

Figure 8.18 The Proud Knight

Knight Fight

In order to impress the king, a knight killed a dragon, thwarting the dragon's goal of staying alive.

Figure 8.19 Knight Fight Episode

used in a slightly different manner. MINSTREL is trying to recall a scene in which some state thwarts a knight's goal of protecting his health. This specification recalls nothing, so MINSTREL applies the creativity heuristic TRAM:Generalize-Actor, and the knight is generalized to another violent character: a monster. The new problem specification is "some state thwarts a monster's goal of protecting his health."

Because the dragon in "Knight Fight" dies rather than merely being wounded, this specification also recalls nothing. TRAM:Similar-Thwart-State is then applied to the specification. TRAM:Similar-Thwart-State is a creativity heuristic that modifies a thwarting state to a similar, related state. In this case, it modifies the knight's wounding to death. The new problem specification is "some state thwarts a monster's goal of staying alive." This specification succeeds in recalling the dragon's death in "Knight Fight."

The Adapt step of TRAM:Similar-Thwart-State adapts the recalled episode by changing the dragon's death back to a wounding. The Adapt step of TRAM:Generalize-Actor changes the dragon back to a knight resulting in the modified episode:

In order to impress the king, a knight wounded a knight, thwarting the knight's goal of protecting his health.

This modified episode is then used to fill in the knight's wounding in "The Proud Knight." Unfortunately, this results in the "knight wounding a knight" and the "In order to impress the king" parts of the modified episode being added to "The Proud Knight."

The problem here is that TRAM:Similar-Thwart-State did not correctly Adapt the recalled episode. TRAM:Similar-Thwart-State knows specifically about states that thwart goals. While this TRAM was able to correctly adapt the thwarting state, it was unable to correctly adapt the extraneous scenes (how the knight was wounded, and the knight's goals). TRAM:Similar-Thwart-State should have stripped off these scenes that it was unable to adapt. This would have resulted in a modified episode of this form:

A knight is wounded, thwarting his goal to protect his health.

In cases where a TRAM does not have the knowledge to correctly adapt some portion of a recalled episode, the TRAM should remove the unadaptable portion. Although this may lose some valuable information, it assures that the TRAM will not produce an incorrectly adapted solution, and is in keeping with MINSTREL's philosophy of TRAMs that are specific and limited in scope.

When TRAM:Similar-Thwart-State was modified to remove extraneous links, MINSTREL was able to tell "The Proud Knight" without error.

8.8 Experiment #2: Adding a New Role to MINSTREL

In the first experiment, a new theme was added to MINSTREL. Although the structure of goals, actions and states used in the theme was new, the theme did not require any extension of MINSTREL's basic representation. As a second experiment, we decided to extend MINSTREL's representation slightly, to see how MINSTREL could handle storytelling involving entirely new concepts.

8.8.1 The King

Until this point, MINSTREL knew of three roles that a character could have: a character could be a knight, a princess, or a hermit. We extended this representation by adding a new character role: the king.

Three things were necessary to add the king to MINSTREL's knowledge of character roles. First, a new symbol was assigned to represent this role: "&king." Second, the new symbol was added to MINSTREL's class hierarchy of roles. Kings were described as violent (as are knights and monsters) and social (as are princesses). Finally, phrases were added to the phrasal generator to tell MINSTREL how to talk about this new concept.

MINSTREL was given no other information about kings. In particular, MINSTREL was not given any episodes or story fragments involving kings. MINSTREL would be asked to tell a story about a king knowing nothing more than that a king was a kind of "sociable knight."

8.8.2 The King in Storytelling

MINSTREL was asked to tell a story about PAT-PRIDE with the main character being a king instead of a knight. Figure 8.20 shows the resulting story.

This story is exactly similar to "The Proud Knight." An examination of the trace shows that MINSTREL created this story in the same way it created "The Proud Knight," with one exception. In this story, MINSTREL used TRAM:Generalize-Actor and its knowledge that kings and knights were both violent to generalize the king to a knight (and subsequently to a dragon).

This story shows how MINSTREL's creativity heuristics can, with a very minimal amount of information about a new concept, use it in a problem solution. Not unsurprisingly, this story is not particularly novel. MINSTREL does not have enough knowledge about kings to invent anything strikingly original.

It was the Spring of 1089, and King Arthur returned to Camelot from elsewhere.

A hermit named Bebe told Arthur that Bebe believed that if Arthur fought with the dragon then something bad would happen.

Arthur was very proud. Because he was very proud, Arthur wanted to impress his subjects. Arthur wanted to be near a dragon. Arthur moved to a dragon. Arthur was near a dragon. The dragon was destroyed because Arthur fought with the dragon. The dragon was destroyed but Arthur was hurt. Arthur wanted to protect his health. Arthur wanted to be healed. Arthur hated himself. Arthur became a hermit.

Figure 8.20 The Proud King

But MINSTREL is able to make use of what it does know to create a competent solution.

8.9   Experiment #3: Learning in MINSTREL

The previous two experiments looked at how MINSTREL's knowledge could be extended from outside the program. But MINSTREL also has the ability to extend its own knowledge through creativity. How can MINSTREL use creativity to extend its knowledge and change its behavior?

In MINSTREL, the basic mechanism for learning is episodic memory. As MINSTREL tells stories and invents solutions to problems, these problems and their solutions are added to episodic memory. These episodes can be used in turn to solve future problems. In this way, MINSTREL uses creativity to permanently extend its knowledge.

Creativity extends knowledge.

MINSTREL also uses episodic memory to judge whether a problem solution is novel or creative. When MINSTREL encounters a problem solution—by recalling it from episodic memory, inventing it, or (hypothetically) reading about it, MINSTREL can determine whether the solution is novel and interesting by comparing it to the solutions in episodic memory. If the new solution has significant differences from all past solutions, MINSTREL recognizes the new solution as creative. And because MINSTREL's episodic memory changes as it solves problems and adds their solutions to memory, MINSTREL's definition of creativity also changes.

What is creative changes with experience.

In creative problem-solving domains like storytelling, this can be used to implement an "artistic drive." When telling a story, MINSTREL can compare the scenes it is writing with past scenes in episodic memory. If a scene is too similar to a past scene, the scene can be discarded on the grounds that it is too "boring." And as MINSTREL tells stories about particular subjects and adds those stories to memory, it's definition of what is interesting will change. Like a human artist, MINSTREL will be driven to be creative.

In this experiment, we look at this issue. The first part of this experiment shows how MINSTREL remembers solutions as they are invented and can then use them immediately—without reinventing them—when asked to solve a similar problem. The second part of this experiment examines how MINSTREL's storytelling behavior changes as it tells stories and is driven to invent new stories.

8.9.1   Learning in MINSTREL

Chapter 2 showed how MINSTREL uses creativity to invent ways for a knight to commit suicide. Using two episodes from memory and three creativity heuristics, MINSTREL invents three methods for a knight to commit suicide. Figure 8.21 shows the reasoning MINSTREL used to invent one of these solutions.

As Figure 8.21 shows, when MINSTREL is first asked to invent a method for a knight to commit suicide, it uses two TRAMS (TRAM:Similar-Outcomes-Partial-Change and TRAM:Generalize-Constraint) to invent an episode in which a knight poisons himself. But once this new solution has been discovered and added to episodic memory, it can be used again without invoking any creativity heuristics.

Figure 8.23 shows a trace of MINSTREL being asked a second time for a method by which a knight can commit suicide. This time, MINSTREL recalls directly the method it had previously invented (&ACT.206). Once MINSTREL has invented a solution and indexed it in episodic memory, it can find and apply that solution quickly, without using creativity. By remembering created solutions, MINSTREL is able to improve its efficiency as a problem solver.

Knowledge extends creativity.

Remembering invented solutions not only extends MINSTREL's knowledge and improves its efficiency as a problem solver, it also extends MINSTREL's creativity. Each remembered solution is the end point of a successful search that used creativity heuristics to find a new solution to a problem. In the case above, the poison solution is the endpoint of a creative process that invented the idea of poison and the idea of a knight intentionally ingesting poison to kill himself, both concepts that were previously unknown to MINSTREL. But now that these concepts have been discovered and remembered, they provide a new starting point for creativity. By starting at this remembered endpoint, MINSTREL can

```
===================================================
                MINSTREL Invention
===================================================
Initial specification is &ACT.105:
 (A KNIGHT NAMED JOHN DID SOMETHING *PERIOD*
JOHN DIED *PERIOD*)

Problem-Solving Cycle: &ACT.105.
 Executing TRAM:EXAGGERATE-SCALED-VALUE.
   Recalling: NIL.
[...]
 Executing TRAM:SIMILAR-OUTCOMES-PARTIAL-CHANGE.
   Recalling: NIL.
    [TRAM Recursion: &ACT.136.]
       Executing TRAM:GENERALIZE-CONSTRAINT.
       Generalizing :ACTOR on &ACT.136.
       Recalling: &PRINCESS-POTION.

Minstrel invented this solution:
 (A KNIGHT NAMED JOHN DRANK A POTION IN ORDER TO
KILL HIMSELF *PERIOD* JOHN DIED *PERIOD*)

Added back to memory as &ACT.206.
[...]
```

Figure 8.21 Initial Reasoning for Poisoning Example

```
===================================================
                MINSTREL Invention
===================================================
Initial specification is &ACT.354:
 (A KNIGHT NAMED JOHN DID SOMETHING *PERIOD*
JOHN DIED *PERIOD*)

ProbLem Solving Cycle: &ACT.354.
   Executing TRAM:STANDARD-PROBLEM SOLVING.
     Recalling: (&ACT.206).
ProbLem Solving Cycle succeeds: (&ACT.358).

Minstrel invented this solution:
 (A KNIGHT NAMED JOHN DRANK A POTION IN ORDER
TO KILL HIMSELF *PERIOD* JOHN DIED *PERIOD*)
```

Figure 8.22 Reasoning After Learning

search further into the potential solution space to find new solutions that it would not have been able to discover previously because of search constraints.

For example, now that MINSTREL has invented the notion of intentional poisoning, it can invent yet another solution to the problem of killing yourself: having an agent poison you. MINSTREL was unable to discover this solution originally because it requires applying four creativity heuristics, and MINSTREL applies at most three creativity heuristics when searching for a problem solution.[16]

But now that the compiled result of previous creativity is available as a new starting point for creative problem solving, MINSTREL can discover this new solution (Figure 8.23).

Remembering invented solutions therefore provides MINSTREL with a mechanism for extending its knowledge, a way to improve its efficiency as a problem solver, and a method for increasing the scope of its creativity.

8.9.2 Learning and the Artistic Drive

In art, a premium is placed on significant new ideas. This drive to create is implemented in MINSTREL as a domain assessment that rejects problem solutions that are noncreative, that is, problem solutions that are similar to known solutions. Consequently, MINSTREL's storytelling behavior changes as it tells and remembers stories. After creating a few stories in which a knight fights a dragon, MINSTREL becomes "bored" with knights fighting dragons and turns

```
========================================================
             MINSTREL Invention
========================================================
Initial specification is &ACT.457:
 (A KNIGHT NAMED JOHN DID SOMETHING *PERIOD*
JOHN DIED *PERIOD*)

[...]
 Executing TRAM:ACHIEVE-VIA-AGENT
    Recalling: (&ACT.206).
ProbLem Solving Cycle succeeds: (&ACT.206).

Minstrel invented this solution:
 (A PERSON FED A KNIGHT NAMED JOHN A POTION IN
ORDER TO KILL JOHN *PERIOD* JOHN DIED *PERIOD*)
```

Figure 8.23 Additional Suicide Solution

---

[16] MINSTREL supposes some limit to the creative search process. This may be a time limit, an effort limit, or some combination of the two. Limiting MINSTREL to a search depth of three implements this type of a processing limit, but is not intended as a theoretical claim.

its storytelling attentions elsewhere. (For this reason, the domain assessment that drives MINSTREL to create new stories is called the "boredom assessment.")

This section looks at how the boredom assessment drives MINSTREL to change its storytelling behavior.

8.9.2.1 Methodology

The boredom assessment operates during the Assess step of problem solving (see Chapter 2). The boredom assessment tests each solution generated by creative problem solving to see if the solution is "boring," that is, noncreative. To do this, the boredom assessment uses the generated solution as an index to the problem solver's episodic memory. If the generated solution recalls more than a small number of similar past solutions, it is judged boring and is rejected.

The threshold at which the boredom assessment rejects a solution is a simple measure of how quickly a problem solver becomes bored with reusing past solutions. In nonartistic domains, this threshold is high, indicating that the problem solver is willing to reuse solutions many times. In artistic domains, this threshold is low, indicating that the problem solver is motivated to discover new solutions. For this experiment the threshold was set to two. With this setting MINSTREL is willing to use a solution twice before beginning to reject it as boring.

To study how this affects MINSTREL's behavior, MINSTREL was repeatedly asked to tell a story about the theme "Pride goes before a fall" (PAT:Pride), in which the main character was a knight. After each story was told, the scenes in the story were added to episodic memory. In combination with the boredom assessment, this causes MINSTREL to tell a sequence of different stories.

8.9.2.2 The First Story

When MINSTREL is initially asked to tell a story about the theme "Pride goes before a fall" it tells the story "The Proud Knight," as detailed in Section 5 of this chapter. In this story, a knight tries to impress his king by killing a dragon, even though he is forewarned that fighting a dragon will lead to trouble.

After this story is told, it is added to episodic memory. MINSTREL adds a story to episodic memory by adding each schema which makes up the story to episodic memory. Although each schema is added individually to memory, the connections between the schemas are retained, so that MINSTREL will recall the entire story whenever a set of recall indices match any part of the story.

This story turns on MINSTREL's recall of an episode in which a knight fights a dragon. This episode is used to create the scene in "The Proud Knight" in which the knight fights a dragon and is injured. After this story has been added to episodic memory, there are two scenes in episodic memory in which a knight fights a dragon: the original scene, and the scene that was used in "The

Proud Knight." Consequently, MINSTREL no longer creates scenes in which a knight fights a dragon, because those scenes have now become "boring."

8.9.2.3   The Second Story

In telling the original story about PAT:Pride, MINSTREL recalled an episode in which a knight fought a dragon, and used that to create the story scene in which the knight suffers his fall. To tell another story about PAT:Pride, MINSTREL must recall or invent a new story scene in which a knight suffers a failure. MINSTREL does this by using a recalled episode in which a knight competes at a joust. The resulting story is shown in Figure 8.24.

To create this story, MINSTREL recalls an episode in which a knight fights another knight (a joust). This episode was not recalled in creating the original "The Proud Knight" story because the episode in which a knight fights a dragon was recalled instead. But now that scene is considered boring and MINSTREL can recall instead an alternate scene. This reveals one aspect of MINSTREL's behavior when using the boredom assessment: As solutions become boring, MINSTREL can discover other, usable solutions which it has known all along, but never previously used because other solutions were preferred.

The second part of the knight's fall is the failure he suffers at the joust. This is created using ALP:INSTANTIATE-FAILURE, which suggests that one way an action can cause a goal failure is if the action itself fails. The overall result is a story in which a knight suffers an unintended loss at a joust. Again, this is added to memory.

8.9.2.4   The Third Story

MINSTREL has now told stories about a knight fighting a monster and a knight fighting a joust. Both these episodes are now considered boring because they have been used twice. (Once in the original episode, and once in the new stories.) There remains one episode in memory that involves a knight, which has not become boring. In this episode, a knight rides his horse to the woods. MINSTREL uses this as a basis for a new story, as shown in Figure 8.25.

MINSTREL invents the important elements of this story in two steps. First, MINSTREL uses TRAM:Recall-Act to invent the action that will lead to the

It was the Spring of 1089, and a knight named Godwin returned to Camelot from elsewhere.

A hermit named Bebe told Godwin that Bebe believed that if Godwin jousted then something bad would happen. Godwin was very proud. Because Godwin was very proud, Godwin wanted to impress his king. Godwin jousted. Godwin lost the joust. Godwin hated himself.

Figure 8.24   The Proud Knight II

It was the Spring of 1089, and a knight named Cedric returned to Camelot from elsewhere.

A hermit named Bebe told Cedric that Bebe believed that if Cedric moved to the woods then something bad would happen. Cedric was very proud. Because he was very proud, Cedric wanted to have some berries. Cedric wanted to be near the woods. He was at the woods because Cedric moved to the woods. He was at the woods but saw that a knight named Arthur kissed with a princess named Andrea. Cedric loved Andrea. Because Cedric loved Andrea, Cedric wanted to be the love of Andrea. But he could not because Arthur kissed with Andrea. Cedric hated himself. Cedric had some berries because Cedric picked some berries.

Figure 8.25 The Proud Knight III

knight's fall. Because the other scenes in memory that involve a knight have become boring, TRAM:Recall-Act recalls the episode in which a knight rides to the woods to fight a dragon. TRAM:Recall-Act adapts this for use in the current story.

The second step is to invent the knight's fall, that is, the events that lead to the knight having a failed goal. When MINSTREL tries to recall some way riding to the woods can cause a goal to fail, it recalls the scene it originally created for *The Mistaken Knight*:

```
Some   time   later,   Lancelot's   horse   moved
Lancelot   to   the   woods   unintentionally,   again
causing   him   to   be   near   Andrea.   Lancelot   knew
that   Andrea   kissed   with   a   knight   named   Freder-
ick   because   Lancelot   saw   that   Andrea   kissed
with   Frederick.   Lancelot   believed   that   Andrea
loved   Frederick.   Lancelot   loved   Andrea.
Because   Lancelot   loved   Andrea,   Lancelot   wanted
to   be   the   love   of   Andrea.   But   he   could   not
because   Andrea   loved   Frederick.
```

This is then adapted to the current story. The end result is a scene in which a knight suffers a goal failure when another knight kisses the princess he loves.

There is one more interesting twist involved in telling this story. After MIN-STREL creates the scenes shown above, it notices that the first scene—in which a knight rides to the woods—is inconsistent, because there is no reason for the knight to do that action. MINSTREL knows of some actions that knights take without specific reason—such as fighting monsters—but riding to the woods is not one of them. Consequently, MINSTREL gives itself the goal of finding a purpose for the knight's trip to the woods.

One reason a knight might travel to the woods is to fight a dragon, but MIN-STREL's previous use of that type of scene and the boredom assessment prevent it from being reused in this context. So MINSTREL must invent a new reason for a knight to travel to the woods. It does this using TRAM:Generalize-Actor. This TRAM suggests that knights might be similar in some ways to princesses (because they are both social characters), recalls that princesses sometimes go to the woods to pick berries, and consequently creates a scene in which a knight goes to the woods to pick berries.

As it happens, this too is inconsistent (knights do not normally pick berries). Again, MINSTREL notices this and creates a goal to add story scenes to explain why a knight would be picking berries. But MINSTREL cannot recall or invent any reason for a knight to be picking berries, so this scene has no further explanation in the final story.

In this case, MINSTREL's initial reasoning (that knights might be picking berries because they share characteristics with princesses, who do pick berries) is sound, and the resulting scene reasonable. In general, MINSTREL does not currently try to judge when a failed author-level goal results in a "bad" story.

It is interesting to note that in creating this story, MINSTREL borrows from a story it had previously created (*The Mistaken Knight*). However, because the scene it borrows must be adapted to the current story, and because various consistency goals change the resulting scene, the resulting story is significantly different from the previous story.

8.9.2.5 The Fourth Story

MINSTREL has now used all the episodes in memory which involve a knight at least twice. To continue to tell stories about proud knights, MINSTREL must begin adapting knowledge about different characters (i.e., monsters, princesses, and hermits). The first result of this is shown in Figure 8.26.

In the first story MINSTREL told about PAT:Pride, a knight fought a monster and was wounded. This story is similar to the first story, but differs in several significant ways: the knight fights another knight instead of a monster, and he is killed instead of just being wounded. And unlike the scenes in the previous stories, these scenes are not based on episodes in which a knight is the main actor.

> It was the Spring of 1089, and a knight named Cedric returned to Camelot from elsewhere.
> A hermit named Bebe told Cedric that Bebe believed that if Cedric fought a knight named Frederick then something bad would happen. Cedric was very proud. Because he was very proud, Cedric wanted to kill Frederick. Cedric wanted to be near Frederick. Cedric moved to Frederick. Frederick was killed because Cedric fought Frederick. Frederick was killed but Cedric was killed. Cedric wanted to protect his health. Cedric wanted to be healed. Cedric hated himself.

Figure 8.26 The Proud Knight IV

Before discussing how MINSTREL creates this story, it is interesting to look at the final scenes of the story. At the end of this story, Cedric is killed, and then wants to protect his health, be healed, and hates himself. Inasmuch as doing anything while dead is difficult, these are storytelling mistakes.

These mistakes arise because MINSTREL's English language generation doesn't make clear the timing of character reactions. In most cases, the timing is irrelevant. But in the case of a character dying, language should be used that makes it clear that the character reactions occur *during* the dying process:

> ...Because he was very proud, Cedric wanted to kill Frederick. Cedric wanted to be near Frederick. Cedric moved to Frederick. Frederick was killed because Cedric fought Frederick. Frederick was killed but Cedric was killed. *As Cedric was dying,* he wanted to protect his health. Cedric wanted to be healed. Cedric hated himself. Cedric died.

The story representation is the same; but the way in which the story is expressed has been changed. This reinforces the complex nature of storytelling: To tell a story successfully requires the careful interaction and cooperation of a variety of complex processes.

To create the scene in which Cedric fights Frederick, MINSTREL uses TRAM:Generalize-Actor to adapt an episode involving a monster to the current story. TRAM:Generalize-Actor suggests that a knight might be like a monster in some ways (they are both violent characters), and this recalls the episode &KILLING-ACT, which is an episode in which a monster fights a knight:

```
A monster fights a knight and kills him.
```

TRAM:Generalize-Actor adapts this episode to the current story by substituting Cedric for the monster, resulting in a scene in which Cedric fights another knight (Frederick), and kills him.

To create the goal failure resulting from this action, MINSTREL again uses TRAM:Generalize-Actor to suggest that knights are like monsters. This time, TRAM:Generalize-Actor helps MINSTREL recall the scene from the first PAT:Pride story in which the monster was killed by the knight:

```
Grunfeld fought a dragon. The dragon was
destroyed, but Grunfeld was wounded.
```

MINSTREL then adapts this to the current story by replacing the monster with Cedric and merging that with the scene in which Cedric kill Frederick:

> Frederick was killed because Cedric fought
> Frederick. Frederick was killed but Cedric was
> killed.

The resulting scene illustrates how fighting a knight can have a bad consequence. There are two revealing points to this story.

Creativity uses old experiences in new ways.

First, this story illustrates an interesting feature of how MINSTREL's creative drive and episodic memory interact. Although the boredom assessment prevents MINSTREL from reusing a scene in a way similar to previously told stories, it does not prevent MINSTREL from making use of a previously used scene in a new way. This is evident in the creation of the second part of this story, in which MINSTREL reuses a scene from the first story (a knight killing a dragon) in a new way to create a scene which passes the boredom assessment (a knight dying as a result of fighting another knight).

Creativity creates new experiences.

The second interesting feature concerns how episodic memory changes during storytelling. When MINSTREL began telling this story, all of the episodes in memory involving knights as actors were considered boring, forcing MINSTREL to invent scenes by analogizing knights to monsters. But after telling this story, episodic memory contains a new scene involving a knight as an actor which is *not* boring: the scene in which a knight fights a knight. Since this scene is completely new to MINSTREL, and the boredom heuristic only considers an episode boring after it has been used twice, this scene is still considered interesting.

The important point here is not the precise setting of the boredom heuristic, but rather the general behavior of MINSTREL. As MINSTREL creates new story scenes in response to story needs and the drive of the boredom assessment, episodic memory grows and changes. New episodes are added; old episodes are found to be boring. Memory and behavior evolve in response to problem solving.

8.9.2.6 The Fifth Story

In telling the next story, MINSTREL makes use of the scene it invented for the fourth story—a knight fighting a knight—and invents a new goal failure for the second part of the theme. This story is shown in Figure 8.27.

The development of this story is straightforward. MINSTREL creates the scene in which Cedric fights Frederick by recalling the similar scene from the

It was the Spring of 1089, and a knight named Cedric returned to Camelot from elsewhere.

A hermit named Bebe told Cedric that Bebe believed that if Cedric fought Frederick then something bad would happen. Cedric was very proud. Because he was very proud, Cedric wanted to kill Frederick. Cedric wanted to be near Frederick. Cedric moved to Frederick. Frederick was killed because Cedric fought Frederick. Frederick was killed but Cedric's sword was destroyed. Cedric wanted to possess a sword. Cedric wanted Cedric's sword to be healed. Cedric hated himself.

Figure 8.27 The Proud Knight V

previous story. The goal failure associated with this scene is created by an author-level plan which suggests that an unintended result of an action which involves an object could be the destruction of that object.

In the previous story, MINSTREL invented a scene in which a knight fights a knight, and discovered one possible bad consequence of that action. In this story, MINSTREL continues to explore this new area, inventing another possible bad consequence. To do this, MINSTREL used an author-level plan that wasn't applicable before creativity had invented the scene of two knights fighting. As this demonstrates, MINSTREL's creativity and domain-specific knowledge can interact to extend MINSTREL's knowledge.

8.9.2.7   Creativity Fails

At this point, MINSTREL's storytelling fails. MINSTREL has exhausted its ability to invent story scenes that meet the constraints of the theme and pass the boredom assessment. Although there are many possible combinations of the episodes in memory, and many more combinations that can be invented using creativity heuristics, only a very small percentage of that space can be used for stories based on PAT:Pride. PAT:Pride requires scenes in which a character is motivated by pride to perform a hasty action that he later regrets. This combination of specific constraints limits the range of MINSTREL's creativity. The eventual failure of creativity is not unexpected. MINSTREL is a finite system. When asked repeatedly to find new solutions to a problem, it will eventually run out of ideas.

An interesting question that can be posed at this juncture is whether the knowledge that MINSTREL acquired in telling five stories about the theme "Pride goes before a fall" carries over into other tasks. This sequence of five stories has demonstrated how MINSTREL's behavior changes as it repeatedly solved the same task. Does this learning carry over into other similar problems? To examine this issue, MINSTREL was asked to tell a story about another theme, PAT:Good-Deeds-Rewarded.

PAT:Good-Deeds-Rewarded is based on a theme from the movie *It's a*

Wonderful Life. It's a Wonderful Life stars Jimmy Stewart as George Bailey, a good, unselfish man who constantly turns away from his dreams in order to do good deeds for others. When it appears that the town tyrant is going to take the Bailey Savings and Loan away from George he despairs and wishes that he had never been born. An angel shows George what the lives of his friends and family would have been like if he had never been born and that experience restores his spirit. At the end of the film, the people he has helped all his life band together to help him save the bank. One of the central themes of this movie is that one should be kindly and help others when possible, because someday that kindness may be returned. PAT:Good-Deeds-Rewarded represents this theme.

When MINSTREL is initially asked to tell a story about PAT:Good-Deeds-Rewarded, it tells the story shown in Figure 8.28.

The first part of this story is based on the scene in episodic memory in which a knight fights a dragon. However, when MINSTREL is asked to tell a story about this theme after telling the previous five stories about PAT:Pride, this episode is not available. It has been used in several previous stories and is rejected by the boredom assessment. Consequently, MINSTREL tells a completely different story about PAT:Good-Deeds-Rewarded. This new story is shown in Figure 8.29.

There are several interesting points about this story.

First, MINSTREL makes an "error of knowledge" in telling this story. MINSTREL does not realize that the goal of achieving love cannot be satisfied by an agent. Consequently, MINSTREL creates the questionable scene in which

> Once upon a time, there was a hermit named Bebe and a knight named Cedric. One day, Cedric was wounded when he killed a dragon in order to impress the King. Bebe, who was in the woods picking berries, did Cedric a favor. Bebe healed Cedric. Cedric was grateful and vowed to return the favor.
>
> Later, Bebe believed he would die because he saw a dragon moving towards him and believed that it would eat him. Bebe tried to run away but failed. Cedric, who was in the woods, killed a dragon and saved Bebe.

Figure 8.28 Initial PAT:Good-Deeds-Rewarded Story

> Once upon a time, there was a hermit named Bebe and a knight named Cedric. One day, Cedric moved to a princess named Andrea. Cedric was with Andrea. Cedric loved Andrea. Because Cedric loved Andrea, Cedric wanted to be the love of Andrea. Bebe did Cedric a favor. Bebe kissed Andrea. Cedric was grateful and vowed to return the favor.
>
> Later, Bebe wanted to scare a hermit named Edwin. Bebe wanted Edwin to believe she would die. Cedric fed Edwin a magic potion that made her appear dead. Edwin wanted to protect his health. Edwin wanted to be healed. Edwin was scared.

Figure 8.29 New PAT:Good-Deeds-Rewarded Story

Cedric's goal to have Andrea love him is achieved by Bebe kissing Andrea. Section 12 of this Chapter discusses in more detail the types of errors MINSTREL makes, and what they have to say about MINSTREL's model of creativity. What is important to note here, though, is that MINSTREL's experiences in telling stories about PAT:Pride force it to create a new solution to the first part of this story. Although the solution MINSTREL invents is not quite correct, it is still indicative of how MINSTREL behavior changes as it learns.

Second, this example illustrates how MINSTREL's learning is not limited to the context in which the learning occurred. As MINSTREL told stories about PAT:Pride, its behavior changed. But that change of behavior has also carried over into a different context. What MINSTREL learned telling stories about PAT:Pride affects the story it tells about PAT:Good-Deeds-Rewarded.

This becomes more evident when one examines *how* MINSTREL creates this story. To create the scene in the second part of this story in which Cedric feeds Edwina a potion that makes her appear dead, MINSTREL makes use of the idea of poison, a concept that was invented during MINSTREL's creation of suicide methods for a knight.

8.9.3 Boredom Assessment

Earlier we presented boredom assessment as a simple heuristic that rejected any problem solution that was similar to two other solutions in MINSTREL's episodic memory. As implemented for the storytelling domain, however, the boredom assessment is more complicated.

Not everything in a story needs to be novel. Familiar events give the reader a context by which to understand a story. Further, to make every aspect of a story new and interesting would require a great deal of effort by the author. Even a human author would find this difficult, and it would add little to the reader's enjoyment of the story. Generally, authors seek to make the important parts of their stories novel and interesting, and are content to use familiar solutions in the supporting parts of the story.

In the case of theme-based stories such as MINSTREL tells, the important parts of the story are the scenes that illustrate the theme (i.e., the plot). Consequently, MINSTREL applies the boredom assessment only to author-levels goals that create the scenes that illustrate the theme. Further, MINSTREL only requires that some part of the plot be creative; it does not require that every aspect of the plot be new.

Each of the five stories MINSTREL tells about PAT:Pride has the opening scene:

```
It was the Spring of 1089, and a knight named
Cedric returned to Camelot from elsewhere.
```

This scene results from an author-level goal to create an introduction to the story that establishes the time of the story and presents the main character to the reader. It is used repeatedly because it is not part of the plot.

However, even scenes in the plot can be repeated. For example, the following scene appears in all five of MINSTREL's stories about PAT:Pride:

A hermit named Bebe told Cedric that Bebe believed that if Cedric did ... then something bad would happen.

The structure of this scene derives directly from the theme and therefore must be the same in all of the stories. But the choice to make the Bebe character a hermit does not derive from theme, and could change from story to story. It does not because other parts of the plot change from story to story, and MINSTREL only requires that some part of the plot change to find a story acceptable.

MINSTREL has implemented a particular drive for creativity - one that looks for novelty and interest in the parts of a story that illustrate the theme of the story. For MINSTREL, this is a reasonable heuristic that produces realistic storytelling behavior. But each artistic problem solving domain and each artist will have different requirements about novelty, and these will change over time. The importance of the boredom assessment is not that it defines precisely when an artist gets bored, but rather that it provides a mechanism for implementing many different creative drives.

By using episodic memory to determine whether a problem solution is creative, MINSTREL provides a dynamic definition of creativity that changes in response to the problem solver's goals, understanding of the problem, and his problem solving history. This understanding of how to judge the creativity of a problem solution provides a basis for implementing many different types of creative drives. Furthermore, by basing judgment of creativity upon episodic memory and not upon static standards of interestingness MINSTREL model has a mechanism by which an author can learn new standards of what is creative.

8.10   Experiment #4: Mechanical Invention

The first two experiments looked at how adaptable MINSTREL's creative problem solving was within the storytelling domain. The third experiment looked at MINSTREL's learning behavior in the domain of storytelling. It is also important to examine how general MINSTREL's creativity model is across problem domains. If MINSTREL can be easily adapted to a problem domain different from storytelling, it is some assurance that MINSTREL's model of creativity is not merely an ad-hoc solution to the storytelling problem.

To that end, MINSTREL was applied to the problem of simple mechanical invention. In this experiment, MINSTREL invents staplers that can handle a thick set of papers. MINSTREL knows about ordinary staplers and some simple mechanical devices, and uses this knowledge to invent several heavy-duty staplers. This experiment illustrates both how MINSTREL's creativity process can be applied to problems outside of the storytelling domain, and how domain assessments can be used to drive the creative process.

8.10.1 Representation

MINSTREL knows about three types of mechanical devices. "Sources" are devices such as motors and hands that generate power. "Sinks" are devices such as brakes and the head of a stapler that use power. "Converters" are devices that transfer and translate power between devices. Levers and pistons are examples of this kind of device.

All of these devices are represented by the &DEVICE schema. The &DEVICE schema has slots for the type of the device, the input power of the device, the input power type (i.e., rotary, vector), and the output power and type. Each instance of a &DEVICE can also have links to an input device and an output device. Figure 8.30 illustrates the representation for a lever that transforms a weak vector input into a normal vector output.

MINSTREL's representation of mechanical devices is obviously very simplified. The purpose of MINSTREL's mechanical device invention is to demonstrate creativity in a second problem domain, not to accurately model human understanding of devices. For more detailed models of mechanical device understanding, see Forbus (1984) and Hodges (1993).

&DEVICE.2

```
TYPE: &CONVERTER
ITYPE: &VECTOR
IPOWER: &WEAK
OTYPE: &VECTOR
OPOWER: &NORMAL
NAME: "lever"
```

Figure 8.30 Representation of a Lever

8.10.2 Episodic Memory

MINSTREL's episodic memory initially contains four devices: a hand-powered stapler, a weak-to-normal strength lever, a rotary motor, and a piston that converts normal-strength vector motion to normal-strength rotary motion (i.e., a car piston). The representations of these devices are shown in Figure 8.31.

8.10.3 Domain Assessments

MINSTREL uses two domain assessments during mechanical invention. The *consistency assessment* examines each device MINSTREL invents to determine if it has a proper power source. If it doesn't, invention is used recursively to invent a power source. The *efficiency assessment* rejects devices that have superfluous components, such as a device that converts rotary motion into vector motion only to convert it back again.

    These assessments are examples of how domain-specific requirements are added to the creative process. Assessing a domain constraint after creation is complete and then repairing any faults, as the consistency assessment does, frees

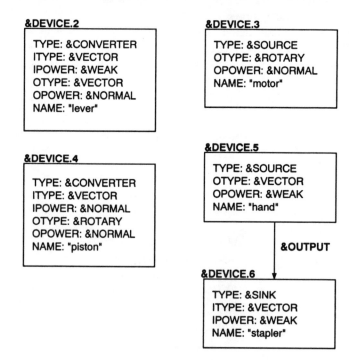

Figure 8.31 Episodic Memory

the creative process from having to exhaustively understand the problem domain and take into account every domain constraint during problem solving. Delaying criticism of inventions, as the efficiency assessment does, gives the creator the freedom to explore solutions that a more strict interpretation of the domain constraints might miss. Delaying criticism is the main feature of brainstorming, a suggested human creativity technique (Osborn, 1953).

8.10.4   Creativity Heuristics for Mechanical Invention

For this new problem domain, MINSTREL was given a small set of Transform-Recall-Adapt Methods: TRAM:Generalize-Power-Source, TRAM:Generalize-Converter, TRAM:Power-Converter, and TRAM:Reversible-Devices. These TRAMs capture simple, commonplace understandings about how mechanical devices can be modified.

TRAM:Generalize-Power-Source suggests that a device that can provide power at one level might also be able to provide power at another level. If weak electrical motors exist, more powerful electrical motors might exist. To prevent overgeneralizations, MINSTREL assumes only small changes in power output, that is, a weak motor generalizes to only a normal motor, not a strong motor.

TRAM:Generalize-Converter makes a similar suggestion about devices that convert power from one form to another. TRAM:Generalize-Converter suggests that a converter that steps up or down the power of a particular input might also be able to step up or down the same amount a different input, that is, a device that converts weak vector power to normal vector power might be also be used to convert normal vector power to strong vector power.

TRAM:Power-Converter suggests substituting a power converter for a power source, and then looking for a power source for the converter.

Finally, TRAM:Reversible-Devices suggests that converters can be run backwards. That is, if MINSTREL knows of a converter that transforms weak power to strong power, then it can guess that the same converter can be used backwards to transform strong power to weak power.

8.10.5   The Problem

In this experiment, MINSTREL is asked to invent a heavy-duty stapler—a stapler head that has a strong vector input. Figure 8.32 shows MINSTREL's representation of this problem. &DEVICE.7 is the stapler head; &DEVICE.6 is an unknown device that provides strong vector input power to the stapler head. MINSTREL's task is to invent a device or series of devices that can provide strong vector power to the stapler head.

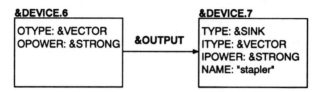

Figure 8.32 Representation of a Lever

8.10.6   Trace

In this experiment, MINSTREL exhaustively invents solutions to the heavy-duty stapler problem. Because invention is used recursively by the consistency assessment, and because MINSTREL follows several reasoning paths concurrently in this experiment, an unedited trace of MINSTREL inventing solutions to the stapler problem is difficult to follow. For the reader's convenience, the trace shown in this section has been edited for clarity. Portions of the trace irrelevant to the solution have been deleted (and marked with "[...]"), and concurrent lines of reasoning have been separated and presented in a serial fashion. MINSTREL's reasoning for one of the four stapler inventions is shown in its entirety. MINSTREL's reasoning for the remaining three inventions is summarized briefly at the end of this section.

MINSTREL begins invention by trying to find a device with a strong vector power output to drive the stapler head (&DEVICE.6 in Figure 8.32). Normal problem solving (TRAM:Standard-ProbLem Solving) fails, because there is no such device in memory. MINSTREL then applies TRAM:Power-Converter to the problem. TRAM:Power-Converter suggests looking for a converter with a strong vector output instead of a power source with strong vector output:

```
==================================================
              MINSTREL Invention
==================================================
Initial specification is &DEVICE.6:
   (AN UNKNOWN DEVICE *COMMA* FEEDING INTO A
      STRONG STAPLER *PERIOD*)

TRAM Cycle: &DEVICE.6.
   Executing TRAM:STANDARD-PROBLEM SOLVING.
      Recalling:    NIL.
   ...TRAM failed.
   Executing TRAM:POWER-CONVERTER.
      Recalling:    NIL.
```

```
...TRAM failed.
```

The new problem description (&DEVICE.11) also fails to recall a device from episodic memory (as indicated by the line `Recalling... NIL`), because there are no devices in memory which convert power to a strong vector output. (Recall that the lever in MINSTREL's memory converts to *normal* vector output.) Since problem solving has failed to find an appropriate converter, MINSTREL recursively applies another TRAM, this time to the converter suggested by TRAM:Power-Converter. TRAM:Generalize-Converter is selected and applied. TRAM:Generalize-Converter suggests that a converter that steps up or down the power of a particular input might also be able to step up or down the same amount a different input. In this case, it suggests looking for a device that can convert weak power to normal power, and then use that device to convert normal power to strong power. This time problem solving succeeds, because the new problem description recalls the lever in MINSTREL's memory:

```
[TRAM Recursion: &DEVICE.11.]
   Executing TRAM:GENERALIZE-CONVERTER.
      Recalling:  (&EXAMPLE-LEVER).
...TRAM succeeds: (&DEVICE.61).
Minstrel invented &DEVICE.101.

(DEVICE &DEVICE.101
   :IPOWER &NORMAL
   :ITYPE  &VECTOR
   :TYPE   &LEVER
   :OTYPE  &VECTOR
   :OPOWER &STRONG
   &OUTPUT <==>  (&DEVICE.102))
```

The initial problem has now been solved. MINSTREL has found a device that outputs strong vector power: a type of lever. &DEVICE.101 is illustrated in Figure 8.33.

However, examining Figure 8.33 reveals a new problem: There is no input power to &DEVICE.101. Solving the original problem has given rise to a new problem: The lever needs a normal vector power source. MINSTREL notices this problem using the consistency domain assessment and calls creative problem solving recursively to correct it:

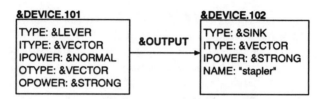

Figure 8.33 Initial Problem Solution

&DEVICE.101 is inconsistent: it lacks a power source.
Inventing a power source for &DEVICE.101.

Note that the power source is being invented for &DEVICE.101, which is
the lever created during the last cycle of invention.

```
TRAM Cycle: &DEVICE.105.
   Executing TRAM:STANDARD-PROBLEM SOLVING.
      Recalling:    NIL.
   ...TRAM failed.
   Executing TRAM:POWER-CONVERTER.
      Recalling:    NIL.
   ...TRAM failed.
   [TRAM Recursion: &DEVICE.241.]
      Executing TRAM:REVERSIBLE-DEVICES.
         Recalling:       (&EXAMPLE-PISTON).
      ...TRAM succeeds: (&DEVICE.248).
[...]

Minstrel invented &DEVICE.253.

(DEVICE &DEVICE.253
   :IPOWER &NORMAL
   :ITYPE  &ROTARY
   :TYPE   &PISTON
   :OPOWER &NORMAL
   :OTYPE  &VECTOR
   &OUTPUT <==>   (&DEVICE.254))
```

There is no normal vector power source in MINSTREL's memory, so
TRAM:Power-Converter is applied to the problem description. This TRAM
suggests looking for a device that converts normal rotary power to normal vector
power. This also fails, because the piston in MINSTREL's memory converts
normal vector power to normal rotary power (not vice versa), so

TRAM:Reversible-Devices is applied. This TRAM suggests that a converter device can be reversed. When this reversal is applied to the problem description, the piston is recalled, and MINSTREL solves the problem of providing normal vector power to the lever by using a piston "backwards."

Once again the domain assessment module notices that the device lacks a power source, so problem solving is called again to find a normal rotary power source. This succeeds immediately when MINSTREL recalls the motor from memory:

```
&DEVICE.253 is inconsistent: it lacks a power source.
Inventing a power source for &DEVICE.253.

TRAM Cycle: &DEVICE.268.
    Executing TRAM:STANDARD-PROBLEM SOLVING.
        Recalling:    (&EXAMPLE-MOTOR).
```

The final device uses a normal rotary motor along with a piston and a lever to power the heavy-duty stapler head:

```
Minstrel invented &DEVICE.273:
    (A DEVICE POWERED BY A NORMAL ROTARY MOTOR
        *COMMA* FEEDING INTO A PISTON INTO A LEVER
        INTO A STRONG STAPLER *PERIOD*)
```

This is the common electric power stapler: a rotary motor driving a piston to power the stapler head. The final invention is illustrated in Figure 8.34.

8.10.7   Additional Invention

As mentioned earlier, MINSTREL invents three other staplers. These are shown in Figure 8.35. The first of these other solutions suggests finding a "strong vector hand" to power the stapler, that is, finding someone stronger than yourself to do the stapling.

The second and third solutions both use levers to generate the force needed to power the heavy-duty stapler. A single lever suffices for a normal strength hand. Two stacked together are needed for weak hands. These are the familiar long-handled extension staplers available in most offices.

In fact, MINSTREL will stack as many levers as needed to generate a required force. In a sense, MINSTREL learns the general rule "The longer the lever, the greater the leverage," although it never represents this knowledge explicitly. Also, MINSTREL does not realize that two stacked short levers can be replaced by a single long lever, because MINSTREL's simple representation of this domain does not include concepts like attachment or length.

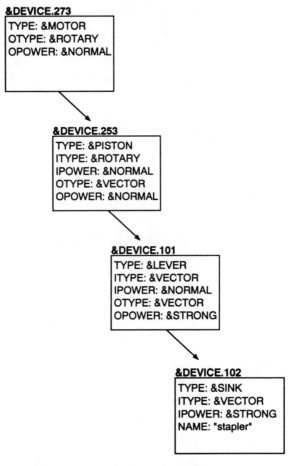

&DEVICE.273
TYPE: &MOTOR
OTYPE: &ROTARY
OPOWER: &NORMAL

&DEVICE.253
TYPE: &PISTON
ITYPE: &ROTARY
IPOWER: &NORMAL
OTYPE: &VECTOR
OPOWER: &NORMAL

&DEVICE.101
TYPE: &LEVER
ITYPE: &VECTOR
IPOWER: &NORMAL
OTYPE: &VECTOR
OPOWER: &STRONG

&DEVICE.102
TYPE: &SINK
ITYPE: &VECTOR
IPOWER: &STRONG
NAME: "stapler"

Figure 8.34 Final Solution

8.10.8 Summary

There are two conclusions to be drawn from this example.

First, the same creativity architecture was able to invent solutions in two very disparate problem solving domains: storytelling and mechanical invention. This indicates that the MINSTREL model of creativity is not an ad-hoc solution to a single problem, but a general model that is applicable across different types of problem domains.

Second, similarities between the creativity heuristics for storytelling and the creativity heuristics for mechanical invention suggest that there might be a class

```
[...]
Minstrel invented this device:
    (A DEVICE POWERED BY A STRONG VECTOR HAND *COMMA*
      FEEDING INTO A STRONG STAPLER *PERIOD*)
[...]
Minstrel invented &DEVICE.716:
    (A DEVICE POWERED BY A NORMAL VECTOR HAND *COMMA*
      FEEDING INTO A LEVER INTO A STRONG STAPLER
      *PERIOD*)
[...]
Minstrel invented &DEVICE.938:
    (A DEVICE POWERED BY A WEAK VECTOR HAND *COMMA*
      FEEDING INTO A LEVER INTO A LEVER INTO A
      STRONG STAPLER *PERIOD*)
```

Figure 8.35 Mechanical Invention Trace Part 3

of "generic" creativity heuristics. Both storytelling and mechanical invention used TRAMs that generalized constraints and TRAMs that substituted different but similar problems. The parallels between creativity in storytelling and mechanical invention suggest that developing universal creativity heuristics might be a useful and productive task.

8.11   Experiment #5: Modifying MINSTREL's Planning Algorithm

MINSTREL uses a queue-based planning model. Each author-level goal is given a priority at the time it is created. Goals are kept on a queue, and at every cycle, MINSTREL takes the highest priority goal off the queue and attempts to solve the goal by applying author-level plans. If one of the plans succeeds, the cycle repeats. If none of the plans succeeds, the priority of the failed goal is reduced, it is added back to the queue, and the cycle repeats. This allows MINSTREL to try goals repeatedly, in the hope that some change in the story will allow a goal that failed initially to later succeed. In this experiment, we modified MINSTREL so that failed goals were never requeued. This allowed us to study the role that requeueing goals played in MINSTREL's performance.

8.11.1   Results

After modifying MINSTREL to never requeue failed goals, MINSTREL was asked to tell a story based on PAT-PRIDE. Surprisingly, MINSTREL told "The Proud Knight" exactly as before. Apparently, requeueing of goals was not used in the telling of this story. This was a surprising result. Earlier versions of MINSTREL had often solved goals on the second or third attempt.

   In light of this result, the traces for stories based on PAT-GOOD-DEEDS-REWARDED, PAT-ROMEO, PAT-PRIDE and PAT-HASTY were analyzed to determine how often MINSTREL had solved requeued goals. That analysis is shown in Figure 8.36. Figure 8.36 shows the total number of goals that MINSTREL attempted in telling ten different stories, the number of those goals that failed (i.e., were never achieved) and the number of goals that were solved on the first, second, or third attempt.

As Figure 8.36 shows, MINSTREL does occasionally solve a goal on the second or third attempt. This occurs when, between the time the failed goal is first tried and the time it is retried, an intervening goal succeeds and as a side-effect changes the failed goal. For example, the failed goal might be "instantiate a scene in which a knight does a favor for some other character." A goal operating on different part of the story might decide that the other character is a hermit. And while MINSTREL could not solve the original goal specification, it can solve the modified specification "instantiate a scene in which a knight does a favor for a hermit."

However, as these statistics show, this happens rarely (about 1% of the time). In this respect, MINSTREL is a very efficient planner: of the goals that it can solve, it solves almost all of them immediately. This efficiency is a direct consequence of MINSTREL's creative ability.

MINSTREL's creativity heuristics permit it to make full use of the domain knowledge in episodic memory. MINSTREL's creativity heuristics make many plausible guesses about how the knowledge in episodic memory can be generalized and applied to different situations. If there is any way to apply an episode to a particular goal, MINSTREL's creativity heuristics are likely to discover it. Requeueing a goal succeeds only when some intervening goal adds information to the original goal that the creativity heuristics could not discover. And the more powerful MINSTREL's creativity heuristics, the less likely this is to happen.

One interesting conclusion we can draw from this is that *a creative problem solver is more flexible than a non-creative problem solver*. Even if goals are poorly stated or attempted in the wrong order, a creative problem solver may still be able to find solutions. Creativity obviously cannot shoulder all of the planning burden. But creativity does make planning a less critical activity.

This also suggests a way to learn creativity. When requeueing of a goal does result in success, the creative problem solver should take note of the happening and analyze it. If the problem solver can determine what information was added that permitted the solution of the previously insoluble goal, that knowledge can be used to invent a new creativity heuristic. Consider the earlier example, in

Total	Failed	Successful Goals		
		1st	2nd	3rd
2466	1262	1191	12	1

Figure 8.36 MINSTREL's Use of Requeued Goals

which a problem is solvable once a secondary character is given a role. This suggests a new creativity heuristic which modifies a problem specification by adding a role for a secondary character.

8.12 Study #2: Analysis of MINSTREL's TRAMs

MINSTREL has a library of twenty-four TRAMs. These TRAMs arose in a number of ways. Some were developed independently of MINSTREL's particular tasks, often by analogy to "creativity techniques" expounded for humans, such as generalization, relaxation of problem constraints, and so on. Other TRAMs were developed in response to particular difficulties in MINSTREL's problem domain. In this section, we characterize MINSTREL's TRAMS by usage, applicability, and function.

8.12.1 Usage of TRAMs

Statistics on how frequently MINSTREL used each TRAM are shown in Figure 8.37. These statistics were gathered on MINSTREL's performance telling stories based on PAT-GOOD-DEEDS-REWARDED, PAT-ROMEO, PAT-HASTY, PAT-PRIDE, and on MINSTREL's performance inventing novel methods of suicide.

Figure 8.37 has been divided into three rough categories corresponding to frequency of use. TRAMs in the first section were used quite frequently, TRAMs in the second section occasionally, and TRAMs in the last section only in specialized situations. Three interesting traits of MINSTREL's TRAM usage are revealed here.

First, TRAM:Standard-Problem-Solving is one of the most frequently used TRAMs. This is no surprise. Most of the problems encountered by a problem solver should be very similar to past problems, and require no creativity. What is more surprising is that creativity heuristics as a whole are used four times *more* frequently than TRAM:Standard-Problem-Solving. It seems unexpected that creativity should be so important to MINSTREL.

In part this is because MINSTREL was purposely given a limited episodic memory. With a broader range of experience, MINSTREL would be able to solve more problems without creativity. Nonetheless, the surprisingly high usage of creativity heuristics may indicate that low levels of creativity are more in use in human cognition than previously recognized.

A second interesting feature of Figure 8.37 is the extensive usage of TRAM:Ignore-Motivations. TRAM:Ignore-Motivations is a heuristic that ignores motivating states when trying to find a plan to achieve a goal. In more common terms, TRAM:Ignore-Motivations says that when you are trying to solve a goal, it doesn't matter why you have that goal. This is "common sense" to a human problem solver. The fact that it is applied so frequently and

TRAM	Number of Uses
TRAM:Ignore-Motivations	62
TRAM:Standard-Problem-Solving	33
TRAM:Generalize-Actor	18
TRAM:Similar-States	10
TRAM:Recall-Act	9
TRAM:Intention-Switch-1	6
TRAM:Limited-Recall	5
TRAM:Favor-Goal	4
TRAM:Generalize-Role	4
TRAM:Similar-State-Outcome	4
TRAM:Achieve-B-Motivated-P-Goal	3
TRAM:Generalize-Object	3
TRAM:Similar-Thwart-State	3
TRAM:Use-Magic	3
TRAM:Generalize-Constraint	2
TRAM:Opposite-State-Achieves	2
TRAM:Similar-Outcomes-Partial-Change	2
TRAM:Thwart-Via-Escape	2
TRAM:Act-Of-A-Favor	1
TRAM:Create-Failure	1
TRAM:Cross-Domain-Reminding	1
TRAM:Exist-As-Precond	1
TRAM:Ignore-Subgoal	1
TRAM:Recall-WO-Precond	1
TRAM:Thwart-Via-Death	1

Figure 8.37 Usage of TRAMs

successfully as a creativity technique indicates: (a) that commonly known, frequently used problem solving techniques may have their origin in the creative process, and (b) that creativity may be involved in day-to-day problem solving to a greater degree than normally suspected.

Finally, Figure 8.37 shows that most of MINSTREL's creativity heuristics get used infrequently. About 80% of MINSTREL's TRAMs were used 6 times or less in all the stories MINSTREL told, and some were used only once. Why is this?

Creativity by its nature is a rare occurrence. The need to be creative arises only when a problem solver cannot find any other solution to a problem. Successful creativity is rarer; and the use of any particular creativity heuristic rarer still. MINSTREL, which has a purposely sparse episodic memory and heuristics to drive it be creative, uses creativity in only 12% of the goals it solved (150 of 1200), and a human problem solver is undoubtedly creative much, much less frequently. Given this, it is no surprise that most of MINSTREL's creativity heuristics are used infrequently; that should be expected of any creative problem solver.

Of course, the infrequency of creativity causes difficulties in the development and testing of a model of creative problem solving. When a creativity heuristic is used only a few times, it is difficult to determine whether the heuristic is general and useful, or an ad hoc solution to a particular, narrow problem. Indeed, one of MINSTREL's creativity heuristics—TRAM:Cross-Domain-Reminding—was added to MINSTREL to specifically look at a particular kind of creativity, and consequently doesn't have any wide applicability. In general, though, MINSTREL's creativity heuristics appear reasonable. Most have been used in several different problem solving situations, and have been used in combination with other creativity heuristics and with different author-level plans, all of which give some assurance that these heuristics are not reasonable initial attempts to codify some of the mechanisms of creativity.

Figure 8.38 shows another analysis of MINSTREL's TRAM usage. We see how often two or more TRAMs were used in conjunction to discover a solution. Figure 8.38 summarizes total successes using one, two, or three TRAMs. (Notice that TRAM:Standard-Problem-Solving is not included in this summary.)

The statistics shown in Figure 8.38 were gathered on 1025 goals MINSTREL achieved telling stories about PAT-PRIDE, PAT-HASTY, PAT-ROMEO and PAT-GOOD-DEEDS-REWARDED (see Section 15.2), indicating that on the average 2.8 TRAMs applied to each goal. With three levels of recursion, MINSTREL applies (on average) 22 TRAMs to each goal that cannot be solved with standard problem solving. With this level of effort, MINSTREL solves a little over 12% of the goals that were not solvable by standard problem solving. Timings indicate that creativity adds less than 20% to the run-time of a typical storytelling session. Based on these numbers, is MINSTREL's creativity productive? Is a 12% increase in performance worth a 20% increase in run-time? We argue that it is, for three reasons.

First, creativity is expected to be less efficient than standard problem solving. Case-based problem solving is simple and efficient: A solution is recalled and applied to the current problem with little or no adaptation. Creativity, on the other hand, is an extension of problem solving that is more powerful at the cost of being less efficient. The creativity problem solver must search memory in inefficient ways, and adapt the solutions it finds. So it is not surprising that a 12% increase in performance has a cost of 20%.

Second, there is no reason to believe that there exists any more efficient method for MINSTREL to gain that additional performance. MINSTREL is

	Single TRAM	Two TRAMs	Three TRAMs
Successes	124	13	10
Attempts	5345	1448	953
Percentage	2.3	0.9	1.0

Figure 8.38 Nested TRAM Usage

very efficient in both (1) searching memory for potential solutions, and (2) adapting those solutions. In fact, MINSTREL is surprisingly efficient. MINSTREL applies only 22 TRAMs on average while searching for a problem solution. Were MINSTREL to apply TRAMs by exhaustively choosing from its pool of 24 TRAMs for three levels of recursion, it would apply 24*23*22 = 12,144 TRAM sequences to each problem!

Finally, the 12% success figure is somewhat deceptive. Many of these successes are key to the stories in which they occur. For example, MINSTREL uses creativity to solve only two goals in telling "The Proud King." But without creativity, MINSTREL cannot solve a single goal in telling that story. The two goals that MINSTREL solves creatively contain knowledge that MINSTREL uses to solve every other goal. So while creativity may directly account for only a small percentage of MINSTREL's success, it contributes indirectly to many other successes.

As with human creativity, MINSTREL uses creativity to solve key portions of the problems it is given. Solving the rest of the problem is often straightforward problem solving. But without the creativity to solve the key portion of the problem, solving the rest of the problem is useless even if possible.

8.12.2   Applicability of TRAMs

In MINSTREL, each TRAM applies to a particular type of representation object, such as an act, a goal, or a state. Figure 8.39 shows how many TRAMs MINSTREL has that apply to each type of representation object.

8.12.3   Functional Distribution of TRAMs

Figure 8.40 shows the functional distribution of MINSTREL's TRAMs into Relaxation, Generalization, Substitution of Similar Sub-Part, Planning Knowledge, and Other categories. Each of these categories represents a particular type of creativity heuristic.

RELAXATION—Relaxation heuristics attempt to find a new solution to a problem by relaxing or removing some of the original problem constraints. TRAM:Ignore-Motivations is an example of a relaxation heuristic. When MINSTREL is attempting to fill in a character goal, TRAM:Ignore-Motivations removes from the problem description any motivating states. This permits MINSTREL to use information from a similar past goal, even if that goal was motivated by a different situation.

GENERALIZATION—Generalization heuristics attempt to find a new solution to a problem by changing the problem into a more general problem, and then adapting any general solutions found to the specific original problem. TRAM:Generalize-Actor does this by generalizing the actor in an action, goal, or state. This permits MINSTREL to generalize knowledge across character

Object	#	Uses	TRAMs (Uses)
Any	4	58	TRAM:Standard-Problem-Solving (33), TRAM:Generalize-Actor (18), TRAM:Limited-Recall (5), TRAM:Generalize-Role (4)
Goals	6	74	TRAM:Ignore-Motivations (62), TRAM:Favor-Goal (4), TRAM:Achieve-B-Motivated-P-Goal (3), TRAM:Similar-Thwart-State (3), TRAM:Opposite-State-Achieves (2).
Acts	9	27	TRAM:Recall-Act (9), TRAM:Intention-Switch-1 (6), TRAM:Similar-State-Outcome (4), TRAM:Use-Magic (3), TRAM:Recall-WO-Precond (1), TRAM:Exist-As-Precond (1), TRAM:Cross-Domain-Reminding (1), TRAM:Create-Failure (1), TRAM:Act-Of-A-Favor (1).
States	5	16	TRAM:Similar-States (10), TRAM:Thwart-Via-Escape (2), TRAM:Generalize-Object (3), TRAM:Thwart-Via-Escape (2), TRAM:Thwart-Via-Death (1).

Figure 8.39 Applicability of TRAMs

types: What MINSTREL knows about monsters can be used to augment what MINSTREL knows about knights, and so on.

SUBSTITUTION OF A SIMILAR SUBPART—These type of heuristics attempt to find a solution by replacing a subpart of the original problem with a similar but different part. This is a specific type of analogical reasoning that guesses that because two things share some similarities they may also share other similarities. For example, TRAM:Similar-States modifies problem descriptions that contain states by replacing the states with other, similar states. This permits MINSTREL to generalize about the results of actions. If MINSTREL is trying to find an action which results in a knight moving to a castle, TRAM:Similar-States lets MINSTREL guess that an action which moves a knight to the woods might also move him to a castle.

PLANNING KNOWLEDGE—Planning knowledge heuristics use specific knowledge about planning to discover new problem solutions. For instance, TRAM:Thwart-Via-Death knows that a goal will be thwarted if the actor of that goal is killed. This specific knowledge about planning can be used to find problem solutions that would otherwise be undiscovered.

OTHER—Three of MINSTREL's creativity heuristics do not easily fit into the previous categories. TRAM:Favor-Goal finds a solution to the goal to do

Functional Category	TRAMS
Relaxation	TRAM:Ignore-Motivations TRAM:Recall-WO-Precond TRAM:Limited-Recall TRAM:Recall-Act
Generalization	TRAM:Generalize-Actor TRAM:Generalize-Object TRAM:Generalize-Constraint TRAM:Generalize-Role TRAM:Ignore-Subgoal
Substitution of a Similar Sub-Part	TRAM:Similar-States TRAM:Similar-State-Outcome TRAM:Intention-Switch-1 TRAM:Similar-Thwart-State TRAM:Opposite-State-Achieves TRAM:Create-Failure TRAM:Similar-Outcomes
Planning Knowledge	TRAM:Achieve-B-Motivated-P-Goal TRAM:Thwart-Via-Escape TRAM:Thwart-Via-Death TRAM:Exist-As-Precond TRAM:Act-Of-A-Favor
Other	TRAM:Favor-Goal TRAM:Use-Magic TRAM:Cross-Domain-Reminding

Figure 8.40 Functional Distribution of TRAMs

someone a favor by finding a solution to the goal that the favor goal is subsuming. This is a syntactic modification similar to the one used by the (failed) TRAM:Switch-Focus. TRAM:Use-Magic is a creativity heuristic specific to the King Arthur domain, which suggests that magic artifacts can be used to achieve almost any goal. And finally, TRAM:Cross-Domain-Reminding is an analogy heuristic that looks for a problem solution by translating a problem description from the King Arthur domain to another domain. Currently, MINSTREL knows only of one other domain—modern life—and of only one episode in that domain, so consequently TRAM:Cross-Domain-Reminding is usable in very few situations.

As Figure 8.40 shows, many of MINSTREL's creativity heuristics fall into categories often described in creativity literature: generalization, relaxation, and analogy. The surprise here is the number of heuristics that use planning knowledge. Why is a technique of obvious use to MINSTREL not broadly acknowledged as a creativity technique?

The lack of mention of creativity techniques based on planning knowledge may be because creativity literature is written both for and about an accomplished, adult audience. As the high usage of TRAM:Ignore-Motivations suggests, human problem solvers may be unaware of their extensive use of some creativity heuristics, or such techniques may be so widely and frequently used that they are no longer considered "creative." In particular, we would expect this to be true for planning knowledge heuristics. By the time of adulthood, humans are such accomplished planners that simple heuristics based on planning knowledge should be so practiced as to be unnoticeable. Where human problem solvers can be expected to have difficulty is in using infrequent creativity heuristics, such as those that fall into the "specialized situation" category of MINSTREL's TRAM usage chart. In addition, adult human problem solvers have such a wide variety of problem solving situations in memory that many problem knowledge heuristics may be unnecessary. This suggests that some of MINSTREL's creativity heuristics may be primarily useful to a planner working in a new problem domain.

Secondly, most creativity work to date has focused on acts of outstanding creativity, such as great artistic works and major scientific discoveries. The model presented in this work explains creativity as a logical extension to problem solving, spanning the spectrum from simple, everyday problem solving to works of outstanding creativity. MINSTREL's planning knowledge heuristics are used primarily to discover slightly different solutions near the problem solving end of this spectrum. For example, TRAM:Thwart-Via-Death is used to discover that being killed can thwart a knight's goal to love someone. This is not outstandingly creative, but because MINSTREL knows nothing of such a concept, neither is it mere rote recall. Because creativity research has previously focused on acts of outstanding creativity, it has overlooked the role of such "day-to-day" creativity in problem solving.

8.13   Experiment #6: TRAMs and Creativity

This experiment looks at the robustness of MINSTREL's creativity model. In particular, we look at how MINSTREL's performance is affected by the loss of TRAMs and of creativity in general.

8.13.1   Loss of TRAMs

As a first experiment, random TRAMs were removed from MINSTREL's library of creativity heuristics. Between 10% and 50% of MINSTREL's TRAMs were removed, and then MINSTREL was given the goal of telling a story about one of the themes it knew, chosen at random. This experiment was performed a number of times in order to develop a general understanding of MINSTREL's performance in degraded modes.

Figure 8.41 shows a typical story told in one of these experiments. This story is based on PAT-PRIDE and was told by MINSTREL with the following

TRAMs removed from MINSTREL's pool of creativity heuristics: TRAM:Similar-States and TRAM:Generalize-Object. A comparison of this story with the original story (given in Section 8.2 of this chapter) reveals that this story is complete except for a missing scene in which Grunfeld travels to the dragon.

This example is typical of the results of this experiment. Removing TRAMs from MINSTREL generally caused MINSTREL to fail to complete one or more small parts of the stories it told. Because MINSTREL's stories have many subparts, because the stories are created by many interacting goals, and because any particular task involves only a few TRAMs, the loss of particular TRAMs usually caused only minor, localized failures in storytelling.

One exception to this did occur. Because MINSTREL has no episodic memories concerning kings, MINSTREL's ability to tell any story about a king turns on its use of TRAM:Generalize-Actor to guess that kings are like knights. Figure 8.42 shows the result of telling the PAT-PRIDE story about a king if TRAM:Generalize-Actor is not available.

"The Proud King II" is a critical failure of MINSTREL's creativity, but there were also situations where MINSTREL achieved a critical success by substituting for a missing TRAM. In the story "The Knight and the Hermit" based on PAT-GOOD-DEEDS-REWARDED, MINSTREL uses TRAM:Thwart-Via-Escape to create a scene where a hermit tries to thwart a dragon's goal of eating him by escaping (the attempt fails):

> ...Bebe believed he would die because he saw a dragon moving towards him and believed that it would eat him. Bebe tried to run away but failed.

It was the Spring of 1089, and a knight named Grunfeld returned to Camelot.

A hermit named Bebe told Grunfeld that Bebe believed that if Grunfeld fought with the dragon then he would be hurt.

Grunfeld was very proud. Because he was very proud, Grunfeld wanted to impress the King. Grunfeld was near a dragon. The dragon was destroyed because Grunfeld fought with the dragon. The dragon was destroyed but Grunfeld was hurt. Grunfeld wanted to protect his health. Grunfeld wanted to be healed. Grunfeld hated himself. Grunfeld became a hermit.

Figure 8.41 The Proud Knight II

It was the Spring of 1089, and a King Arthur returned to Camelot from elsewhere.

A hermit named Bebe warned Arthur.

Arthur became a hermit.

Figure 8.42 The Proud King II

If TRAM:Thwart-Via-Escape is removed from MINSTREL's available creativity heuristics, MINSTREL will invent a different method of thwarting the dragon's goal by using TRAM:Thwart-Via-Death:

> ...Bebe believed he would die because he saw
> a dragon moving towards him and believed
> that it would eat him. Bebe tried to kill
> the dragon with his hands but failed.

In general we conclude that because MINSTREL has a large library of TRAMs, because problem solving goals are typically localized, and because MINSTREL can sometimes discover alternate solutions, MINSTREL's performance degrades gracefully as TRAMs are lost. Sometimes, a single TRAM is critical to an important decision, and loss of that TRAM will consequently cause a major failure.

8.14   Study #3: MINSTREL's Common Failure Modes

In describing MINSTREL's attempts to tell a story about PAT:PRIDE, we noted one of MINSTREL's common failure modes. This section further discusses that and other common failure modes. By looking at how MINSTREL fails, we hope to cast some light on the creative process and discover new areas for research.

8.14.1   Recovery From Bad Decisions

In its standard configuration, if MINSTREL is asked to tell a story about PAT:PRIDE, it chooses to make the main character a hermit. As it happens, this is a bad decision. PAT:PRIDE requires the main character to perform an action that has unintended bad consequences, but MINSTREL cannot recall or invent such an action for a hermit. Consequently storytelling fails.

Being unable to continue a story because of a bad decision earlier in storytelling is a common problem for MINSTREL. MINSTREL has a very simple planning model, and no effort was made to give MINSTREL the ability to recover from bad planning decisions. So when MINSTREL makes a bad decision that prevents it from successfully completing a story, it cannot recover from that decision. To recover from bad decisions, three facilities would be needed.

First, MINSTREL needs the ability to detect when storytelling fails. This is easily implemented. By checking the status of its important storytelling goals (primarily whether the theme has been instantiated) MINSTREL can determine how successful storytelling has been. MINSTREL can even make simple judgments about whether a story has been told well or in a minimal fashion, by checking the status of its author-level writing goals.

Second, MINSTREL also needs to be able to trace storytelling failure to a bad decision. This is a more difficult task for several reasons. The first difficulty is that MINSTREL does not maintain a history or memory of the storytelling process itself, and so has no way to examine what it has done in the past. The second difficulty is in determining which of the many decisions involved in the storytelling process is the critical bad decision. This is very much an open research question. One can imagine various simple heuristics (such as finding the last successful goal previous to a long string of goal failures) but the efficacy of such heuristics is unknown.

Finally, MINSTREL needs to be able to retract a bad decision. The simplest method for achieving this is to throw out the entire unsuccessful story and start anew, avoiding the bad decision. But that's potentially very wasteful. A better method would be to recover from a bad decision by repairing the failed story. MINSTREL does not currently have any plan repair abilities.

MINSTREL's inability to recover from bad planning decisions is a consequence of MINSTREL's simple planning model. Were MINSTREL able to backtrack away from failed solutions, explore multiple solutions in parallel, or detect and repair bad decisions as outlined above, it would avoid most failures of this type. This type of failure reflects more upon MINSTREL's planning model than its model of creativity.

8.14.2 Errors of Knowledge

A second type of failure that MINSTREL encounters is due to inadequacies in MINSTREL's knowledge of the problem domain. An interesting example of this occurs when MINSTREL is asked to tell a story about PAT:PRIDE in which the main character is a princess. As with the hermit story earlier, MINSTREL is unable to complete its storytelling. The failed story is given in Figure 8.43.

This story is particularly interesting because it *appears* to fulfill the theme. The hermit predicts that something bad will happen if Jennifer drinks the potion and it does: She gets buried in the woods. But this is misleading.

The bad consequence of drinking the magic potion—being buried in the woods—is actually created by MINSTREL to resolve Jennifer's fate, not to resolve the theme. One of MINSTREL's author-level writing goals is to resolve loose ends at the end of a story by determining the fate of the characters in the story. Dead characters are buried and mourned, characters who have brought tragedy on themselves or others may change their roles, and so on. In this case,

Jennifer was a lady of the court. One day a hermit named Bebe told Jennifer that Bebe believed if Jennifer drank a magic potion something bad would happen.

Jennifer was very proud. Jennifer drank the magic potion and appeared to be dead. Jennifer was buried in the woods.

Figure 8.43 Failed PAT:PRIDE II

MINSTREL mistakenly believes that Jennifer is dead at the conclusion of the story, and buries her as a way of resolving her fate. This error occurs because MINSTREL's author-level plan that achieves the goal of resolving character fates lacks the knowledge to correctly interpret MINSTREL's representation of deceptive states.

MINSTREL represents deception by two states of the world. The true state of the world is "shadowed" by the deceptive state. In this case, Jennifer's good health is shadowed by her death. A graphic representation of this is shown in Figure 8.44.

However, MINSTREL's author-level plan for determining a character's fate does not have the knowledge to correctly interpret shadowed states. When this plan examines the story, it notices that Jennifer is dead, without noticing that Jennifer's death is in fact a deception state. Consequently, the author-level plan assumes that Jennifer is truly dead and decides her fate on that basis.

Of course, it would be interesting if MINSTREL had intentionally reasoned that Jennifer's deception might result in a premature burial. But in this case, Jennifer's burial is an error that occurred because MINSTREL's knowledge of the problem domain was incomplete.

This type of error does not indicate any shortcoming of MINSTREL's planning or creativity models. Errors of knowledge can be made by the most sophisticated planners and problem solvers when their knowledge of a problem domain is incomplete. MINSTREL has a very rudimentary knowledge of the King Arthur and storytelling problem domains, and can be expected to make errors of knowledge.

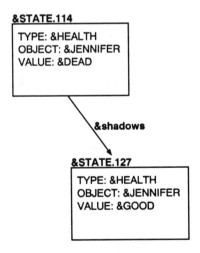

Figure 8.44 Representation of Deception

8.14.3   Creativity Errors

A final type of error that can occur in MINSTREL is a creativity error. The philosophy of MINSTREL's creativity heuristics is to make small, incremental changes. Many of these heuristics will never make an error. For example, TRAM:Intention-Switch changes intended actions into unintended actions. That's a problem modification that is always reasonable. But many of MINSTREL's creativity heuristics are guesses about what might be "reasonable" about the world. And sometimes these guesses are wrong.

One error of this type occurs when MINSTREL tries to solve a knight's goal of feeding himself. Because MINSTREL does not have any episodes in memory in which a knight feeds himself, TRAM:Generalize-Actor is applied. This TRAM generalizes the knight to a monster, because both knights and monsters are violent characters. This recalls a scene in which a dragon captures a princess and eats her to assuage its hunger. When applied to this problem, the result is a scene in which a knight kills and eats a princess. Oops!

This particular error occurs because MINSTREL has a simple-minded understanding of the similarities between knights and monsters, and modifying MINSTREL to avoid it would be trivial. But it is indicative of the types of errors that creativity heuristics can introduce.

The importance of these types of errors are that they validate MINSTREL's creativity model. A creative problem solver *should* make errors, because being creative requires the problem solver to extend the limits of his or her knowledge. By making good use of what is already known, a problem solver can often make accurate guesses about what is not. But sometimes he or she will err. One of the challenges of creativity research is to find a model of creativity that limits errors while still being powerful enough to meaningfully extend the limits of a problem solver's knowledge. MINSTREL's creativity model, which incrementally extends the problem solver's knowledge in small steps, has this characteristic. By making small changes near the border of its knowledge, MINSTREL is assured that what it invents is likely to be reasonable. But because MINSTREL can apply many creativity heuristics to a single problem, it also has the power to make bigger leaps when necessary.

9 | Future Work and Conclusions

9.1 Introduction

Storytelling and creativity are broad topics. Creating a computer model that can tell stories has required addressing many issues from a variety of disciplines: cognitive science, psychology, computer science, and art. The preceding pages have examined a large number of disparate and seemingly unconnected topics: memory, creativity, themes, the artistic drive, foreshadowing, and so on. Each issue has been viewed from a variety of angles: as a cognitive model, as a computational model, as a psychological model, as it interrelates with other issues, as a part in a complex system, and as part of a storytelling machine.

Because of this wide variety of issues, this research is of interest to many different types of scientists:

- **Cognitive Scientists:** MINSTREL defines a model of creativity and storytelling that can be studied for insights into how these processes can be modeled.
- **Psychologists:** MINSTREL is based on current psychological understanding of human creativity. It provides a possible explanation for human creativity that can be used as a tool for exploring human psychology.
- **Computer Scientists:** The MINSTREL creativity model suggests a basis for implementing computer systems with new levels of flexibility and robustness.
- **Artists:** MINSTREL defines certain artistic concepts—the artistic drive, creativity—in process-oriented ways. The understanding of these

processes could lead artists to new self-awareness and increased productivity, as well as new ways to teach and execute art.

Neither scientists nor artists will find a complete answer to their questions about creativity and storytelling in this volume. There is still a long way to go before computers will be built that can compete with human authors. But MINSTREL does make many important contributions to understanding these topics. The following sections summarize MINSTREL's contributions to our understanding of creativity and storytelling.

9.2   Creativity

The introduction to this book identified a number of challenges that a model of creativity faced. We return now to those challenges and examine how MINSTREL has addressed them.

The Challenge	The Answer
Explain the relation of creativity to ordinary problem solving.	*Creativity is an integral part of the problem solving process.*

One of the principal questions a researcher must face about creativity is: Is it understandable? Great works of creativity do seem almost miraculous, and it is tempting to deduce from these that creativity is a mysterious process beyond our comprehension. But this ignores the day-to-day creativity that each of us exhibit in our own lives. MINSTREL provides a model of creativity not as something entirely different from problem solving, but as an extension to problem solving that can explain both mundane, noncreative problem solving, day-to-day creativity, artistic creativity, and great works of creativity. MINSTREL provides an explanation of creativity as a process that can be understood, analyzed, and studied.

The Challenge	The Answer
Explain how a problem solver can find and adapt old knowledge to create new solutions.	*The fundamental process of creativity is integrated search and adaptation.*

Among the challenges a model of creativity faces is to explain how a creative problem solver can find useful knowledge to apply towards creating a new problem solution while still adapting the knowledge he finds in an efficient way. How does one know what old knowledge can form new solutions? And how can one know what combinations will lead to something useful? By combining the search for knowledge with process of adapting that knowledge once found, the MINSTREL model of creativity explains how the creative problem solver can find useful knowledge and apply it without being overwhelmed by an intractable adaptation problem. MINSTREL's Transform-Recall-Adapt heuristics discover useful knowledge by transforming the problem description, and eliminate the adaptation problem by bundling a specific solution adaptation with each problem transformation.

The Challenge	The Answer
Explain great leaps of creativity.	*Leaps of creativity are composed of many small steps.*

One of the fundamental concerns of creativity is whether a continuum exists from noncreative problem solving to great leaps of creativity. Is it necessary to posit a different process to explain great leaps of creativity? MINSTREL's claim is that great leaps of creativity can be explained as many small steps. Although each of MINSTREL's creativity heuristics makes only a small change in discovering a new problem solution, MINSTREL can combine many of these heuristics to make great leaps of creativity.

The Challenge	The Answer
Explain how people can be creative in a variety of problem domains and cognitive processes.	*The integration of creativity with memory makes creativity transparently available to all cognitive processes.*

MINSTREL's integration of creativity with the process of recall to create an *imaginative memory* explains how creativity can be a domain-independent cognitive process. All cognitive process must rely upon memory to store and recall the knowledge they use to understand and solve problems. If the memory itself is capable of inventing new knowledge, then creativity becomes transparently available to all cognitive processes.

9.3 Storytelling

Creativity is a fundamental cognitive process. Consequently, MINSTREL's important contributions about creativity concern the process model of creativity: how it achieves creativity, how it integrates with other cognitive processes, and how it explains human creative behavior.

In contrast, storytelling is a problem task which makes use of cognitive processes to achieve a goal. More so than with creativity, MINSTREL's contributions to the area of storytelling focus on the specifics of this problem task: what knowledge is needed, what processes are used, and what the specific difficulties are in solving the storytelling problem.

Storytelling is problem solving.

A major thesis of this research is that there exists no difference at the process level between artistic problem domains and nonartistic problem domains. Because creativity is integrated into the problem solving process and because the artistic drive can be modeled as a domain assessment, MINSTREL can use the same processes to solve problems in the artistic domain of storytelling that it uses to solve problems in the domains of planning and mechanical invention. Art can be understood in terms of the same cognitive processes that explain problem solving in domains like science and day-to-day living.

Stories are created through the interaction of many simple author-level goals.

As MINSTREL demonstrates, interesting, complex, and cohesive stories can emerge from the interactions of many, small, simple author-level goals. No particular author-level goal or plan in MINSTREL understands a story in its entirety. Each author-level plan is a simple, easily understood method for achieving a simple and narrow problem. Yet together these goals solve a very broad and complex problem: creating a story. Both by this behavior and by the use of many simple creativity heuristics to make great leaps of creativity, MINSTREL demonstrates that complex, difficult-to-understand phenomenon can often be understood as emergent behaviors of many interacting simpler processes.

Important goals for storytelling include: theme, consistency, drama, and presentation.

For the types of stories that MINSTREL tells, four classes of author-level goals emerged as essential to the storytelling problem. Whether the particular author-level goals and plans MINSTREL uses have applicability to other types of storytelling is an open question. But the classes of author-level goals MINSTREL identifies and their interactions with one another to create a story are the basis for an understanding of the storytelling process.

Instantiation is a fundamental storytelling process.

A final, unexpected result of MINSTREL was the importance of instantiation to the storytelling process. Instantiation—the process of taking an incomplete description and filling out its details—surprised us by emerging as an important process in nearly every step of the storytelling process. A further surprise was that instantiation could often be achieved by imaginative memory. The importance of instantiation to storytelling and its relationship to imaginative memory argue that instantiation may be a fundamental process to artistic problem domains or perhaps all types of problem solving.

9.4   Final Retrospection

What stands out most in my experiences creating MINSTREL?

The first impression is of overwhelming complexity. To tell even a simple story, MINSTREL must make intelligent, creative use of an enormous amount of knowledge. MINSTREL knows about knights, horses, princesses, places in the world, swordfights, jousts, monsters, love, revenge, anger, death, magic and a host of other facts about King Arthur's knights. On top of that, MINSTREL knows about stories: themes, foreshadowing, characterization, story structure, paragraphing, consistency, language. And to make use of all this MINSTREL implements a variety of cognitive processes: memory, planning, problem solving, creativity. The complexity of the storytelling task is staggering.

And yet paradoxically the second impression is of elegant simplicity. Case-based problem solving is a simple idea that answers a number of difficult questions about how people solve problems. TRAMs encapsulate creativity in an understandable way and answer the challenge of inventing new knowledge without making endless mistakes or being overwhelmed by complexity. Imaginative memory provides an elegant integration of creativity into the larger cognitive model. The problems MINSTREL addresses are complex, but the answers it finds are simple.

I find this paradox oddly comforting. I believe that intelligence must, in the final analysis, be based on simple but powerful mechanisms. Although the mechanisms that MINSTREL proposes may someday be shown to be totally incorrect, they do show that complex behaviors can arise from simple mechanisms. Therefore I have hope that someday we can understand intelligence, and hence ourselves, a little bit better.

References

Alvarado, S. (1989). *Understanding editorial text: A computer model of argument comprehension* (Tech. Rep. UCLA-AI-89-07). Artificial Intelligence Laboratory, Computer Science Department, University of California, Los Angeles.

Arens, Y. (1986). *Cluster: An approach to contextual language understanding.* Doctoral dissertation, University of California Berkeley (Report No. UCB/CSD 86/293).

Bickham, J. (1992, June). Step 6: Revising your story. *The Writer's Digest.*

Boden, M. (1991). *The creative mind.* New York: Basic Books.

Callahan, S. (1986). *Adrift, seventy-six days lost at sea.* New York: Ballantine Books.

Carbonell, J. (1981). *Subjective understanding, computer models of belief systems.* Ann Arbor, MI: UMI Research Press.

Cohen, G. (1989). *Memory in the real world.* Hillsdale, NJ: Lawrence Erlbaum Associates.

De Camp, L. S., & De Camp, C. C. (1975). *Science fiction handbook, Revised.* Englewood Cliffs, NJ: Prentice-Hall.

Dolan, C. P. (1988). *Tensor manipulation networks: Connectionist and symbolic approaches to comprehension, learning and planning.* Unpublished doctoral dissertation, University of California, Los Angeles.

Dyer, M. G. (1983). *In depth understanding.* Cambridge, MA: The MIT Press.

Dyer, M. G. (1987). Emotions and their computations: Three computer models. *Cognition and Emotion,* I(3), 323-347.

Flower, L. S., & Hayes, J. R. (1980). The dynamics of composing: Making plans and juggling constraints. In L.W. Gregg & E.R. Steinberg (Eds.), *Cognitive processes in writing* (pp. 30-47). Hillsdale, NJ: Lawrence Erlbaum Associates.

Forbus, K. D. (1984). *Qualitative process theory.* Cambridge, MA: The MIT Press.

Hammond, K. (1988). Case-based planning. *Proceedings of the Case-Based Reasoning Workshop.* Clearwater Beach, FL.

Hammond, K. (1990). *Case-based planning: Viewing planning as a memory task.* Boston, MA: Academic Press.

Hodges, J. (1993). *Naive mechanics: A computational model for representing and reasoning about simple mechanical devices.* Unpublished doctoral dissertation, University of California, Los Angeles.

Koestler, A. (1964). *The act of creation.* New York: Macmillan.

Kolodner, J. L. (1984). *Retrieval and organizational strategies in conceptual memory: A computer model.* Hillsdale, NJ: Lawrence Earlbaum Associates.

Kolodner, J. L. (1987). Extending problem solver capabilities through case-based inference. *Proceedings of the Fourth Annual International Machine Learning Workshop* (pp. 167-178). Irvine, CA.

Lebowitz, M. (1985). Story telling and generalization. *Proceedings of the Seventh Annual Conference of the Cognitive Science Society* (pp. 100-109). Irvine, CA.

Lehnert, W. (1982). Plot units: A narrative summarization strategy. In W. Lehnert & M. Ringle (Eds.), *Strategies for natural language processing.* Hillsdale, NJ: Lawrence Erlbaum Associates.

Lenat, D. (1976). *AM: An artificial intelligence approach to discovery in mathematics as heuristic search* (Memo AIM-286, doctoral dissertation). Stanford AI Lab, Stanford University, Dept. of Computer Science.

Meehan, J. (1976). *The metanovel: Writing stories by computer* (Tech. Rep. #74, doctoral dissertation). Yale University, Dept. of Computer Science.

Miyamoto, M. (1982). *The book of five rings* (Victor Harris, Trans.). Woodstock, NY: Overlook Press.

Mueller, E. T. (1989). *Daydreaming in humans and machines: A computer model of the stream of thought.* Norwood, NJ: Ablex Publishers.

Muller, H. J. (1956). *The spirit of tragedy.* New York: Alfred A. Knopf.

Oatley, K., & Johnson-Laird, P. (1987). Towards a cognitive theory of emotions. *Cognition and Emotion,* I(1), 29-50.

Osborn, A. (1953). *Applied imagination; principles and procedures of creative thinking.* New York: Scribner and Sons.

Poincare, H. (1913). Mathematical creation. In *The Foundations of Science Series* (G.B. Halsted, Trans.) New York: The Science Press.

Price, R., & Stern, L. (1958). *The original Mad Libs,* Los Angeles, CA: Price Stern Sloan.

Propp, V. (1968). *Morphology of the folktale* (Laurence Scott, Trans.). University of Texas Press.

Rees, E. (1966). *Fables from Aesop.* New York: Oxford University Press.

Reeves, J. (1991). *Computational morality: A process model of belief conflict and resolution for story understanding.* Unpublished doctoral dissertation, University of California, Los Angeles.

Reeves, J. (1989). *The Rhapsody phrasal parser and generator* (Tech. Note UCLA-AI-N-89-14). Artificial Intelligence Laboratory, Computer Science Department, University of California, Los Angeles.

Reichenbach, H. (1938). *Experience and prediction; an analysis of the foundations and the structure of knowledge.* Illinois: The University of Chicago Press.

Reisbeck, C., & Schank, R. (Eds.). (1989). *Inside case-based reasoning.* Hillsdale, NJ: Lawrence Erlbaum Associates.

Reiser, B. J. (1983). *Contexts and indices in autobiographical memory* (Tech. Rep. 24). Cognitive Science Program, Yale University.

Reiser, B. J. (1986). Knowledge-directed retrieval of autobiographical memories. In J. Kolodner & C. Riesbeck (Eds.), *Experience, memory and reasoning.* Hillsdale, NJ: Lawrence Erlbaum Associates.

Reiser, B. J., Black, J. B., & Abelson, R. P. (1985). Knowledge structures in the organization and retrieval of autobiographical memories. *Cognitive Psychology, 17,* 89-137.

Roberts, E. V. (1977). *Writing themes about literature.* Englewood Cliffs, NJ: Prentice-Hall.

Schank, R. C. (1979). Interestingness: Controlling inferences. *Artificial Intelligence, 12,* 273-297.

Schank, R. C. (1982). *Dynamic memory.* Cambridge, England: Cambridge University Press.

Schank, R. C., & Abelson, R. (1977). *Scripts, plans, goals, and understanding.* Hillsdale, NJ: Lawrence Erlbaum Associates.

Slade, S. (1991). Case-based reasoning: A research paradigm. *AI Magazine,* Spring, pp. 42-55.

Smith, F. (1982). *Writing and the writer.* New York: Holt, Rinehart, and Winston.

Tchudi, S., & Tchudi, S. (1984). *The young writer's handbook.* New York: Charles Scribner's Sons.

Tulving, E. (1972). Episodic and semantic memory. In E. Tulving & W. Donaldson (Eds.), *Organization of memory.* New York: Academic Press.

Turner, S. (1993). *MINSTREL: A computer model of creativity and storytelling.* Doctoral dissertation, Artificial Intelligence Laboratory, Computer Science Department, University of California, Los Angeles.

Turner, S. (1985). *MINSTREL, A story invention system.* Unpublished master's thesis. University of California, Los Angeles.

Turner, S., & Reeves, J. (1987). *The RHAPSODY Manual* (Tech. Note UCLA-AI-87-3). Artificial Intelligence Laboratory, Computer Science Department, University of California, Los Angeles.

Wallas, G. (1926). *The art of thought.* New York: Harcourt, Brace.

Warren, D. (1978). *WARPLAN: A system for generating plans* (Memo No. 76). Edinburgh University.

Weisberg, R. W. (1986). *Creativity: Genius and other myths.* New York: W. H. Freeman.

Wilensky, R. (1982). Points: A theory of the structure of stories in memory. In W. Lehnert & M. Ringle (Eds.), *Strategies for natural language processing*. Hillsdale, NJ: Lawrence Erlbaum Associates.

Wilensky, R., & Arens, Y. (1980). PHRAN: A knowledge-based natural language understander. In *Proceedings of the Eighteenth Annual Meeting of the Association for Computational Linguistics (ACL-80)*. Philadelphia, PA.

Zernik, U. (1987). *Strategies in language acquisitions: Learning phrases from examples in context* (Tech. Rep. UCLA-AI-87-1). University of California Los Angeles.

Author Index

Subject Index